THE   PRESIDENTIAL   PLOT

THE PRESIDENTIAL PLOT

The Map, the Story & the Conspiracy

To

Elect a President

P. ANDREW COSTELLO

STORYWISE PUBLICATIONS

2008
Washington DC

Copyright 2008 by P. Andrew Costello

Library of Congress Cataloging-in-Publication Data
P. Andrew Costello

The Presidential Plot: the Map, the Story and the Conspiracy to Elect a President
By P. Andrew Costello

ISBN 978-0-615-25449-4

1. Narrative Analysis, 2. Political Campaigns, 3. Media Ethics, 4. Storytelling

Cover Design: Simon Lloyd-Lavery
Editor Assistance: David Russell

Published in the United States of America by
Storywise Publications, Washington DC

DEDICATION

To Senator McCain and Senator Obama for their inspiring stories

To the memory of our friend and mentor, Michael White (1949-2008) the Founder Father of Narrative Therapy, gone too soon

To the people of Washington in Congress, in Government, business and the wider community for allowing me to be a part of your story

To the Washington Ireland Program and its Founders and the community of graduates for the chance to test these ideas

To Mark Shields and David Brooks and all the people at Public Television for the invaluable service they render

To my big sister, Sue, for her courage and her enduring legacy and to all my family Down Under

To Ben and Tess and Imogen and Matilda

TABLE OF CONTENTS

A NARRATIVE ANALYSIS OF THE PRESIDENTIAL ELECTION

What Obama knows, what McCain needs to know and what Hillary didn't know!

TABLE OF CONTENTS

TABLE OF CONTENTS

"The media want stories, and the Candidates want to get elected and the people want the truth. The people only count for the media if they are potential viewers, and the people only count for Candidates if they are potential voters, and consequently, nowhere in the Presidential Plot do people count as people. What if we restored "We the People" as the hero of the Democracy story?" Page 136

PROLOGUE

WHY THE BOOK?

We are all suckers for a good story; it's not just that people lie to us. We lie to ourselves. We are the willing confabulators of our fictions and if you don't believe me, let's remind ourselves of a few recent stories.

Remember Iraq? There were no Weapons of Mass Destruction (WMD's) but most of us wanted to find them because we knew Saddam was a baddie! He should have had them. It <u>so</u> fit the story. Now we are blaming the Government, so we don't have to blame ourselves, but even 65% of Democratic voters originally bought the horror movie of "Smoking gun to mushroom clouds."

Remember how Enron was re-inventing the energy business? All the Harvard business gurus were lauding it for setting new standards of excellence and profitability. We didn't want to know about any bottom line finagling until they ran out of money. But big business, who are paid to know, and government, who are paid to regulate, bought it big time. Ken Lay was a White House VIP, a member of the Board of Harvard Business School no less.

And lest we forget Katrina-FEMA was a great agency. They knew how to handle hurricanes and were doing one "heckuva of a job," because our President told us so. Then we saw the bodies floating and the people abandoned on housetops. The images didn't fit the story, though 'heck,' as a euphemism for "hell" was at least accurate!

Katrina-Enron-WMD's, I am sure you can name even more-the Boston Archdiocese, Pat Tillman, Jessica Lynch, AIG, Fannie Mae, Freddie Mac. Corporations now produce stories as an industry, and whether they be the military, the White House or Wall Street,[1] they wield enormous power over us, until sometimes, reality has its revenge and firms go bust, wars go bad, and levees break. But by then, it's too late. And we are left to wonder: Why were we suckers for the story in the first place?

With so much damage done through the deliberate use of stories to deceive or confuse, you would think we would have wised up by now, but the Story Industry out there is more formidable than ever.

---

[1] Think of what a story did to United Airways in September,*2008* where a 6 year old story was recycled by mistake and the company almost disappeared in 60 minutes of frantic selling, before someone realized, it was only a story!

They know they don't have to change the reality. They just have to tell their stories better by adjusting the image. Make sure next time, the President is visiting the hurricane-damaged communities on the ground, not from 3000 feet up. Long distance compassion doesn't play well to a media who crave good close-ups!

And what if greater zeal goes into telling "The President Really Cares" story next time? It may have nothing to do with a more effective emergency response. Who is concerned about being able to tell a better story of effective prevention and relief?

Many narrative specialists are selling their skills to business, politics and government to help them tell their stories better and it's a lucrative game. But that's hardly a consoling thought. Sure, the stories of government and business are badly broken. But what about us? What about the ordinary citizens who bought them and are still paying the price?

How can we detect the next big "con" and save ourselves from another Enron or Katrina or Iraq? It feels like an impossible task. The mortgage meltdown could be another Enron? How would we know? Global warming might produce a dozen Katrina's. The EPA wouldn't tell us. A nuclear plant in Iran might be another "bogus WMD," a pretext for another war. But "to protect national security" we will be asked to trust the President, the Pentagon, and even the *New York Times*, trust anything but our own gut instinct that's screaming at us, "Suckers! They are feeding you another story!"

We are about to decide the next President of the United States. If politics is nothing more than one big con game, and we remain suckers for a good story, then we are in big trouble. What chance do we have of selecting the right candidate?

Campaigns are now huge parts of the Story-Industry. They know that people vote for the best story, rather than the best candidate. They know that the candidate who wins is the candidate whose story best fits the voters' story for the future of America. We have already experienced the primary campaigns, but we ain't seen nothing yet!

In the next few months, we will face an unprecedented display of untrammeled narrative power, targeting us to get our money first and then, our vote. Obama will raise over 400 million, and he spent 26 million alone in June,[2] most of it selling us his autobiography.

---

2 Jeanne Cummings Politico.com 7/21/08

The week I write this, close to the 4th of July, it happens to be 'The Patriotism story'. Next week, it will be "The story of Obama as foreign policy expert', and next month, 'Obama the good economic manager.'

It's no less true for John McCain who spent 27 million in June. [3] This week, his theme was "I want free trade with Columbia,' and though he will only have a little over 100 million to play with, McCain will take public funding of up to 85 million and most of that will go towards tearing holes in the Obama story. Stay tuned for Story-wars to rival Star-Wars.

The brains behind the campaigns, Rick Davis and Charlie Black, David Axelrod and David Plouffe, are the most accomplished narrative practitioners in the business, though they would hardly call themselves that.

They are ruthless in the way they pull the levers of narrative power. Anything that gets in the way of the storyline must be edited out. Anyone who distracts, overshadows or threatens to disrupt the plot is "thrown under the bus." It's getting a little crowded down there. Ask Rev. Wright, and Rev. Hagee, and Mr. Johnson. Who's next? It's like a brutal military campaign-shock and awe-the Presidential Election, the Biggest Story there is!

Most of the big events that capture the world's imagination every four years, like a summer Olympics or a Soccer World Cup are stories so big that the networks compete for exclusive coverage. But the events themselves are the story, a team wins, someone breaks a world record or someone fails a drug test, and they amount to no more than a few weeks of intense coverage.

In a presidential election cycle, the actual result comes from one day's voting-November 4th, which is hardly an occurrence to supply two years of news! But the unfolding and the unraveling of the Presidential Stories is the main event. And election News covers the co-generation of these Stories. By co-generation, we mean that the media are no longer reporting the news; they are in symbiotic relationship to it. They have to sell it, so they get to shape it. They deliver what the customer wants and so, they cater for the viewer, not the voter!

Elections now have to compete with the drama of "Survivor" and "The X-Factor." Yet, an election is hard to package as a show. It has to be done as a serial, with banners that tell us "Choice 2008"

---

3 *Op Cit*

3

or "America Decides," and most of it is what Karl Vonnegut calls "persuasive guessing"[4] because, despite all the stories, not much actually happens in an election before the election. Newsmakers have to be creative artists in a relentless pursuit of what's new. They are like modern day novel-ists.

In former times, we could be watching Charles Dickens' writing 'Great Expectations," (a good title for the Presidential election.) How exciting it would have been to watch this great epic unfolding before us live from the pen of a master storyteller. We could read over his shoulder and be sucked into the vortex of steamy emotions between Pip and Estella and what happens next? Or we could step back to concentrate on the author, and watch the drama of the story creation rather than the drama of what is created. This second way is the narrative way. It's what allows us to read and take an aesthetic pleasure in the Presidential Plot and understand a Presidential election in a new way.[5]

To think of the election as this unfolding literary process explains aspects that might otherwise appear redundant or just plain silly. Remember Hillary's laugh? Or Obama's flag pin? They have nothing to do with electing the next President but they are the small things Hemingway or any good novelist will use as a cipher for character. It's because they get recruited into this made for TV mini-series that they then become part of the election saga.

And perhaps, we are politely inferring that campaigns and the media are making it up as they go along, just like Dickens did. It is a closed, self referential and self-reverential process, or some would even say, a self-cannibalizing process. The candidates work the media and their sources. The media work the candidates and their sources. And the two feed off each other in a prime-time frenzy of story-generation called "news." That's our Presidential Plot.

Then, comes the reality of November 4th, and we remember that these two years of relentless coverage come down to something strange. It's called voting! We are puzzled-Is that all there is? At least someone wins and someone loses, and the story is over.

---

[4] Karl Vonnegut A Man without a Country Random House 2007 p. 82

[5] "As a novelist, I am jealous of the present national moment. I'd love to have invented it-what author of thrillers wouldn't? The fate of the nation is at stake. Powerful characters vie for the chance to save it, and each one's supporters contend loudly that the others are being manipulated by the malevolent forces that secretly run Washington...We have war; we have religion, we have race, we have gender, we have class, and we have confusing subplots galore. What reader could resist?" Stephen L Carter "Fate of the Nation" Washington Post May 4 2008 p.B2

But not so fast! The story factory will continue churning out the post-mortems, and "Who stole the election?" and an obligatory Florida 2000 Redux. They will also rewrite the victory story to say, 'McCain gets out of Prison again-War Hero wins Against All Odds,'- because he had the experience-or 'America tells Obama Yes We can-African American Hero wins in landslide'-because he had the charisma. And on to "The First 100 Days" and "The Honeymoon is Over," and "President reneges on election promise," etc.,

Elections are amazing feats of industrialized storytelling that would even dazzle a Henry Ford. At least he was forced to change his models a few times in 40 years. The Presidential plot is stuck in a formula that hasn't changed much since 1968.

Before we begin our exploration, let me say a few words about our title "The Presidential Plot" and how it applies to at least three meanings: plot means a conspiracy, and it is part of a story, and it involves reading a map.

CONSPIRACY

First "plot" means something sinister, something underhand or conspiratorial. The campaigns are spending over half a billion dollars between them (at the last estimate) and they are up to something that they don't want you to really know about it. Their money is used to

- work out our narrative vulnerabilities, (polls) and their narrative vulnerabilities (vetting)

- determine what story we most want to hear, (focus groups).

- measure their candidates' narrative capacities and character to package for prime time (the five minute biography plus all the campaign slogans and ads.)

Their job is to pull all these together into a solid plotline and make it all fit together in one seamless story, and dress it up in the red, white and blue of Campaign camouflage. Once they have that, they flood every media market and pull every PR trick in the book to tell it to us again and again and again-on TV, internet, YouTube, print media, MySpace, Yahoo groups, etc so we internalize it and can tell it to others. Once we do that, they assume we will vote for them, and we might even be inspired to donate money towards furthering their calculated story infection.

Yet for all that, they still cannot guarantee a result, because finally (and thankfully) it's not their story. It's ours! Senators McCain or Obama will only win if they win us over. And they can only do that if we decide to cast them into the lead role of the movie our imaginations are running entitled, "The Hero who can save America."

What they think is a marketing exercise is actually an audition. We don't expect their stories will be exactly true, but we need the candidates to convincingly perform the part our plot calls for. Bush was elected and re-elected because despite the policy disasters, his character has been a better narrative fit for our American story these past eight years. It's hard even now to imagine a President Gore, or a President Kerry.

STORY

The second meaning is the traditional sense of the role of the plot in a story. Peter Brooks calls it:

> "The principle of interconnectedness and intention which we cannot do without in moving through the discrete elements-incidents, episodes, actions-of a narrative." [6]

A plot, to be meaningful, has to conform to a familiar design, one that we can recognize well enough to anticipate. Just as we can guess how a story that begins, "Once upon a time" is going to have princes and goblins, so too the Presidential Plot is equally predictable. It's a story that begins, "After eight long, and challenging years, the nation decided it was that time for change, time to find a new President." Like any genre, it has a narrative necessity to it which means we can get ahead of it to chart its progress.

It has a promising and crowded beginning, a messy middle and two definitive ends, one heroic and one tragic. It has audiences that will make or break the show. (New Hampshire-Ohio-Iowa) It has villains and turning points, and complications, and it ends with crises and climaxes. It has narrative vulnerabilities and possibilities that will mirror our own convictions and our own confusions.

And finally, it will emerge as a somewhat peaceful yet nonetheless ruthless plot to overthrow a government, and anoint a new head of state, to crown a new Caesar. It is the French Revolution minus the

---

[6] Peter Brooks <u>Reading for the Plot</u> Harvard Press 1984 p. 5

guillotine, the Easter Rising without the GPO, the Russian Revolution with its own slightly milder versions of Lenin and Trotsky as plotters. (though Karl Rove as character would fit into the Russian epic quite easily)

MAP

Thirdly, the Presidential plot is also the map or playbook that the campaigns don't want you to read because it might reveal where they have positioned their troops, or disclose the secret behind their plotters' magic. Or to shift metaphors, it might mean we get to see how they keep pulling rabbits out of hats, or issues out of misquotes. But with this playbook, we can more fully enjoy the majestic literary effort going on, with all its theatricality and melodrama, its bizarre creativity and improv. We can even play it forward and read it back. Instead of campaign 2008 putting us to sleep, we will wake up to the delicious con game which is this Plot to change a president, change a government, change a country, and change the world.

A COUNTER-PLOT LED BY THE PEOPLE

At the end of the book, I hope you might even be inspired to join us in hatching a counter plot where, invoking a Thomas Jefferson and a John Adams, we might conspire in our own scheme to restore the people as the hero of the democracy story, not the lobbyists, not big business, not the parties, not the media. What would it take to release the narrative power of citizens all over the country? Imagine 300 million Studs Turkels! How would that challenge the hold of industrialized storytelling that recycles the old stories and prevents America from telling its own best stories?

Our mantra is not to tell the same story better, which is what we will argue the campaigns are all about, but to tell better stories. And in the process, we will find 'better stories about stories' that reveal their power both to inspire us and to corrupt us. Ultimately we need new stories about America. We need to think of it as a Republic of Stories, the stories that work best for its people. And then, elections will better reflect our choice about what stories we want to shape our national destiny. That is what we are voting for; not the best candidate, not even the best party, but for the best story, one that works for the future.

So, as you read this book, imagine you are boarding the Straight Talk Express or the Obama's Train to Triumph. You are all fired up, ready to go, yes we can, yes we will, with the leader you can believe in, the change you can believe in. Once you have your T-shirt on and flag pins attached, fasten your seatbelts, settle back. You are stepping on to the Storytelling Express. With our map, our story and millions of fellow conspirators, we are plotting the route to 1600 Pennsylvania Avenue.

CHAPTER ONE

INTRODUCTION

"Whoever can give his people better stories than the ones they live in is like the priest in whose hands common bread and wine become capable of feeding the very soul."[7]

It's Friday night. It's Washington DC. Anyone who is a bit of a news-junkie tunes into the public television station for the weekly shot of Washington politics. Overdose more likely. How can anyone endure three to four solid hours of chat? But this is the evening to catch every nuance, every morsel of gossip told by people who still value conversation as an art, and not a contact sport. Why, they even use subordinate clauses in sentences!

Every other channel-Fox-MSNBC-CNN during the week and over the weekends in particular, sound like Hardball on steroids. Shouting matches between people each wearing their Red or Blue Party hats but more often needing helmets. They decry the malaise of the day including the disease of partisan politics that they themselves so tragically demonstrate. No one expects it to be fair and balanced, but it is not even mildly entertaining save for the occasional perverse pleasure a viewer might get watching a heavy-weight ego contest between George Stephanopoulos and Hillary Clinton.

Hardball, McLaughlin, The O'Reilly Factor, it is all World Championship Ego Wrestling without the brawn and with brains, if working at all, working on remote or repeat. King Kong Bundy at least knew how to entertain. But on Friday night, at least for now, there is still this oasis. On the NewsHour, you can rely on Mark Shields to drop his regular bon mot like, *"I was reminded of what Mario Cuomo said 25 years ago, "We campaign in poetry. We govern in prose."* At what other cocktail party will you hear someone say that? And David Brooks will reply in kind.[8] Gwen Ifel takes it from there in her panel show that is so "Not over the top" that it makes all the others sound like *Aida* on acid.

---

[7] Hugh Kenner

[8] Analysts Mark Shields and David Brooks Originally Aired: April 27, 2007 *Newshour*

Then there's *Inside Washington* with Evan Thomas' cell phone going off or Nina Totenberg gently chiding Charles Krauthammer not to be such a bully. "But Charles, but Charles..."and Gordon Petersen coaxing Colbert King to speak out.

Friday night Public Television might be the one caveat to a lot of what I am going to write about in this book about a craven media. Yet even tonight, what originally triggered this book project showed up again, tripping lightly from the lips of Mark Shields talking about something that would "shift the Obama narrative."

"Narrative?" Even Mark Shields is using the term. Then two nights later, it's Richard Wolfe of *Newsweek's* turn, when he says that people have realized Obama's "two competing narratives." Ugh! And so it has continued. E.J.Dionne Jr. "What Obama still lacks, they say, is a compelling narrative..."(*Washington Post* August 22) "For the first time, there is a consistent narrative...in the McCain team." (August 21 *Washington Post* Lois Romano) "But positions are one thing and narratives something else,"(Harold Meyerson *Washington Post* Aug 21) And if you turn on most other commentators, you realize it has become *de rigeur* to use the term "narrative" for everything and nothing.

Clearly it is time that someone who has spent a career studying narrative and teaching narrative practice to enter the fray and rally to protect the word, the discipline and the practice from becoming another Friday night cliché.

If 'narrative' becomes a Washington buzz word, it is basically dead on arrival. It will go the way of WMD's and "I did not inhale" and "no controlling legal authority." Words regularly take a pounding here but someone using "narrative" always sounds to my ears as if someone is talking about my Mother. (And she is still the greatest storyteller I know.) I am immediately on the defensive.

Narrative exploded into my world twenty years ago when I had the privilege of studying with the late and great Michael White, the founding father of Narrative Therapy. He taught that people were never the problem. It was their problem-saturated stories. The solution was always to find a better story.

I have studied, written, and applied narrative method for over 20 years to peace and reconciliation programs in Northern Ireland, to the homeless in Australia, to African-American communities in Miami, to kids from Georgia and Abkhazia, to emerging leaders in Uzbekistan, to communities in South East DC and all manner of organizations from Malibu to New Mexico. But in all that, I never thought "narrative" would be the new election word, or that I would be inspired to write a book that applies narrative analysis to the Presidential election of 2008.

What do I know about politics? I am not even from here, but I can name-drop with the best of them. Washington is such a small town, and it seems that if you hang around long enough, you can get to meet the Clintons and Chief Justice Roberts, and you can get insights into how Hillary and Obama and McCain run their offices. I am not an insider, but I can credibly talk like one, which matters as much in Washington. I have worked with members of Congress and the Clinton White House and their interns for the last ten years. I know legislative mark-ups from legislative make ups. But I don't often talk about it. It's where the luck of life has brought me, not something I have earned. But now, for the cause of narrative, it seems timely to tell this part of my story.

I imagine my retirement years in a home for seniors in my native Australia telling stories that will so disturb the nursing staff that they will call my family to say, "Your old man has finally lost it-he is talking about advising Chief Justice Roberts in his chambers and of President and Senator Clinton gate-crashing his party, and even saying Congress voted an official Tribute to his work. We want to up the meds." And my son, Ben, saying," Go right ahead. Mind you, the old man's not making it all up." So I do know Washington. At least to tell some good stories.

And I know narrative, and that's more to the point!

This is not going to be a book about the latest polling trend. It's not going to compete with the Peter Hart's of this world and their focus groups, nor with my weekly inspirations on WETA TV. But I want to show that narrative can offer so much more than the cheap cliché that is being thrown around increasingly in this election. It always sounds as if it is being used as a substitute for analysis rather than offering any new insight. I want to humbly offer Washington (is that an oxymoron?) and anyone else interested, the explanatory power of narrative analysis, a new way of looking at the world of politics, and especially during these intense times of an election.

I am a founding member of a group of story consultants in Washington DC called the Golden Fleece who run an annual conference on applying stories to organizational change. It includes luminaries from the World Bank like Stephen Denning, Seth Kahan and Madelyn Blair and managers from NASA and IBM and Government departments like GSA and the Treasury. They know their stuff. Earlier this year, I ran a short workshop for Golden Fleece on "A Narrative Approach to the Presidential Elections." At the very least, I expected it would generate an engaging political debate, and at best, we would have some fun trying out some of my crazy ideas.

Why I call them crazy is because in a town where nothing is left unsaid by way of political analysis and opinion, no one else in Washington was saying the things I wanted to say about Obama and Hillary and McCain. I proposed that the issues didn't matter, but the stories did, and that Obama and McCain were characters in a story that had already been scripted. They were our two try-outs for the one part. I also offered that Hillary had a compelling story and she might well have triumphed had she decided to tell it, but she didn't.

The workshop was a blast-not one argument!!! When it ended all too soon, the response was overwhelming. Participants assured me, 'You are not crazy,' or maybe "Not that crazy!" They said it helped "illuminate the election process as a story process', and they accusingly asked, 'Why wasn't I writing about this?' So thanks to you folks, I have nailed myself to the computer and here is the result. I can blame you.

So let me give you a map of what lies ahead, and what my purposes are. 'Narrative' or 'Story' are words I use fairly interchangeably but I am talking of story as a system of meaning-making, not just the usual, "Did you hear the tale about the three legged dog?"

It is 'story as strategy' and 'story as a species or a language system.' It is about how our world of meaning-making increasingly gets organized into a narrative logic of beginnings, middles and ends, and of characters entangled in and driven by a dominant plot. I maintain that narrative logic is overtaking rational logic. We don't deal in syllogisms anymore, we deal in stories. And we use the bigger stories to understand the smaller stories. It's a dynamic system of narrative interconnection.

I am speaking of 'narrative' as a literary term that encompasses the literary critical skills of interpretation that are normally applied to literature-the sort of concepts that Ricoeur and Foucault and Le Man theorize or obfuscate about, and the set of concepts you might use when writing an essay on the character of the Whale in

'Moby Dick.' What narrative analysis does is take those same practices normally applied to the dead letter of a classic text, and applies them instead, to the living stories of a corporation or, in this case, an election process.

Imagine an essay topic on "Explore the use of the word 'honor' in Senator McCain's biography and its impact on his election campaign." Or "How well did Hillary exploit the end of her campaign to invite us to re-interpret her failure as a new milestone for women?" Or "How is Obama's campaign an extension of his quest narrative for the absent parent in "Dreams from My Father?'

They may sound academic but when one realizes that one of these story-sets will become the shadow and the light of the nation in the next four years, I believe it's highly relevant. Imagine if in 2000, we had written about "The measure of the son is what he has yet to prove to the father- Discuss in relation to what Bush 43 has to prove to Bush 41." Who knew that that would have been an essay on Saddam Hussein?

The same question could be asked of McCain and Obama as America is once again being thrust into a choice of conflicted paternities, between dominant or absent father stories. Life, as we like to say, is a literary art not because we are wannabe writers, even if we are, but because we make meaning through language and language gets its oxygen from stories.

I am not affiliated with any party, and I am not writing in the genre of the great linguist George Lakoff[9] or of brilliant neuroscientist Drew Westen[10] because their works feel partisan. They are trying to wake the Democratic Party up to delivering a more emotionally resonant message. Nor am I trying to restore the conservative agenda, or redeem a brand that everyone says in 2008 is degraded. Sounds like soap to me. One book that started to explore this theme is The Power and the Story by Evan Cornog[11] whose basic thesis agrees with mine. But where he takes up story in an historical survey, my aim is to demonstrate a practical narrative method that can be immediately applied to this election now unfolding before us.

I belong to the narrative party that wants to see better stories because better stories can inspire new meanings which can in turn

---

9 George Lakoff, Howard Dean Don't Think of an Elephant!: Chelsea Green, 2004

10 Drew Westen The Political Brain Public Affairs 2007

11 Evan Cornog The Power and the Story Penguin 2004

re-inspire the nation. Surely that is what leadership is about at this, the highest of levels. I am going to take critical and sometimes savage aim at both the media and at the campaigns for industrializing the story-telling business, and for their manipulative adoption of the power of story for political ends.

And I have a dream of empowering the normal citizen, Mom and Dad and the local sheriff and the McDonalds manager and the taxi driver, the normal person who is bombarded with stories that aren't his own and yet, has little choice but to use them to make sense of his or her own life.

Once we buy into someone else's story, we are in danger of becoming the agent of intentions other than our own. I say this not to scare people or write a tirade of how bad things are. We already have an army of pessimists coming at us. Rather it is to invite us to think of stories as products we consume. And to think that some stories work for us, and some of them don't, and some are dangerous, and some are even deadly. Like cigarettes, all stories should come with a consumer warning label to say: "Stories have been proven to be harmful to your health. So be sure that this story works for you and not for someone else."

We are unconscious consumers of stories that don't work for us at all, but they have preemptively invaded our imaginations, and we don't seem to know how to determine which story is which. Yet I will argue that deep down, we do.

I want to speak to the natural narrative intelligence that anyone who goes to a movie or reads a book or listens to his kids when they come home from summer camp has in spades and, somehow, never transfers to the stories of candidates and parties. We use our narrative IQ in personal life, so why not in public life?

I believe we are suckers for a good story, and that is good in so far as we know it. Stories can move us to tears, and they can ennoble the human journey. But having worked in Northern Ireland, I also know stories can kill and maim and paralyze a generation who, though they want peace, are so traumatized by the memories of hatred that violence seems the only way out.

And then there are other stories such as the rumors that spread like wildfire in East Berlin late in 1989. Word was that the Berlin Wall was open and unguarded. By the time the border guards moved to secure it, thousands were already streaming through. There was no going back. The final act that brought the Berlin Wall down was not the global politicking; it was one simple story spread by its citizens.

We have to choose better stories, stories that inspire us, that challenge us to break through barriers, that open alternative windows onto reality. If we remain suckers to the stories that exploit and demean and coldly calculate our narrative vulnerabilities, then we will continue to fear every foreigner with a beard, or lose sleep worrying about economic insecurity. Fear is a story infection, but so is hope. It's time to wake up! It's time to take America's story back as the story of its citizens rather than the stories endlessly manufactured to make us buyers, voters, and viewers.

The narrative work that my colleagues[12] and I began in Washington 13 years ago at the Center for Narrative Studies coalesced under the name of Storywise, at www.Storywise.com, and our summary goal was **'shaping the stories that shape us.'** We teach people a process *Living Stories* which helps communities find their best stories to renew and inspire their shared life, and *Narrative Room* which is a listening laboratory that teaches listening as a way of getting critical distance from the story to disarm its power over our imaginations. We have always had three aims:

- To help people understand the power of stories

- To teach people how that power has real effects in shaping their identity and destiny

- To teach people to apply this understanding in a practical way to communities and organizations undergoing change, dealing with conflict, or seeking renewal.

Those aims have not changed. But in the supercharged climate of the next few months leading to a Presidential election, it seems more urgent than ever for us all to become storywise as distinct from story-stupid.

Then and only then, the media and the campaigns and the commentariat will have to stop treating us as suckers. And our vote in November will be for the story that we choose to help us shape the nation's future. One new Senator whose profession

---

[12] I must recognize the inspiration and collaboration of Harry Rieckelman and Kathie Hepler in those early years developing Narrative Room and Living Stories and their continued support of this work.

before politics was writing successful novels agrees. Senator James Webb in his latest book, <u>A Time to Fight: Reclaiming a Just and Fair America</u> writes

> *"And to American voters, I would offer this small piece of advice. Be just as shrewd and ruthless in your demands on leaders as the political wizards who are running these campaigns are in their strategies designed to get your vote."*
> [13]

We are hot on the trail of these political wizards and their narrative strategies.

---

[13] Jim Webb <u>A Time to Fight: Reclaiming a Fair and Just America</u> Broadway 2008

CHAPTER TWO

DISCOVERING THE GAME PLAN

"We American workers are more beguiled than we are oppressed."[14]

Though there are so many great books and blogs on the election, it's hard to know which ones to rely on for an unbiased account. And of course there are the campaign web sites that are their new secret weapons. I recently stumbled across these pieces of campaign rhetoric. See if you can guess the sources.

> A-*"Never has so much military, economic and diplomatic power been used so ineffectively…And if after all this time and all of this sacrifice and all of this support there is still no end in sight, then I say the time has come for the American people to turn to new leadership-not tied to the politics and mistakes of the past. I pledge to you, we will have an honorable end to the war."*

That's pretty easy. Who else is offering an honorable end to a failed war? OK, let's try this one.

> B-*"There's uneasiness in the land. A feeling that things aren't right. That we're moving in the wrong direction. That none of the solutions to our own problems are working. That we're not being told the truth about what's going on. The trouble is in Washington. Fix that and we're on the way to fixing everything."*

I know you think this is way too obvious, but let me give you a few more just so you are sure.

> C-*"America is in trouble today not because her people have failed but because her leaders have failed. What American needs are leaders to match the greatness of her people."*

It's too easy, I know, but try one more.

> D-*"The American voter, insisting upon his belief in a higher order, clings to his religion…"*

---

[14] Curtis White <u>The Middle Mind</u> Harper San Francisco 200, Page 8

It sounds as if we have lifted a few talking points from Team Obama but we would be dead wrong. Excerpt A is from 1968 and its Nixon's central campaign message about the Vietnam War.

Excerpt (B) 'America is in trouble and Washington is broken' sounds like Obama and it could also be McCain. The polls are saying this is the certainly the mood of the electorate with the approval ratings of Congress close to single digits. But no. It's the Nixon Campaign of 1968. Again! Though Obama keeps saying much the same. ``For eight long years," he said recently, *"Washington hasn't been working for ordinary Americans."* He used it as his excuse for opting out of public funding, "declaring his independence from a broken system." And more recently, Senator McCain has been thundering the same message and re-enforced it with his surprise selection for Vice President.

It remains a delicious irony for Nixon to be campaigning on the issue of "Washington is broken" because he was the President who broke Washington, and we are still trying to pick up the pieces. Whatever "broken" meant back then, he made sure it meant something different after Watergate blew up in 1974.

But a 'Broken Washington' is an equal-opportunity slogan, because Romney for President-2008 said "Washington is broken" and before him, John Kerry for President 2004 said "Washington is broken." You get the idea. It's a script from the Presidential Plot, and it's a very old script.

And finally, who is the person who accused the American voter of 'clinging to his religion.' That has to be Obama. OK, but even before Obama, it was Joe McGinnis, the writer of "The Selling of the President"[15] from which I have taken all the other campaign quotes.

When you read a book about the 1968 elections and it sounds like the 2008 contest, or you see the headlines of history re-appearing on the front pages of the *New York Times*- for instance June 2008- "Character is the issue," and June 2004 "Character is now the issue," you wake up to the fact that the Presidential Plot is a genre, on its four yearly visitation.

"Genre" technically means a convention of discourse whose recognizable patterns signal to us how we should interpret it. But I just think of the local Borders or Barnes and Noble and their

---

15 Joe McGinniss The Selling of the President Penguin 1969 A-Page 90 B-Page 173 C-Page 95 D -page 26

18

shelves stacked with genre fiction, such as Romance or Chick Lit or Memoir, or History or Biography. We know where to look for a book because instinctively we know the genre, and each genre carries "implicit meanings, associations, and expectations." [16]

We tend to forget that we have heard the election genre before because, though an old story, it is made new by a fresh cast of characters, each of whom is trying to reprise an old lyric that might fit the mood of the nation.

Recognizing this allows us to draw up a story map, with a definite time-line. And the show-flow goes something like this, each setting off its own chain of stories.

- Candidates are contemplating running and setting up exploratory committees, and publishing their own or "as told to" biographies
- Primaries and caucuses are held that usually end by February but this year, by popular demand, ran till June
- The end of the primary season results in a Candidate winning the nomination and the candidate becoming the 'presumptive nominee,' which is worth it just for the sound of the title
- There is the July 4th breather with obligatory sermons on patriotism
- Summertime and no one pays attention, so Candidates try a trip overseas to a war zone or to nations who send the USA mobs of immigrants who might just vote for you
- The formal nomination of each party's candidate is made official at the conventions: August/September (which are also a convention in genre terms)
- We begin the obligatory debating season
- Next the October surprises
- We expect the 'widening the gap' stories
- We expect the 'closing of the gap' stories
- Election Day dawns, the race is on, and we are treated to a day of special drama
- Early predictions tell us someone is up here and down there
- Someone wins Ohio or Florida, Michigan, and California comes in late

---

16 Murray Chamberlain, Paul Thompson editors, <u>Narrative and Genre of Communication-Contexts and Types</u> New Brunswick 2004 Page 10

- The declaration of the winner, the APP poll now projects "that Gore will win Florida" etc.
- Next the challenges, revisions
- The voting scandals
- The calls for recounts
- Maybe, but hopefully not, the chads or the counting machines
- Florida again! Iowa,
- Finally, with or without the Supreme Court, we have a new President-elect, though he is not called Presumptive anymore
- We have a break to get ready for Thanksgiving and Christmas and get ready for winter and Inauguration fever
- Maybe we watch a few pardons in the waning days of the old administration, as the soon to be ex-President is allowed to get all misty eyed and merciful
- We have the compulsory stories of what the old admin staff left and how they stole-the "d" key on all the White House keyboards maybe?
- The new team sweep in like a team of pest-exterminators
- The new President re-decorates the oval office and gets ready for the campaign to be re-elected in four years since this has been so much fun!

The story has symmetry of ascending and descending cycles of suspense and surprise. It has a definite beginning and a definite ending, it has celebrity and it has various levels of participation and various peak viewing times so that, like a good soap opera, even if you miss six episodes straight, the villain is still trying to tempt the heroine, and there are two would-be heroes still wanting to run the country. It's reminiscent of a folk puppet show in Java where Obama went to school called the *Wayang Gulang* that he must have watched. It goes for 6-8 hours and people wonder in and out as they please, knowing that the story will keep on repeating.

Election 2008 is a story that we watch unfold and it's unfolding and its unraveling is the drama. Remember that front-runner for the Republicans? What was his name? Yes, Rudy Giuliani. Or that great actor who was hunting for Red October, Fred Thompson? And then, what about Jo Biden and the other John, John Edwards? Remember them? Was Biden named VP or was that just a rumor? And there was Romney and Gilmore and Paul and Richardson and Dodd and Hunter and Nader. How unforgettable they all were then, even if we don't remember them now. What a story?

A narrative analyst enjoys the saga as much as anyone else, but the extra pleasure derives from reading the play as if you were a writer/director and anticipating all the story's possibilities, and knowing that we have heard most of it before.

A book like McGinnis's even 40 years later still carries the shock of revelation and in the end, it reads as a disturbing prophecy. It was Watergate 'in utero.' Reading it makes you feel you are eavesdropping not only on Nixon's campaign, but on the current one. When the book came out in 1969, it became a best-seller and people could read not only how Nixon got elected, but how they were duped. Journalists apparently read it and were ashamed at how Nixon and his gang of tricksters had fooled them. And one is left wondering: would America have elected Nixon if some of the stories had come out <u>before</u> Election Day?

Here is a sample of how his handlers strategized their campaign.

> *"Nixon has to come across as a person larger than life, the stuff of legend. People are stirred by the legend, including the living legend, not by the man himself. It's the aura that surrounds the charismatic figure more than it is the figure itself, that draws the followers. Our task is to build that aura." So let's not be afraid of television gimmicks. get the voters to like the guy and the battle's two thirds won."*
> *(McGinniss: 36-37)*

'Aura' and 'Nixon' look strange even in the same sentence. Team Nixon knew they had their work cut out, but they were film-makers, specialists in the art of illusion. We watch them go to work like one of those "make over" TV shows. Let's give you the new Nixon, but what do we have to fix? Where to start?

They worried that Nixon had little humor and a decided lack of warmth. So, *"Give him words to say that will show his emotional involvement in the issues."* (McGinniss, 37)

He lacked humor. They can fix that." *If we're going to be witty, let a pro write the words."* And he appears on the best comedy show of the 1960's, Rowan and Martin's <u>Laugh-In</u> and speaks his immortal lines, "Sock it to me." (McGinniss, 37) and people laughed, probably at the total incongruity.

What about the thorny issue of "Integrity" given that Nixon came into the race as "Tricky Dickie", with a history that led many to deeply distrust him. Here is Nixon's chief advisor, Harry Treleaven's memo of November 1967 about how to handle it.

21

"Integrity-Although there were some doubts in the past, these have been dispelled by the years. Richard Nixon is now generally regarded as honest, a man who levels with the people. (The way he is handled from now on should strengthen that impression-particularly in light of credibility issue." (McGinniss, 173)

And he's looking puffy and pale. *"An effort should be made to keep him in the sun occasionally to maintain a fairly constant level of healthy tan." (McGinniss, 74)* This is for Black and White TV! What would they do with HD?

The history they had to disarm was that Nixon was a loser, having failed twice to get elected, and that he "feels" like a loser. But that needn't be a problem. Operative Ray Price writes in his memo:

"Let's leave realities aside-because what we have to deal with now is not the facts of history-but an image of history. The history we have to be concerned with is not what happened, but what's remembered, which may be quite different. Or to put it another way, the historical untruth may be a political reality." (McGinniss, 191)

It would appear that campaigns were signing out of the "reality based community" way back then. It wasn't new at all when Karl Rove was quoted in 2004 as saying to a journalist that "reality is not the way the world works anymore, that we (those in power) create our own reality" for you, the press, to judiciously study.[17]

In 1968, Treleaven was joined by Roger Ailes, later the genius behind Fox News, and other team members were Pat Buchanan and William Safire and even Alan Greenspan. (Does this already sound like a conspiracy, or perhaps just the genealogy of the modern campaign?)

What Treleaven and Ailes realized before anyone else was that television changed forever the way politics would be conducted. People say that 1960 was the first TV election, but it was nothing compared to the thoroughly calculated media strategy of 1968.

These guys were students of media guru, Marshall McLuhan. They understood that a TV election was about image and story, not about issues and substance. A young Roger Ailes was quoted as saying, *"This is the beginning of a whole new concept. This is the way they'll be elected forevermore. The next guys will have to be*

---

[17] Ron Suskind "Without a Doubt"_New York Times Magazine October 17, 2004

performers." (McGinnis, 155) Ronald Reagan, Fred Thompson and Arnold Schwarzenegger must have overheard him.

They did not have to change Nixon; they had to manage how his image was projected because TV distorts reality, both positively and negatively. Price wrote emphatically on this:

> *"We have to be very clear on this point that the response is to the image not to the man...Its not what's there that counts, its what's projected....It's not the man we have to change but the received impression. And this impression often depends more on the medium and its use than it does on the Candidate himself." (McGinnis, 38)*

When you realize that both Ailes and Treleaven helped run Bush 41's winning campaign in 1988, and other key Bush and Reagan elections, you can follow a trail from 1968, where they were inventing a new genre of Presidential campaigns, to 2008 where, though smarter and slicker, they are essentially using the same techniques. But where once image was king, now they speak about "narratives."

McGinnis's book is especially disturbing in hindsight when one realizes that all these talented media and image experts worked to elect one of the most despised presidents in history. A criminal, in fact. And even more disturbing is that their 'sophisticated' or some would say cavalier approach to truth and to reality, the managed "integrity" and all the rest, were not disconnected from the culture and the morality that made Watergate possible. They "checked out of the reality community" to package a crook to look compassionate, to be someone who will level with the citizens. If a liar can be made to look like the Truth, then the Republic is in danger. It was back then.

But of course, that was 40 years ago and we aren't at risk now. Oh, if only that were so. Even if the campaign methods have got more sophisticated with the internet/YouTube generation, the basic McLuhan premise holds; the media can so distort what is there to create an image of reality more powerful than the reality itself.

The McCain we see could be a total bore or a total idiot, someone with PTSD from his Vietnam days, (as Bush supporters intimated in their smear campaign of 2000) but our image suggests he is an incorrigible old warrior, with a twinkle in his eye and loads of conviction and compassion. But what is real, and what is the "reality" that the campaign wants us to imagine Candidate McCain to be? They are serving up for us *the story of McCain* which

23

remains just that. The Story of McCain is the Story of McCain, it is not John McCain! But the story will be told so well that it feels real, even though we know it's not, once we become aware of the narrative manipulation.

The gap between *the story* and *the real* is where we need to stay if we want to stay connected to the "reality community." The job of the campaigns is to make us think there is no gap, and make sure no one gets behind the scene to expose the facade. The start of McGinnis's' book takes us to the scene of Nixon taping ads, retake after retake after retake, to get that natural, spontaneous feel, and the press were barred. So rest assured they are not going to make the same mistake today, and let some 26-year-old journalist, as McGinnis was then, into the backrooms, or see the bloopers and the furious memos and emails zipping back and forth between campaign organizers. But we can imagine an email in the McCain camp,

> "Who put that lime green puke wallpaper behind him? It's not St. Patrick's day for God's sake. And can we make the text on the teleprompter 20 point? It's too small. He can't read it. That's' why he is always squinting. And next time, he has to rehearse the speech. He fluffed his punch lines and instead of a lead, all we got is Comedy Central and You-Tube replaying them overtime as Funniest Home Videos."

Or take the Obama image. Along with his being young and handsome, he could be arrogant, superior, haughty and prissy and highly strung, but the image we see suggests an intelligent, warm, young Dad and ebullient law professor with energy and natural instincts for leadership. What is the package? What is the real person? One hears that at campaign meetings held right after losing Pennsylvania, John Kerry told Obama that he was too aloof, and needed to connect with blue collar workers. Obama was coming off as too intellectual. So the next week, we saw more Obama in more photo shots with the workers.

Again, let's stay in the gap and remind ourselves that the Story of Obama is the Story of Obama. It is not Obama. But the campaign wants us to elide the gap by flooding the screens of our imaginations with the images of their seamless, polished performer. What would we give for more snippets from inside their campaign war rooms, because judging by the productions, the same narrative manipulation, or creative scripting is happening, as always.

Remember Obama was being accused of not being patriotic? So what to do? David Axelrod has about two years of video footage from trailing the candidate in every conceivable situation, so he has plenty of good images of the candidate waving flags on previous 4th of July's and kissing babies and embracing the veterans in time for Memorial Day. Get into the editing room and add some text for Obama to read, add some resounding music and send out the message, 'Obama the Patriot.' It's the classic Treleaven touch from the Nixon days.

Or take the issue of McCain being 72 years old and how to handle the age issue when it inevitably arises. His campaign will already have prepared to show McCain moving, pacing, showing signs of vigor, as in town meetings, and perhaps have him do a parachute jump, or catch a football. It will be reminiscent of all those images that Kennedy used of the boys playing football at Hyannis. And remember JFK had a back disease and had to wear braces and took painkillers every day. He was anything but the vibrant, fit young President, except for his libido.

In earlier days, it was truly about image. But today, it isn't quite as simple, because the 24 hour media means much more exposure. Think of how many debates the eight Democrats or Hillary and Obama had. It makes it hard to massage every shot, because Obama is bound to come off looking pouty when Stephanopoulos asks a stupid question, or Hillary can't disguise her gloating look as she seems to enjoy Obama's discomfort a little too much.

Remember Gore groaning, or Bush Snr. looking at this watch? And now everyone with a cell phone is a potential journalist, who can send voice and image instantly. "Hey guys, listen to what Hillary just said to Bill." Or remember Bill's recent comments about his not so favorite journalist, or here is Jesse Jackson cutting up on Obama.

The image is now part of a larger unit of meaning which is why the campaigns now talk about 'narratives.' It's a more complex package. They know that the image only works in as much as it evokes the story, and so it has to fit the story. Those images must be linked up to create a larger narrative, as if the images are now part of a movie. They only make sense in a moving picture. Image alone is not enough, and in fact, an image that suggests a contrary story is deadly. For instance, remember John Edwards preaching about the 'haves and the have-nots' and his supposed 30 million dollar house! A dissonant image can wreck a story. Yet a powerful story can also re-frame or re-contextualize a negative image. Remember Obama and his speech on race after the first Rev. Wright flare-up and before the Rev. Wright meltdown. The speech repaired the breach, at least for a while. Or we can recall the image of the Katrina flood and the image of Bush at 3000 feet that didn't add up to any story of Presidential concern. An image can break a story open so its meaning drains away.

Campaigns and candidates have to weave all these elements into a coherent story, tight enough to withstand all the inconsistencies, digressions and contradictions. And more importantly, to withstand the counter-attacks, given that campaigns have increasingly become defensive games.

The "Narrative" also needs to anticipate the unguarded moment, the Makkaka slip up, or the "Clinging to guns" eruption which is as threatening to the "narrative" as any bimbo eruption was in the Clinton campaign. The narrative imperative is to tightly package and promote your storyline, cut out any fat, edit out the dross, reduce complex to simple, and throw any threat under the bus.

If the handlers can't manage a disciplined story, the campaign falls apart because the story will fragment into so many alternative plots that your opponents will seize upon. This is what happened to Hillary. She offered "Experience" and then "Change," until she morphed into "The Workers' Champion" before ending up for "Women's Lib." What was her story?

Obama, in image and voice and staged action must be the change candidate, even if his policies end up being the same old John Kerry and Clinton-Gore doctrine of clinging to the security of the center. It's the image, and the staged action and the story that all have to fit together to distract us from inconsistencies or ensure we disqualify any narrative gaps, contradictions or vulnerabilities that will inevitably emerge because stories and reality never quite coincide. Reality is prone to have its revenge eventually.

The poet Mark Doty was writing a memoir about his father when he realized that we all face this choice between an honest story and a coherent story. Campaigns do 'coherent' because they are story-shapers and manufacturers. "Honest" often comes across as too confusing, and too complex to fit into a sound bite or a five minute infomercial.[18] Reality never quite conforms to the dramatic perfection of the well crafted story. There is always some artistic license. But how much? Howard Kurtz back in 1995 said *"It's*

---

18 Mark Doty writes "But when it comes to talking about my father and my memoir, I have to choose between honesty and coherence" Mark Doty 'Return to Sender, Memory, Betrayal and Memoir' *Writers Chronicle Oct Nov 2005 P 17*

*possible for a candidate to go though a whole campaign and never
have one story written about him which is totally true."[19]*

He explained, *"Candidates must turn their lives into compelling
narratives to get elected."* That means that we are dealing with
story construction and story deconstruction, as one side tries to
dislodge or undermine the other's story. This is where the narrative
analyst sees the real drama, which is the story of the stories, if we
can step back long enough to watch it all unfold.

The real Obama and the real McCain are much more and much
less than their stories, as we will find out. And the New Orleans
experience is prophetic, in its way, of all stories. The levees break
to not only devastate a city, but to break a story and discredit an
entire administration. As veteran White House correspondent
Helen Thomas told a Literary Conference in April 2008[20], Katrina
pulled the final plank of credibility from under an administration
usually so tightly in control of its message.

So can the levees hold? Can the stories of the candidates hold their
coherence and substance to resist the hurricane force of the media
from now till November? That's the compelling drama for the
narrative analyst. Or will reality make a late comeback?

We will return to the McGinniss book to amplify the brilliant story
sense that Ailes and Treleaven had back in 1968. And what we will
be referring to is less McGinniss's text and more the appendices
that make up the last 80 pages of his book. They deliver the plan of
presidential elections that remain a primer of the modern
campaign. You can be sure that the campaign directors have read
them, or are thoroughly schooled in this approach.

But what <u>The Selling the President</u> does not have is an informed
insight into how stories work. Nor does it anticipate modern media
access where anyone with a computer can make a clip of McCain
or Obama and all their broken promises and post them on a
YouTube site and attract millions of viewers.

The campaign technology is now within reach of normal citizens,
which means that campaigns are much less in control of the storylines of their candidates and much more at the mercy of active
media-savvy citizens.

---

19 *Washington Post Magazine* July 16th 1995 Page 10

20 Bethesda Literary Festival April 2008

Everyone and anyone can be the trickster now. So we are in a different media environment. It feels like we are on the verge of another campaign revolution. That means that more than ever, we need a map to read how stories are made, how they are fitted with images and voice and staged actions to have us buy or reject the manufactured candidate. Narrative is the new aesthetic of manipulation.

Yet, for all the bells and whistles, it is still *story*. It is still the basic building blocks of what you need to tell a story. Technology makes them more available, more seductive and more sophisticated, but if the technology was altering the total pattern, then we would not be still so focused on candidate speeches, interviews and debates.

McGinnis's opening line is *"Politics in a sense has always been a con game,"* (McGinnisss, 26) and that is no great revelation. But the tragedy is that we keep on allowing ourselves to be conned. The Presidential Plot wants to make sure we aren't as easily conned this time.

CHAPTERS THREE THROUGH FIVE

BEGINNINGS, MIDDLES, AND ENDS

"A whole is that which has a beginning, middle and an end."
Aristotle

"Politics is just like show business. You need a big opening. Then you coast for a while. Then you need a big finish." Ronald Reagan[21]

Aristotle's *Poetics* talks about a story having a beginning, a middle and an end, and though that sounds pretty basic, it offers one of the more powerful tools a narrative analyst can use to understand the dynamics of a story as it applies to the Presidential Plot. We will give it the shorthand of BME.

Aristotle was on to something when he said that a sense of the whole demands a progression through time from a beginning, through a middle, to a recognizable ending. A sense of completion is less a feature of reality than it is of the story that we tell of it. And the sense one gets of a "fullness of time" comes in the way that a good ending arches back to a promising beginning. The beginning predicts and anticipates the ending, and the ending recapitulates the beginning. Like a good novel or a good piece of classical music, the finale resounds with a familiar theme so that our narrative logic intuits that this is where we were meant to end up. It is completing the circle, or closing the circuit of story logic.

If you are the candidate wanting to present your best story to the voters, you have to be very careful how you craft your beginnings and your endings, as Ronald Reagan knew, and you have to protect yourself from the predictable malaise of the middle.

Life is never so neat because we arrive in this world without anyone asking our permission, and most of us exit whether we want to or not. Life is no respecter of any larger story than birth and death when it comes to the pure biological facts, and whatever part of the middle we are in now, it grows shorter by the minute. But in our world of meaning-making, only in this middle passage do we get time to reshape our beginnings and design our endings, as we try to impose a template of time and place on the raw factuality of life and so map it into navigable space.

---

21 Robert Ornstein Paul Ehrlich New World, New Mind, Touchstone NY 1989 Page 5

A beginning is only a beginning because it has an ending and an ending is nothing unless it already had a beginning. And without a middle passage, there is the sense that either something has ended too soon or begun too late. A sense of completion comes from a sense of proportion, between how we distribute the middle between its end and its beginning. This is what one might call the deep structure of our story minds, long before we get into content or issues.

With this narrative sensibility, let us explore how the Presidential Plot is a negotiation of beginnings, middles and endings, and how the candidate's ability to shape these three key unfoldings of their story will help determine the success or failure of his or her attempt to get elected.

CHAPTER THREE

A SENSE OF A NEW BEGINNING

"Nourish the beginnings, let us nourish beginnings. Not all things are blest, but the seeds of all things are blest. The blessing is in the seed." [22]

"There is a magic in every beginning," wrote writer Herman Hesse and in those few words, he captures one of the allures of the Presidential Plot. It is always about change because America is about change, the land of immigrants, the land of fresh starts, always in search of a more perfect union. And change means endings and beginnings. Election time means we get to start again literally and more importantly, metaphorically. America, it appears, can be born again.

As a raw fact, one president leaves and another takes over. But what that change means in any larger sense is up to the storytellers. Is this the New Age? The New Frontier? The New Deal? Or is it continuity, the passing of the torch from the elder to the younger? No one campaigns on "Vote four more years of the same." Unless, as that astute political commentator, President George Bush explained, you are in mid-term.

> *"Let me start off by saying that in 2000 I said, 'Vote for me. I'm an agent of change.' In 2004, I said, 'I'm not interested in change --I want to continue as president.' Every candidate has got to say 'change.' That's what the American people expect."* [23]

One might be a lucky candidate following a successful presidency where the need for a change at the White House does not signal any great national malaise, and the people want the new leader to be sure to keep the good times rolling. But "change" is still the coin of the realm. If we were paid a dollar for every time a candidate used the words, 'Change' and "New' and 'Future' we could probably pay down the deficit. As even President Bush knows, there are things that the American people expect. Give us your "New Beginning" speech, we ask of Obama, or we ask McCain to give us your 'Change" speech. It's expected and it is what plays out at the Conventions.

---

22 Muriel Rukeyser

23 George W. Bush, Washington, D.C., March 5, 2008

But 'Change' and 'New' are empty words and an election is an empty event that begs for content and context. We know we are at the beginning, but the beginning of what? No one is going to say that this change won't mean much, or this is just your constitution at work, and it's no big deal.

No, every election in living memory has been billed as the most decisive vote in history, or in our lifetime, or this century. One wonders if one lives long enough, how many historic votes one can possibly register without exhaustion from the awesome responsibility thrust upon voters every four years. Perhaps that's why some years, we sit it out, just to recover from the weight of our duty to history.

Yet it is the irresistible temptation for every candidate to cast themselves into the role of a new Lincoln or the next FDR and aspire to define a new epoch of change. At least the new president knows that his name will be given to a stretch of at least four years and possibly eight. What will the Obama years be like? What will the Republican revival of McCain achieve?

Historians are already sharpening their pens to dissect the legacy of the Bush-43 years, and compare them to the Clinton years of Enlightenment, or the Golden days of Reagan, or the dark days of Richard Nixon.

When you look at the Presidential plot, you soon realize it is a book of beginnings, each interlocking and radiating out from the other.

- the beginning of the thinking you are running. Remember the Fred Thompson candidacy story, "Will he or won't he?" Or Al Gore?

- the announcement of your candidacy, which is a beginning that Obama held at the Illinois State House, where Lincoln was a Senator before he came to Washington to be President, and Hillary announced through an intimate webcast from her lounge room. McCain announced from New Hampshire, where in 2000, he very nearly beat Bush for the nomination. All that is carefully thought out, because the campaigners know this is the launch, this is where there is fresh energy, a new hunger for their story. They want to start with a surge.

- In the speeches at the end of each primary, Candidates have to keep redefining endings as new beginnings, whether they have won or lost, because beginnings keep excitement in the story, and where the end, even when it appears obvious, is delayed, waiting for a last minute miracle. "So it's on to Iowa…"

- The story of when it becomes clear you are the presumptive nominee, which is a mouthful in itself, but you have to have a story of what you are going to begin to begin to do, now that you are basically the chosen one.

- Then, there is the beginning of the campaign proper and the formal beginning at the Convention, in a speech that embodies the vision and the promise of your presidency.

- Then between the Convention and the elections, it's time to get down to business, when it really, really begins and the gloves come off.

Hence, candidates need to brush up on their commencement addresses and master the art of at least six beginnings on the actual campaign. And there is another beginning story you also need. As campaigns increasingly become exercises in preaching biography as destiny, you also need an Annunciation story, "What were the humble, childhood beginnings of this great man or woman?"

IN SEARCH OF YOUR OWN ANNUNCIATION STORY

If your name is to be a candidate for the hallowed halls of heroes, you need a story of the early manifestation of your destiny to be Chief Executive. One needs an epiphany story like a Buddha who journeys outside of the palace and sees the suffering poor, or a Jesus born in a Bethlehem stable visited by three wise Kings. The burden of the story is to inspire the nation and make them believe that this candidate was chosen by destiny to renew the American dream.

The locally tried and tested template is that of Abraham Lincoln, reared in a log cabin, never went to school, never went to college, a self-made and a self-taught man who lifted himself out of poverty and the nation out of slavery.

IN SEARCH OF LOG CABINS AND STABLES

Obama went to Harvard and McCain went to Annapolis, so neither were exactly reading by candlelight in a tent on the prairies, but we already see how they seek to appropriate that "Log Cabin" staple of the beginning story. Obama grew up in the heartland, in plain town

Kansas, (along with Honolulu and Java) and McCain grew up as a navy brat, always in trouble at school and in Annapolis, and one of the kids you expected to get into trouble rather than run for President.

It's endearing, and of course, it has to have some basis in verifiable truth. "I cannot tell a lie" goes the tradition. And even though George Bush Jnr. hardly grew up on a ranch, and Al Gore hardly cleared and planted the tobacco fields of Tennessee, they each spent enough time to turn a chapter of childhood into a volume called "My Early Rural years," when we lived on our wits and shot wild deer and channeled Daniel Boone. These are stories for children, because they are stories about children.

Recently archaeologists have discovered the site of George Washington's childhood cottage, so we are still digging into the childhood of Presidents. If Freud and the Jesuits are right and the child is indeed father to the man, then the child story is important. But it is another novelistic device of the Presidential Plot. It's Dickens in *Great Expectations* deciding we will know Pip better if we start him off as a kid lost on the marshes and terrorized by the runaway convict. This story of the personal beginnings has to fit the national myth in some rudimentary form. And remember, while history requires truth, myth only needs the minimum because it has the power to stretch facts to fit.

Imagine a candidate telling us that he never had to cook or wash or worry about anything, and that his mansioned childhood had nannies and servants and endless pleasures and holidays and an adoring mother as a personal coach and mentor. Would he be selected let alone elected? No, probably not, or at least not now because that was the childhood that resembles FDR's at Hyde Park. But he was a private man back then and could remain one, even to the extent of covering up his polio and dying in the company of his mistress, without Eleanor or the press knowing (until later.)

In modern elections, the Candidate's private childhood is floated on the public register of stories, and if the opponent or the press can find someone he bullied, or the girl he stole a kiss from, or a teacher who said he was an over-sexed little brat, then be assured they will. But more likely, they will wheel out Sister Immaculata from her retirement home to say that she always knew that little Johnny would be president. It's a scene lifted straight from the bible. Jesus as the babe in arms being taken to be blessed and the pundits at the Jerusalem Temple of the day saying, "Hey Mary, your little guy will go far."

34

One does not intend to demean this or suggest it is wrong but rather to say that it is just the Presidential Plot and a requirement of its syllabus. Someone like a Clinton knew that and made sure he had that iconic picture with JFK. He knew even as a teenager that he was consciously creating the story of prologue to his future Presidency.

PROMISE AND VISION

Hidden within the Candidate's beginning story is an underlying sense of promise, because this is no blind or automatic start up. This is a beginning with the promise of something unseen and unprecedented, and that expectancy casts its glow into the future with an almost messianic hope. Perhaps this is the one born to save the nation, and perhaps this is the time we can embrace a fuller sense of possibility than ever before. Obama's election book is called it "The Audacity of Hope" but it describes the energy of any beginning story because they all begin with hope. The miner hauls his wagon out to California in 1849 in the hope of finding gold, or the young woman marries the young man in the hopes of a happy life together. Hope is the starter fuel of the future.

Senator Obama has the narrative intelligence to cast himself in these terms, but they are the classical themes of Presidential elections that mark the possibility that people always sense in the end of one era and the beginning of another. It was just as true for McGovern as for Robert Kennedy as for Howard Dean.

While Obama's high rhetoric of hope has so excited the voters, it is less an expression of policy and more an expression of his narrative intelligence, and his ability to capture the energy of what he represents, a New Beginning, a Fresh Start. And it only stands to reason that he will cast his opponent as the "Stale ending" the "More of the same," the Bush Mark 3, to re-enforce his own narrative position.

If promise is twinned with hope, the other requirement is vision. It doesn't have to be detailed, or made up of a raft of policy statements on all the burning issues. No, it is more an image of where we are headed that evokes possibility and creates new energy. Ironically, Obama's adviser David Axelrod gave Clinton his catchy 1996 campaign slogan of "Building a bridge to the 21st Century." In this campaign, we seem to have an abundance of promise but a decided lack of vision. Neither candidate has broken through the level of the mundane in terms of any one image that radiates the promise they hope to represent. They could do well to listen again to the masters of the narrative of beginnings, such as

JFK who at his Convention speech, the formal beginning of the campaign, said, "We *stand today on the edge of a new frontier*"[24] And six months later, at the Inaugural Address, which is the end of a long series of beginning speeches, Kennedy deftly demonstrated how all the earlier beginnings were but a rehearsal for this real one:

> *"All this will not be finished in the first 100 days. Nor will it be finished in the first 1,000 days, nor in the life of this Administration, nor even perhaps in our lifetime on this planet. But let us begin."*[25]

ASSESSING NARRATIVE CAPACITY FROM THE TELLER'S POSITION

Aristotle's map of stories across the span of beginnings, middles and endings (BME) also provides us with a useful tool to assess the narrative capacity of each candidate from his or her telling position on the life span. We can all situate our life on that tri-scale, of young, middle age and old, and similarly, we can situate each candidate. Are they a Beginning, a Middle or an Ending in terms of their own life story? The answer will tell us how much narrative material they have access to in terms of life lived, obstacles overcome, goals achieved. When we use the same inquiry on the electorate, we can explore what their mood is and assess their receptivity to a candidate who is either a Beginning, or a Middle or an Ending and thereby, interpret the narrative matches and mismatches.

OBAMA AS A BEGINNING

Obama is a beginning. At 47, he is one of the youngest ever to run for President. (JFK was 43) He is just starting out, has a young family and has had less than four years as a Senator. He is new and untried even at the Senate level. If he doesn't succeed, he has a good twenty years to launch other attempts, and if he is successful, he will be an ex-president at 56. (Or 52)

HILLARY AS A MIDDLE

Hillary is a middle. At 61, we know her as First Lady and celebrity New York Senator with her family all grown up, husband retired, sort of, and a checkered history that is our history too. She fell

---

24 John Fitzgerald Kennedy, Democratic presidential nomination acceptance speech, July 15, 1960

25 John Fitzgerald Kennedy, in his inaugural speech, January 20, 1961

short this time but she can run again, and probably will. She remains one of the most powerful woman brand names in the world.

McCAIN AS AN ENDING

McCain is an ending. He is well known, has run before, and at 72, he is the oldest ever candidate to run for president. Reagan ran at 69 and retired at 77. McCain was a naval aviator, and then a long serving Senator, and now, his chapter three could be as the next President. But if he fails, it is unlikely he will run again. This is his last shot. He is defying the odds even to run at his age, and if he wins, he will have the last laugh on President Eisenhower who once said," *No one should ever sit in this office over 70 years old, and that I know.*"

So, let's try to tease this out a little.

Obama as a beginning story means that the drama and the excitement lies ahead of him and ahead of any nation that elects him as its leader. He will be only 56 when he steps down, meaning the nation will be hard-wired to his maturity curve. We will grow up with Obama, from a young, untested politician to hopefully, a seasoned and wise President. All the energy lies in the future, and he has barely begun to fight. He can't creditably argue that 47 years has made him the wise old man who knows it all, and has seen it all. David Axelrod, his chief advisor, knows this implicitly and that is why he has cast the Obama campaign as an election about the future. It couldn't be about anything else.

The beginning story generates high energy as it moves to the middle, into the uncharted, the unknown. Supporters are recruited to be fellow adventurers, and they, like their leader, will learn as they go. Any great ideas for reform will be the exploratory ideas of a young idealist. In other words, there isn't enough story material in the Obama file to pretend that this person has got all the experience. And though this has become the wedge issue for Obama opponents, accusing him of being too callow, it is a trap for Obama if he tries to over-correct in response. You can't be both fresh and new, but also tested and experienced, as Hillary learned.

The energy of his narrative depends on his sticking with the "new." He might deftly and humorously admit that experience rightly belongs to his middle and end opponents, but the election need not get hung up on experience if it's about a fresh start. What the beginner has is the openness to new learnings, fewer scars, someone less risk averse, and presumably with fewer lessons to unlearn. Change goes with new, not with old.

A younger person starting out has a date with destiny and a fresh slate to shape that destiny on. Beginnings don't have to be too specific and therefore, the demand for details is less a requirement for this story to work, and Obama knows that. But he needs a larger vision to flesh out the promise of what he is beginning.

Christopher Columbus on his journey of discovery didn't need to tell his crew the specifics because he didn't know them himself, but he invited them on the adventure to find the new world. Similarly the beginning story is more about the skill of the captain to sail the ship and navigate through the shoals and keep the excitement alive about what lies ahead, about what is over the horizon rather than be worried about what is left behind. The dominant themes are to 'explore and discover,' to 'create and learn.'

When you match up the stories of the candidates with what the electorate hungers for on this BME scale, Obama comes up trumps. The electorate wants a new beginning, and Obama is a new beginning.

Hillary had to 'begin again' if she was to fit, and somehow, McCain has to convince the nation either that America's new beginning is to go back to an old tried and tested warrior, or he has to so undermine Obama by proving that his new beginning is far too risky. McCain needs to cast Obama as too hollow and ambitious and untried. McCain would then win by default. There could be more electoral percentages in this narrative strategy than polishing his own story. It's the tactic of the spoiler, in that if you can't win on your own, make sure your opponent doesn't win, which means you win by not losing.

Hillary's campaign adjudged on this scale reveals a major mismatch. In contesting against Obama on the message of experience, she made a disastrous narrative choice, and didn't read the electorate's openness to Obama or anticipate his power to make the theme of change stick. But what else could he make it? What else could the Clinton campaign have expected?

Hillary went to the primaries as the middle, someone who had been there waiting in the wings, and who was now ready for the 3am phone call, but it was a classic narrative mismatch. She was running as if she was in a mid-term election, (experience) whereas she had to run as a new beginning to have any chance.

But she was not alone in a fundamental misread of the narrative necessities of an election. Think back to Gore v Bush in 2000.

After eight years of progress and reform, and success overseas in bringing peace to Northern Ireland and the Balkans, the nation for once, did not want a radical new beginning. They were not saying as they are today, that the nation was going the wrong way. Yet for all that, Gore presented himself as the change candidate, allowing Bush to position himself as the status quo. Bush would change the tone, by restoring honor to the Oval Office etc, but George Bush did not win on a platform of change so much as his vision of "compassionate conservatism." His was the story that Gore should have worn like an old suit, and he was entitled to since he was Clinton's anointed heir. But the Lewinsky escapade made Gore a little squeamish in proclaiming himself the next CEO of Clinton Inc. and it cost him. He made the classic mismatch of offering a New Beginning when people wanted a Middle, meaning less change and more continuity.

This may sound all a little too simple, but that is precisely the point. Occam's razor applies in that while we will tend to look for more complex explanations if our livelihood depends on it, at a more basic level, there are some simple assumptions implicit in the Presidential Plot as a narrative construct around beginnings that must be honored. If you get that wrong, nothing else is likely to save you.

WHAT'S WELL BEGUN IS HALF DONE

If you want to run for the Presidency of the United States, you need to have a good beginning story in your own biography, and you need to read the mood of the American voters who usually want a new beginning when they vote for their new president. Once you have assessed your own story, and whether you are a beginning or a middle or an end, you had better recast your story, no matter how old, into something compellingly new, because the voters will invariably choose the new beginning story that most appeals to them.

If you are a budding 18 year old thinking one day that you want to run for President, build your story now, and get that iconic picture with Clinton and with Bush, who will by then probably be redeemed as one of the great Presidents, and one with President Obama or President McCain. If you live in the city, find an uncle who has a farm in the south so you can at least have some story that will win the southern rural votes. You need a Kansas or Tennessee or Crawford, Texas story. And if you don't have tough or missing or alcoholic parents, then find some obstacle you have to overcome, or save someone's life or stick up for that gay friend, or get a black eye for defending the Mexican kid. You know what I mean. You will need that story one day as prologue to your Presidency, so get ahead of it. Live it now, to tell it later.

As environmental prophet, Paul Ehrlich,[26] points out, the narrative zones of highest energy are beginnings and endings. America is the New World, the land of the American Dream, the New Deal, the New Frontier. Every product that wants to grab out attention has to shout its newness. So, America has both a huge capacity and just as huge a vulnerability for beginnings and fresh starts. F. Scott Fitzgerald said America had no second acts, but even he had his second act as famous novelist turned screenwriter. Though America will boast of being the oldest democracy in the world, it still thinks of itself as a young country. It is that middle aged man of a nation that still thinks it is 18 and can do anything and be anything.

Such is the narrative framework into which all candidates have to fit their campaigns. If you have come to the end of something, what happens next? That is the narrative gene, or the Demonstrative Narrative Affinity (DNA) in our brains. So what now, and what next? The President is leaving office. And by statue, we have made it mandatory that every 4 or 8 years at maximum, we enter the story of new beginnings or a fresh start, or if it is not a fresh start, a new start. We get another chance, or the second chance of the redemptive arc that promises we can do it better or faster or fairer next time.

If a candidate is going to exploit this narrative landscape that is handed down by both the Constitution and history, he or she must somehow couch the story as to why I am a new beginning, why I am the promise of a fresh start and what is it I am beginning, what is the promise of your vision?

For the candidate who is already a known, it means some measure of re-invention such as the Nixon campaign did in 1968 and what the Hillary campaign this year never seemed to understand. She had to reinvent herself to fit the story of a new beginning and a fresh start, whereas Obama is a fresh start by definition. He personally embodied that, not because of what he said but because of who he was. His image told the story without words.

26 Paul Ehrlich, Robert Ornstein New World New Mind Touchstone 1989, p.4-5

In this election, narrative has turned the tables on traditional political wisdom. What would normally seem to be Obama's political disadvantage, of being a total unknown, has worked to his narrative advantage because a story of new beginnings can tolerate, even embrace, an unknown. The political advantage of Hillary, of being so well known, was a narrative liability when she had to be forced to fit into the compulsory plot of being a change candidate in a country deeply dissatisfied with its current leadership. You can't run on experience, and at the same time, effectively hook into the script for change. Or if you do, your experience better be the story of you as the "Change-agent," the "Maverick."

Political intelligence is not the same as narrative intelligence. Yet as campaigns become more and more based on narrative strategies, political intelligence has morphed into narrative intelligence because what is politically paramount is what serves the story. As Gore-the VP and Kerry-the famous war hero, and Hillary-the Celebrity First Lady- all learned the hard way, political assets can become liabilities when 'newness' becomes the most powerful narrative asset. Elections are normally new beginnings to tried and tested stories of patriotism and promise, but if a candidate can be both a new beginning to a brand new story of what America might yet become, that candidate might have an enormous advantage for wining the story contest that is the election.

CHAPTER FOUR

NOT GETTING LOST IN THE MIDDLE

"Beginnings are usually scary and endings are usually sad, but it's the middle that counts. You have to remember this when you find yourself as the beginning." [27]

"In the middle of my life, I lost my way," said Dante and he wasn't even running a presidential campaign. His hero was on his way to hell and perhaps for some candidates who get lost, it feels like just such a journey. No wonder that we have middle age crises and we have middle men, and we only feel "fair to middling," which all sums up a 'neither here nor there' sensibility about middles.

These are the risky parts of any journey because you are out in the middle of the ocean, a thousand miles from land one way and maybe a thousand miles away from the landfall ahead, and you have to trust your compasses and your reading of the stars at night because you have no other way of reckoning. In fact, you don't quite know if you are going forward or backward or anywhere.

Somehow or other, it's where we all live our lives unless we are a crying baby or someone breathing their last breath. If we aren't busy being born, according to Bob Dylan, we are busy dying, but Bob thankfully is still with us, and like us, he is still in the middle of his life, *in media res*. In the plot to be President, middle moments are those where there are no milestones to check off. There are a multitude of such middle passages in any campaign.

McCain about a year ago thought he was at the end, no money and staff deserting the ship, and yet, somehow, he turned that into a tough middle and came out of the trough. Or remember the more recent Hillary campaign team who were at the end though they desperately wanted to redefine it as a middle, that it was not over yet.

As we look ahead to the trajectory of the Presidential elections, there are middle passages behind and ahead where the captain of the ship needs to caution the crew that this is not the end, as when Obama won the nomination finally, or when McCain's poll numbers predictably tank in October. Then there is the pre-Convention slump, the distraction of the summer and the holidays and the foreign trips and the over-exposure of Obama in Berlin, Obama in

---

27 Sandra Bullock

Paris, Obama in London, or McCain attacking this and attacking that, and getting his own trip to Paris with Paris Hilton.

Leaders in a story of well defined endings and excited beginnings have to exercise real leadership in the middle, to re-orientate their troops by constantly injecting hope, by hanging tough, when the winds die and there seems to be no signs of movement or life.

One of the greatest exponents of this was Winston Churchill who was always redefining ends as beginnings and beginnings as ends to make sure that his British people kept the long view during World War Two and stayed inside the story he wanted to tell them.

When the troops safely retreated from Dunkirk without the Germans decimating their defeated force, it was time for Britain to celebrate their escape, but Churchill reminded his people that as great as it was, battles are not usually won by successful retreats. When the Allied forces finally pushed back against Germany's greatest General, Field Marshall Rommel, in El Alamein in North Africa, again the mood was to celebrate. Yet, Churchill cautioned in the much quoted phrase, "This is not the end nor is it the beginning of the end, but the end of the beginning."

When a candidate like Hillary loses a primary and the media says, 'It's over,' or when a candidate like McCain wins in New Hampshire in 2000 and everyone says, 'He's our man', the candidate with the narrative IQ knows that having a vivid sense of the middle will inspire patience, and the all important spirit of perseverance.

MIDDLES- WHERE REALITY LIVES MOST OF THE TIME

Middle passages are treated as fillers between beginnings and ends. They are dramatically not where the big pay off is, nor where the orchestra swells and the sun sets. Nevertheless it is where the real work gets done. It's easy for a candidate to name beginnings, or ends, 'Let's end the war in Iraq,' 'Let's begin to reform Washington,' 'Let's end our dependence on foreign oil,' etc, but the greater leader also needs to know what we are in the middle of right now.

Are we in the middle of a recession and a collapse on Wall Street? Are we in the middle of a global warming and weather meltdown? Are we in the middle of a peace dividend in Iraq? Are we back to a new Cold War having to deal with a resurgent Russia? Is China emerging as the new power?

The critical point about middles is that once you locate you are there, you can adjust, you can take corrective action. For instance, did 'No Child Left Behind' work? If it did, are we in the middle of an important educational reform that the next President needs to carry forward? If it didn't, what do we need to change to make sure it does? Already Obama seems to be demonstrating that he can read the middle with his own ideas of faith-based initiatives that would extend the work of President Bush.

Our biology[28] is wired to detect endings and beginnings, as to when the fire rushes through the house or the earthquake shakes the roof or the expectant mother groans with labor pains. We know that beginnings and endings call forth an extra special effort for which our bodies pump out the adrenalin. But the undeclared middles will leave us silently breathing in the poison before we know about it, or being effected by other changes that are invisibly incremental. Unless we have the canary in the mine shaft, we won't even know that we are under threat. Global warming has been such a case.

READING THE MIDDLE- "WHAT ARE WE IN THE MIDST OF?"

A powerful way to read the middle is to suspect that it contains endings that haven't become apparent yet, and beginnings that no one is paying much attention to. Though the mantra of the Presidential Plot is change, what candidates often pass up is the opportunity to identify the changes that are already happening, rather than the changes they themselves are going to bring. Bill Clinton was an expert at this, defining the times and re-describing the present as the platform for the future he was promising because it was already happening.

We might be in the era which spells the beginning of the end of newspapers and bookshops and Starbucks, but we can't be sure. And we might be at the beginning of an Internet.3 that becomes the new pub, the new disco, the new social and political glue of a community, with the explosion of the social networking sites. We might be in a middle that is the last days of broadcast journalism as we know it, with the rise of citizen journalism and potentially a whole new way of running elections and governing.

The place that most attracts savvy innovators and investors is the middle, because it will always be un-storied or under-storied. As Howard Kurtz writes, "Steady progress and decency in someone's

---

[28] Paul Ehrlich Robert Ornstein <u>New World new Mind</u> Touchstone 1989 p.5ff

life is boring."[29] Check out how many headlines that read, "Still in the middle of the peace talks," or "Still in the middle of fixing the Environment." Not sexy enough, and not enough dramatic movement.

But the middle has movement that is invisibly precipitous. Somewhere the snow is piling up and one last flake will bring the avalanche down, and someone is cooking the books and is overreaching and some accountant is starting to scratch her head as she adds up the financials that don't add up! Somewhere, someone is sitting on a story about the candidates and deciding if they should tell or not. (We wrote this before the John Edwards revelations.)

A story gestates like a baby in the womb, and though conception and birth can be wildly dramatic, the real miracle happens in between, as sinews and bone and blood form little feet and attach exquisite fingers to tiny hands. We all need and our candidates especially need an expansion of their Narrative IQ to read the middles. They are essential to mastering the Presidential Plot.

Reading the middle might have saved us from rushing into Iraq, if we had more patience with the weapons' inspectors. We display an almost childish impatience with a story, "Get to the point" we demand, or "Tell me the ending, quick! so I don't have to read it all." The media's rush to arbitrarily declare beginnings or endings, and politicians' appetite for pre-emptive headlines like "Mission Accomplished" can lead us to disastrous decisions. Being Storywise, we know ends and beginnings hold the narrative energy, but we should also keep reminding ourselves it is not necessarily where reality is. Most of the time, it is where we are, in the middle passage.

Science in its attempt to apprehend reality knows that it's always in the middle, that the latest experimental finding serves as a temporary ending, acting as a place marker on the forward journey towards the next break-through. If we can change the DNA of a mouse to create cancer immunity, we know that it might take 10 years for that to play out in possible human cancer treatments because it took possibly 10 years to get to this result. This end result becomes the middle of a potentially more expansive or focused search.

---

[29] Howard Kurtz *Washington Post* July 16 1995 Page 28

In contrast, politics is largely a story of impatience, generated by unreal narrative expectations, and by the finite electoral cycle itself. The false urgency of, 'If we don't get it done now before the next election, we won't be re-elected," works against our long term progress. Crisis mode is a hugely dramatic but largely misguided and a costly way to run a country.

The Presidential Plot has an un-storied middle that the nation needs to hear more about right now. Some of the problems that have taken us decades to create won't be fixed in one term, or in one electoral cycle of one Presidency, but you would never think that if you hear the candidates. How many candidates offer us that larger promise that they will build a platform so that at the end of their term, we will be ready to attack overdependence on oil, that they will work with the energy and car industries and take the first steps? That might be sensible and reasonable but who will vote for someone who promises to get ready to do something? That is clearly not a man of action though it might be the only kind of action that is achievable. You can't change whole economies overnight by simply changing the leader.

The story demands beginnings and ends, but the real work is done in the middle, like the enduring work of a Senator Ted Kennedy or a Chief Justice Rehnquist, people who have been around long enough to know that both Rome and Washington weren't built in a day and that significant achievement in public service usually demands a life commitment, not pretending that the nation's ills all can be fixed in one election or with one messianic candidate.

OBAMA- CAN HE LEAD US INTO THE MIDDLE?

In this campaign, Obama has the power of a beginning, and not much experience to offer us, to lead us through the middle passages. Less than four years in the Senate doesn't give you much to boast about. The Beginning leader must excite the base to stay with him through the middle passages, when the romance of the beginning has worn off. This is a man who has not even reached the 'chronos' of middle age, so he will dangerously overreach if he pretends to the nation that his election will provoke the 'kairos" or defining moment of the century. It might, but he can't promise that without getting above himself, and stepping outside his story. Visits to Berlin and London had the reverse effect for some voters because it seemed to show Obama getting way ahead of himself. He is a candidate who has more grace than gravitas, and he will get that soon enough, if he is going to succeed.

McCAIN AND CLINTON LEADING FROM THE MIDDLE

Senators McCain and Clinton had middle stories in spades. Hillary lost her chance to tell us about her "middle age" crises and what she learned. McCain has lots of wisdom being an elder of the Senate. He can see what we are in the middle of, and how like Churchill, we need to keep resisting the narrative impatience of offering short term solutions to solve long term problems such as global warming or the war in Iraq or the economy.

When endings look too fraught and beginnings too stressed, it pays to declare a middle. It gives candidates or a nation a chance to take a pause and work out where they are. It's a chance to consult the map. A middle means we are somewhere in between where we set out from, and where we are headed. If we feel lost, it is because we have lost our bearings by either forgetting what the journey was about at the start, or we forget what the destination was going to be.

Unless we revisit those two narrative anchors at the heart of our quest, our origin and our destiny, then we will drift and the Presidential Plot will unravel into mutiny or a sense of betrayal. Like a Columbus, the leader needs to keep telling us where we came from, and why we set out, and keep telling us where we are going. Then we can contain the anxiety of the undefined middle passage. But if you or your people forget origin or destiny, your story loses its power to shape the journey and your campaign falls apart.

WHAT HILLARY DIDN'T GET ABOUT LEADING FROM THE MIDDLE

Hillary Clinton has a gripping story of growing up, marrying the ambitious young Rhodes Scholar from Hope, and taking the torturous road to the White House. Hers is an epic story in itself, and being First Lady was already a peak of achievement and recognition. She could have served out her time in the Senate and retired with a story that would be a remarkable American story without any addition. But what else did Hillary want that she didn't already have? That remained the vital question, and most people answered the same as they did back in the 1990's, that this lady wants power-full stop, just like her partner.

If Hillary or Mark Penn had read and taken heed of the book <u>The Selling the President</u>, they might have decided that America needed to meet a new, more real Hillary, (as I have a few times) a Hillary minus Bill. We would meet the Hillary who would tell us why she messed up the health care reform and what she learned about what she did wrong, and why next time as President, she would get it right. Or about the inner story of why she stayed with Bill through her Lewinsky humiliation and link that story to her new story of her as a woman ascending to the pinnacle of power, the last unconquered Everest for women to climb.

There were many obstacles Hillary had to face, among them the second-guessing of motive as to why she, as a woman, would stay with an unfaithful husband, as so many women do, or why she was seeking to be President? The old narratives that portrayed her as grasping and manipulative would have to be tackled head on. But had she told us more of this inner story, you could guarantee that no cable TV and no magazine anywhere wouldn't carry this new Hillary story to the world. Obama or any other candidate would have struggled for air, because the Hillary brand is universal, and our fascination borders on an obsession.

She needed to exploit her telling position from the middle realizing that this was her best chance for reinvention, to declare a new beginning, and how her new story had grown out of the old, scars and scandals and all. But what we saw in image and action was the old, rigidly programmed Hillary. Though she could speak of her deep sense of a call to serve, she did nothing to disrupt the old story of Hillary's quest for Power with a capital P. The messes of the Clinton years which had her fingerprints all over them were not only not recanted but aggressively defended, even now. The health care fiasco was someone else's fault, and she was not wrong on Iraq back then. The Hillary that had built amazing Senate alliances across party lines hardly got any airplay.

Her story inevitably became entangled with sexism and a gender bias, but that was the given of the landscape she had to traverse because she was leading from an enigmatic middle. Middles can't totally change the story their history locks them into, but they can soften the edges, and there was a well tested playbook for doing precisely this.

In 1968, Roger Ailes and company were intent on creating a new image for Richard Nixon. They knew he hadn't much changed but they knew that with his record as Tricky Dickie, they had to show growth and maturation and wisdom. Hillary certainly came across as smarter, smarter than even Obama, but was she any wiser? If the Nixon Tricksters were advising her, they would have said that there was no dividend in defending her past. Hillary had to show

how she had grown through these experiences. Here is how Nixon did it.

> *"The natural phenomenon of growth...The great advantage of the growth idea is that it doesn't require a former Nixon-hater to admit that he was wrong in order to become a Nixon supporter now. He can still cherish his prejudices of the past; he can still maintain his own sense of infallibility even while he shifts his position on a Nixon candidacy."* [30]

What America soon realized was that the Clinton show had not changed at all. Bill won the academy award for playing the best supporting actor in a distracting role and that wrecked the deal. Here was Bill with what appeared to be his overweening ambition for her which got translated by the hostile media into Clinton's third term. He allowed himself and the media to so thoroughly upstage her that he demonstrated precisely why the new story of "A Woman as president" wouldn't work. She was too much of a threat to powerful men!

The Bill Clinton "Character" became an unattractive symbol of male dominance and patriarchy that Hillary had to beat in order to win. Had she sent him to Africa for six months to work on his AIDS charities, it might have been a better idea. But the ultimate tragedy of her defeat was that though she did have the story, she did not have enough confidence or courage to tell it. It was finally her own failure, and Bill's. History might unkindly claim that the Bill Clinton Story helped ruin the chances of two future candidates whose chances for becoming President were compelling precisely because they were uniquely placed to leverage the glorious successes of his own presidency. His legacy is laced with such ironies.

Why the Clinton campaign lacked the narrative insight to recognize they had a story to change, if not a candidate, is one mystery. But more amazing is how they squandered the advantage of their candidate who could mine the wealth of the middle for a veritable goldmine of stories that the media and the public would devour because they were our stories too.

Instead, the campaign began by recycling the old story of experience, and when that unraveled, it became whatever story was poll popular or expedient. The tragedy of the Hillary campaign was

---

[30] Joe McGinnis <u>The Selling of the President</u> 1968 p. 192

that Hillary had a much better story to tell and she only got to tell it at the end when, because it didn't matter, she could be honest.

When the country wants a new beginning, they certainly do not want an unrepentant middle who seems to have learnt nothing from the defining events that have shaped the nation's opinion of her. Perhaps the nation was not even ready for a new reformed Hillary but she never gave them that chance to decide.

CONCLUSION-THE MIDDLE IS NOT THE CENTER

The country is in the middle of an election, and it is in the middle of a war, and it is in the middle of an economic downturn. You would think that because reality likes to hide in the middle, that we would have a larger set of narratives at hand to story the middle, but we don't. What we have instead, as voters and Candidates, is the story of the Center. We cling to the Center as our preferred place of compromise, but the Center is not going anywhere fast. It's the point in the middle of a circle and the center is static whereas on a straight line, the middle is what you pass on the way to the end.

A story or a campaign that is fixated on the Center is not going anywhere as a story. You can offer the people your safe, poll tested Centrist position on abortion or on energy or on Iraq, which means you have weighed up both sides and come down in the middle, but that kind of middle signals that you have stopped moving, that this is the end, and a dead end at that. The rediscovery of the middle in the political story is a narrative way to get the story of Washington moving again.

Where are you on Abortion? I am in the middle, working towards reducing the number of unwanted pregnancies. Where are you on Iraq? I am in the middle, working towards an end that protects our troops and the future of Iraq. Where are you on the economy? I am in the middle, sorting what we need to do now to stem the crisis, and how we make sure it never happens again.

The middle position is the path that defines itself by the goal, whereas the Center is a stasis defined by and surrounded by a circle of compromise. And since we know how circles move, it is the very quintessence of spin, offering a position on an issue which seems to signify conviction or integrity but which comes out of a static view of reality that went out before Galileo.

51

We should be asking Candidates, "Where are you moving on the war?" or "Where are you moving on energy?" not 'Your position,' because as quantum physics tells us, every time you measure a position, you have to pretend you aren't moving yourself. If politicians give us positions instead of stories, we should be asking, "Why have you stopped moving on that issue? Is it dead or have you decided that you have apprehended the totality of its reality?"

Stories capture the dynamic of a flowing life, and the middle increasingly gathers to itself a revelatory force because life's meaning rarely discloses itself in one-hit epiphanies. Rather, meaning unfolds as life unfolds. If we aren't busy being born, if our lives aren't unfolding and we aren't embracing more and more of reality as it discloses itself in the middle, then we are zombies, the living dead, and is it any wonder that our politics is moribund?

CHAPTER FIVE

A SENSE OF AN ENDING

We seek closure not simply for healings' sake but because we can only tell the story when it has an ending and without an ending, we can't even be sure of what it all meant.

As Ronald Reagan knew from his film days, many a bad movie is saved by a great ending. What you experience as you leave is what is most likely to stay with you, compared to what you experienced on arrival, and even if the start was poor, it can still be salvaged. But a great beginning deserves a great end and sometimes endings do no justice to a great story. Just as a candidate who wants to win an election has to know how to do beginnings, and how to work from the middle, he or she must also know how to do endings because what a story means is usually how a story ends. If the cop catches the bad guy, we know it's a "Who done it," or if the ugly frog becomes the handsome prince and marries the princess, we know it's the romance of a fairy tale. Ends and endings are the narrative wrappings of goal and purpose, and what we are all about.

Just as we listed the number of beginnings that a Presidential campaign demands, so we add another list for the Book of Endings that have to be mastered, or endured or exploited, as in

- The end of the unsuccessful minor candidates in the primaries
- The end of the major candidates, and the winners who end their primary contest in victory, and the losers who exit stage left and get a cameo return to endorse the victor
- The end of the silly season of campaigning and the real contest
- The end of the campaign
- The end of the election for the loser
- The end of the campaign for the winner
- The end of the incumbent presidency and his government

Let's have a closer look at three endings that will exemplify the power of a narrative analysis. We have only one candidate whose telling position on the life map is from the ending, his chapter three of honor and service. We will begin by looking at how Senator McCain can bring an intuitive narrative sense to the story he tells. Then, we will examine the dramatic end of the Hillary Clinton campaign and what a great ending can salvage for posterity. And

53

lastly, though everyone seems to have wanted to forget, the ending of the current Presidency of George Walker Bush.

JOHN McCAIN –AN ENDING FOR A BEGINNING

John McCain has 72 years of stories, and what stories! If anyone has narrative capacity and advantage, it is Senator McCain. He is like your granddad with all those great yarns, which, whether they are all true or not, he knows how to truly tell them. "When I was a lad," and "When I started my first job," "When I was shot down," "When I was in prison," and "When I met your mother." All engaging tales. And it's not just because Senator McCain has more to tell. but because he comes from a long line of warriors who exemplify the very best in the American ideal.

If this ending is the narrative last stand of this candidate in public life, then this surely is the way to crown a life, to use all that wisdom in one final act of service to the country; that's a story totally in keeping with the McCain family epic.

It reminds one of the Tennyson's poems, *Ulysses* that was said to be JFK's favorite and quoted by Teddy Kennedy at his ending, his final 1980 concession speech, after losing the nomination. Homer's aging hero speaks about one final journey:

> *Come, my friends,*
> *'T is not too late to seek a newer world...*
> *To sail beyond the sunset, and the baths*
> *Of all the western stars, until I die...*
> *Tho' much is taken, much abides; and tho'*
> *We are not now that strength which in old days*
> *Moved earth and heaven, that which we are, we are,*
> *One equal temper of heroic hearts,*
> *Made weak by time and fate, but strong in will*
> *To strive, to seek, to find, and not to yield.* [31]

One can almost hear the voice of a Senator McCain, "Come, my friends," as he loves to say, "*T'is not too late to seek a newer world.*" But what gives it power is that this last journey is a reunion of the old crew and a re-enactment of the earlier adventures. This is no hero setting out on a virgin quest. Its pathos is in the return, and in the faithfulness of friends to the undying quest, to what Senator Kennedy said at the Denver Convention as he reprised his 1980 speech, "The hope rises again, the dream lives on." An aging hero is

---

[31] Alfred Lord Tennyson *Ulysses*

not a character we expect to bring about revolutionary change. Leaders like the aging Mao who tried it in the Cultural Revolution almost ruined China, and more recently, the aging Mugabe's and Fidel Castro's of this world too easily forget that young revolutionaries are prone to grow into oppressive reactionaries.

The only recent examples of leaders of senior age who have wrought great change even in their later years are Popes, people like John XXIII and John Paul II. As an 80 year old, Pope John Paul II visited his beloved Poland for the last time and thousands of young people took up the chant, "You are young, you are young." If John McCain had that sort of charisma, he might be able to fit the recipe for change, but it's a tough act apart from that. We simply don't have these sorts of elder stories in our cultural memory.

Since the Senator's telling position is from the end of the Life Story Cycle, not the beginning or the middle, he has to cast his message of change like a Ulysses, as a recapitulation of the themes of his life. He most of all can tell us the story of "experience" and the story of "wisdom" which is not as authentically available to younger candidates. And what lends pathos and urgency to it is that this is the last chance for an aging character, that this is his final summons to the country that urgently needs to renew itself through a return to the time tested values that have guided McCain's own life. That's the powerful change story that Senator McCain can coherently carry in his narrative.

When we look at ancient epics like Homer, we will see similar patterns to what Ulysses voices in the poem. It is a loyalty to the past that inspires one final journey to the future, *to strive, to seek, to find, and not to yield.* Hence, McCain to fully claim the power of his story position needs to connect running for President to his life story and his Life position as a Teller heading towards Life's glorious end. He can leverage the emotion of his final mission to serve and to restore honor and peace and prosperity to the nation.

It will not work to pretend to be hip or new or to be a new beginning. He can never portray that. The fact that he doesn't do email or use all the latest gadgetry of modern life is a signal of his quaintness, his grandfatherly status. But also, it re-enforces his message of a return to fundamental decency, to old fashioned civility, to honor abroad and to fairness at home. We will flesh this out in a later chapter when we come to explain how Senator McCain can win by winning the best story competition that is the election.

As a veteran and survivor, he might well take an inspiration from the Vietnam memorial in Washington DC that honors his service and the service of 56,000 of his dead comrades. The beginning and end of the Vietnam Wall rests at the deepest part of Maya Lin's "slash in the ground" where 1957 links to 1975 and the Alpha connects to the Omega. The ending reconnects to the beginning, and the story finally feels whole, and complete.

That is the epic nature of the grand story that McCain can offer his nation now, and just as he and John Kerry worked so tirelessly to bring the last soldiers and MIA's home, John McCain's mission as President is to repatriate the nation to its timeless values, to bring the nation out of the prison of its pessimism and its waste and restore honor and the honor code to our culture too easily corrupted by deceit and greed.

AN ENDING TO CHANGE THE BEGINNING- HILLARY'S END

If we want a perfect example of the power of an ending to change the story, we need look no further than the definitive end of the Hillary campaign. She wasn't going to play the gender card just as Obama was not going to play the race card and both were not going to play the ageism card against John McCain. It was always going to be a boring old card game at that rate, if you are not going to play your best hand.

But Hillary's campaign veered and swerved like a drunken bowling ball, narrowly avoiding the gully until it finally zeroed in on Obama's wizened view of the working classes whom he typecast as lost souls "clinging to guns and religion." There she found her voice and her second chance.

When that did not win the super delegates the way it was winning the voters, and more particularly, when it was not winning the money to compete with Obama, Hillary's speeches started to sound like a public television fund drive. Send money to hillary.com. We all realized that she was in a tricky middle passage beset with an Obama perfect storm that she was unlikely to survive. While Obama was speaking triumphantly about the audacity of hope, Hillary was living audaciously on the edge of defeat.

To the end, she remained the enigmatic candidate. She remained trapped inside the story that had dogged her for a decade, the Lady Macbeth of endless ambition, with a will to power so brazen as to be breathtaking. The electorate had a sense that someone who wants to wear the pants and be President that much might not be the best person to put there. She was cocky and she was entitled, but no more than a Bush or a Kennedy. But being a woman with such ambition did not befit our stultified womanly stereotypes because, in many men's eyes, she was no lady!

A healthier criteria for national leadership and for an electoral process that could enthrone a megalomaniac, would be to never elect anyone who wants it that bad. Our modern process means that, by definition, we only elect egomaniacs. Gone is the old modesty, the pretense of the good old days when men were gentlemen, and where, to grasp at power was to appear unseemly. Today the Presidential Plot demands the opposite. To even qualify, you have to display an almost pathological desire for power, for how else would anyone spend so much money and endure the rigors of a campaign and its exposure. It becomes 'Elect me because I want it,' not 'Elect me because the people want it.' The engine of a story, the *jouissance*, the desire is perverted or misplaced. It is supposed to be the desire of the people that drives the story, but in our media saturated world, it has come to be driven by the desire of the candidates.

And then, on that same fateful Tuesday evening in June, Senator McCain was decked out in front of the lime green monster and showed he truly was in the Bush league of champion line fluffers and slogan manglers. Meanwhile, Obama was stamping his headline of "The end of Hillary-the beginning of Obama," on the night by rallying his troops back in Iowa where he had first won the white vote to become the third apparition of the Come-Back kid, only he was not named Clinton.

But Hillary did not go gracefully into the night, as the media had demanded. No, she was still raging against the dying of the light or at least, she was going to sleep on it, to think more about "What does Hillary want?" Freud must have been smirking in his grave, because his unique contribution to male's incomprehension of females was entitled, "What do women want?"

The fact that a candidate was going to stop and think about it, that she did not have the instant sound bite or the talking points was quite a radical notion for this campaign, and actually for this country come to think of it, if we do come to think of it, which we often don't. But Hillary did, and her narrative IQ kicked in big time with her impending sense of the end. She was going to take back control of the story because she would get to tell the ending.

Friends I know who attended Hillary's finale at the Building Museum in Washington went to rage, and console and do anything but surrender, but they came away angry because Hillary had to shush them, so that she could praise and thank them. Under the spacious atrium of the Old Pension Building, she offered them a symbolic victory, by declaring 18 million cracks in the glass ceiling and re-titling her story as, 'The prologue to the first woman President.' She attached her valiant campaign, its doggedness and its resilience to the annals of the suffragettes and to Elizabeth Katy Stanton and at the end, pledged her undying fealty to the man who beat her for cash and super-delegates, but not the popular vote. (And in case we forgot-it was 18 million.)

For the media who have made an industry out of attacking Hillary, you would have thought this would have been heard as another shameful pander, to rewrite history, to shift not only the goal posts as she was accused of doing in demanding disqualified Florida delegates be counted, but actually shifting the playing field, that you thought we were playing a footy game of experience and "I will be your champion" and "I will get health care through for the workers" but it was not about that at all. It had become "This was the woman's suffrage movement 60 years later, and I was fighting for women all along." This wasn't football with the lads, it was women's lacrosse.

The upshot was that the media bought it. Only columnist George Will thought she was substituting vindication for victory, but no matter. She knew the narrative energy field was there for an ending, as it always is. How come John Kerry and Al Gore and Ted Kennedy all gave their greatest speeches at the end, when it didn't matter? Because the end zone is the narrative territory with the charge. It's where you rush on to the field to get the emotional interviews, "How do you feel?"

Endings are super-charged for history, for the final headline, the obituary, and she gave it to history, which will forget most of the campaign, but it will remember how she ended it, and as smart commentators suspected, the "I'll be back" undertones. Here was Hillary trying out the next story, should she decide to run again. Her narrative sense that had deserted her all campaign finally kicked in because she realized an ending can also be a beginning. Perhaps next time, she will play the gender/equality card and be who she is, not whom she thinks people or the media want her to be.

There is another ending that is critical to assess if you are a presidential candidate. It's the handover story, the President who goes before you. Recently someone in the aviation industry told me about the new generation of jets that will carry 800 passengers, and how the back draft of these gigantic craft after take-off is so powerful that the next aircraft has to delay a few extra minutes to not get swept up in the vacuum.

Call it a backdraft, or a wake, but you are following before you are leading and whatever party you are in, you are applying to enter the Presidential story, a story that pre-exists you in the particular incumbent you replace. Therefore, you have to connect to, or speak to the space now left vacant and waiting for you to fill. Bush told the nation he would restore dignity to the Oval office, no more hanky-panky with interns, and he seems to have at least kept that promise. But for the rest, you know if you are McCain or Obama, that you won because your greatest asset was probably your family name was not Bush.

You enter into the White House as a house of tattered ghosts, with the voices of Rumsfeld and Karl Rove and George Tenet and Brownie and Colin Powell, and all the rest still echoing in the corridors. The country will be suffering a kind of Post Traumatic Bush Disorder and like every other presidency, the golden rule seems to be, whatever they did, we won't do it like that anymore. If they create a huge department of Homeland Security, we will break it back into separate departments. If they had dogs as pets, we will have cats. If they had blue carpets in the Oval office, we will have green. And for the first twelve months, or longer, you can easily justify any policy by saying, it is not doing what your predecessor did and that will immediately make it right. But more critical than the window dressing of office, you will have to assess, 'What is the shape of the listening that Bush has left the country in?'

Think back to early 2001 when Clinton and his team briefed the Bush administration and warned them of a resurgent Al Qaeda and Osama Bin Laden. Of course, the body politic in 2000 was charged with the electricity of Kenneth Starr's pornography and the stains on a certain dress, and the press fed our excited appetite for salacious politics right up till September 10th when the big news was an intern who had gone missing, feared murdered, and a Congressman under suspicion. Meanwhile, Bush was following in the wake of a two-term Clinton and showing no willingness to listen to a Party that he and Cheney had just removed from office.

Could it have been any different? The 9-11 Commission and other reports suggest a fatal disconnect in the Bush-Clinton handover and some lessons to be learned. The new President might win an election repudiating his predecessor, but once elected, his responsibility is to serve the bigger story of his office. And the two Presidents have to so conduct an ending and a beginning that connects the assumption of power with the ongoing affairs of state and the awareness even if they are from different parties, they are now in the same story.

BUSH'S POWERFUL ABSENCE FROM THE CAMPAIGN

Assessing the wake of your predecessor is part of the point of entry decision a candidate makes. Bush is not ending but he has ended, he has gone, people aren't paying any attention to him and he is not paying any attention to us, there is a vacuum the size of a Jumbo Jet. It's like we have already quit this guy, and can't wait for his lease to be up on 1600 Pennsylvania Avenue. Even his supporters feel the country is stale because the Bush ending is going on too long. Go already! The longer he stays, the more storytellers come out with their confessions and their "Don't blame me" memoirs.

What is unusual in this cycle is that the president is essentially absent from the narrative landscape, and that opens up enormous opportunities that usually aren't there. Clinton was not popular with the Gore team but he was still an effective executive and his approval ratings were high and getting higher. Bush had to target him as he entered the fray. One of the signs of a failed presidency is that the president has no power to even sway the vote for his successor, except that any plausible candidate will have to show that he is NOT Bush to win

That is surely a sad way to exit the Presidential Plot. Our last experience of Bush as president is as an absence, as someone who couldn't even generate an audience of his band of brothers. He has to go to Liberia to be greeted as a savior. The show flops if no one is clapping at the end, or only clapping politely. Presidents are supposed to leave and go to the garden of heroes and enter the pantheon of Mt Rushmore, or on the other hand, leave in disgrace as a villain a la Nixon. Either way, you still have a story to tell. But this second term ends with a whimper and a whine, well actually; it ends with a loud yawn, and the next election is about waking people up and turning them back on to the possibility that we can have a President who is effective. What does that feel like?

The fate of every President is that he can become the same story he condemned in order to get elected. You become the person your mother warned you about not to mix with. You say Washington is broken, and then, move to Washington and people will say after a few years, you broke it. You came as a Uniter and you end up dividing. You promise no more nation building, and you end up smashing and then trying to rebuild at least two, to the neglect of the nation you were supposed to be running.

As we speak of the narrative power of endings, we should note that if Bush is not evident and not spoken about, he is the silent force who has shaped the landscape and created a hunger for something vastly different. Whatever we want, America seems to be saying, we don't want any more of that. Please! And it is the power of a bad and sad ending that adds voltage to the hope for a new beginning.

BUSH'S REPUTATION IN POSTERITY?

Our narrative understanding of Presidencies alerts us to the fact that the Bush story will not end on January 20th 2009. Rather, it will all depend on the success of his successor for one thing, and secondly, it will also be subject to the continuing unfolding of events that were triggered in these last eight years and are still "Unfinished Business."

If Bush was a stellar success with the economy and in foreign affairs, the Clinton years would have retained the stigma of personal scandal and wasted opportunities. However, the worse the Bush team seemed to perform, and the greater secrecy and perfidy lately revealed by a finally vigilant press and Congressional oversight means we find ourselves thinking back to the Clinton years as the glory days. Bush in the short term helped the Clinton reputation immeasurably. In the longer term, it is not quite as easy. Clinton is now more likely to be the anomaly, the interim between the end of the first Cold War and the beginning of perhaps the second Hot War or the next Great Depression.

What is predictable is that time will be kinder to the second Bush administration than the media or the polls are at the moment. He will become the elder statesman, and as the situation in Iraq inevitably reaches some sort of status quo, (as it seems to have already) and the drama of terrorism is perhaps swallowed up in the greater drama of economic or energy crises and a revival of old fashioned balkanization in Europe, we will look back nostalgically to the moral certainty of a President who acted decisively and took his chances.

It doesn't seem likely now, but President Bush's last year, when he has been all but neglected by the media and considered a lame duck, might be considered his best year when he achieved more than his previous seven in slowly and determinedly seeing through to the end the course of his muscular diplomacy.

If the economy picks up and the oil price drops, and the dollar continues to recover, the new President might be inheriting an improving situation even as he wins office by declaring that the nation is in dire straits. (as JFK and Clinton did.)

The irony of history is that every President gets at least one or two more terms to rule in posterity, where the successful ones have to suffer the humiliation of revisionism before they establish some stable spot in the pecking order of good, better and best of presidencies. Even the worst performers get the same second chance. The point with George Bush is that he will be remembered more fondly as an ex-president simply because we will have a new President to blame, and because when you are that far down, the only way to go is up. In a strange way, he has had a greater impact on the world than William Jefferson Clinton and, for good or ill; his presidency has set new benchmarks that will be the measure of future presidents, either to repudiate or to return to.

History might be able to ignore the Clinton years because not much happened and because success is boring, but it will speak of the Bush years as some sort of watershed, a high water mark of Government power and a low water mark of America's moral leadership in the world. His story will live on, and George Bush won't suffer the fate of his predecessor who felt compelled to re-insert himself into public life to get his wife elected. He not only did not succeed, but he also reminded America of the worst of the best years they had with him in the last decade of the 20th century.

Perhaps, as some critics have said, President Clinton has never quite recovered from his recent heart surgery. But the lessons for past presidents are to let the mystic chords of memory do their mythologizing work, and don't do anything but the expected acts of a senior statesman to protect your growing reputation as an esteemed ex-president. George Bush's father is the perfect example. What admirable restraint he has shown these past eight years, and he never tried to get Barbara elected to anything.

If a limited but belated redemption could happen to a Richard Nixon, our beloved crook of a president, whose actions at Watergate and the cover-up look rather tame compared to WMD and Abu Ghraib, it can happen to a George Bush too. His place in history is assured, and he only has to live long enough to experience the natural narrative vindication of time. It is harder for all of us as we age to not look back with a mixture of nostalgia and forgetfulness, and therein lays the prospect of forgiveness.

OCCASIONAL COLUMN

HOW TO LOSE IN A WINNING WAY

The sad end of a great lady and a lousy campaign

The beginning of a story and the end of a story is where it has the most chance for traction. It is where the energy fields are created. It's the middle where the story can easily get lost, or attention can drift. Last week and the weeks before, the commentariat were calling for the end, for Hillary to quit, to surrender, give it over to the new kid on the block. But of course, Hillary wouldn't be Hillary if she didn't do it her way, showing scant respect for those cable talking heads who always talked as if they, not her, were running her campaign. Yet they too were drawn into this energy field of the narrative end zone. How a story ends helps us decide what the story meant. And if it was the cable TV's story, they would have ended it five weeks ago, but alas it was not their story; it was the candidate's and her people. And how she ended it revealed a grace and sense of occasion otherwise lacking from the campaign. There are precedents for such times.

On the deck of the *USS Missouri* in Tokyo Harbor, General Douglas Macarthur took the declaration of unconditional surrender from the Japanese Government in 1945. Flanked by his Admirals, including Admiral McCain Snr, it was a formal, brief and dignified end to what had been one of the most barbaric and undignified wars in living memory. But MacArthur, with his ear for history, his eye for the catching photo op and his sense of occasion, briefly accepted the instruments of surrender with a few words that did not even try to capture the meaning of this ending. He simply declared the war in the Pacific over.

At Appomattox Courthouse, Robert E. Lee negotiated with General Ulysses Grant so that his Confederate Army would retain some dignity. Grant allowed them to keep their horses and their side arms and dismissed them to go home to their former civilian lives. He did not even ask for Lee's ceremonial sword.

In World War One, Germany signed the surrender in the infamous train carriage at Compiegne that Hitler resurrected in June 1940 to take the surrender of France and later, had the carriage destroyed.

History warns us forcefully that any surrender that robs formal dignity from the defeated is likely to become the first act in the undeclared war of the future. You can accept losing your stake if you have to, but not your status or your standing.

Hillary did not concede on Tuesday and she wanted to end it on Saturday surrounded by her supporters and with pride and dignity. She wanted to lose like a winner, and not like a loser. She was not going to simply slink away like some defeated football team at the Super Bowl. Nor was she going to surrender her sword, because that sword is the weapon Obama now needs. The media covered it like a State Funeral, speculating on what she needed to say in concession, and whether her supporters' grief could be assuaged. Hillary gave one of the greatest speeches of her life and turned a carping media into awe-struck witnesses to a piece of history that will remain one of the more memorable moments of presidential politics.

Hillary may have had a presumptive beginning, and got totally lost in the middle, but she certainly knew how to end it. In that alone, we saw a greatness that redeemed the rest by giving it a new meaning that alas, had Hillary discovered 18 months ago, might have made a different ending altogether possible.

POSTSCRIPT

"Begin at the beginning and then go on till you come to the end: then stop." [32]

To practice what we are preaching, we need to return to the beginning, and to what Aristotle told us in his *Poetics* about the sense of the whole being a function of beginnings, middles and endings. The Presidential Plot works as a Three Act Play, and whatever the content, this BME axis is a central spine to which we must attach the flesh of specific meanings, and which allows us to follow the path of the Candidate's journey. Without these clear markers, the story will have no direction and suffer from a sense of confusion or even feel out of sequence.

---

[32] Lewis Carroll <u>Alice in Wonderland</u> Ch 13

The chaos of any political campaign is formidable enough for managers and Candidates to impose some control over, because no story can fully accommodate the unpredictable world of hurricanes, Wall Street collapses and Russia invading its former satellite states. In Chapter Ten, we call these Wild Card entries. But a narrative analysis will look for how strong a campaign's sense is of their Beginnings, Middles and Ends, and their power to weave a story that allows for the unpredictable without at the same time becoming unpredictable or incoherent or falling apart because it is forever changing to fit the latest polling result.

WHY REALITY LAUGHS AT THE TRAGIC ENDING

Because of our lust for heroes, American culture sets up every presidential candidate for tragic ends, because heroes only inhabit tragedy. Think of Lincoln or FDR or JFK or MLK, our faculty of giants in the American story are all of them, tragic giants. Perhaps only George Washington escaped the fate of the gods and probably because he was the first President to eschew any of that personality cult that was usually part of the sovereign's tools of power and influence. To this day, his Presidential Library is still his modest study at Mount Vernon.

Perhaps the Presidential Plot is not meant to end in tragedy. Film critic Frank Pittman, who writes in *Psychotherapy Today*,[33] has a theory that the goal of therapy is to turn tragedy into comedy, and that as far as stories go, comedy allows for so much more reality than tragedy. Comedy embraces the mistakes and the hypocrisy, and can absorb the egotism with a knowing wink, refusing to take anything too seriously. Perhaps *Comedy Central* and Jon Stewart and the *Colbert Report* have much to offer to inspire a healthier and less tragic sense of an end, and deflate the chronic seriousness that so pervades the electoral realm. Yet if Washington developed a sense of humor and the media were able to laugh at their own ridiculous sense of self-importance, *Comedy Central* would be out of a job. Even if the writers guild goes on strike, so long as Washington is up and running, comedy and satire will have more than enough to feed on, until we find a better story to pick a president that isn't so epic and isn't so tragic.

---

33 Frank Pittman MD *The Family Therapy Networker* 1995 "T. S. Eliot has told us that 'human kind cannot bear very much reality.' But we can bear far more in comedy than in tragedy, because in comedy we don't have to be perfect, we are not alone in our suffering and we get to change in time to not die from our hopeless emotional position. If we are fully embedded in our comic perspective then we can bear all the reality life has to offer."

CHAPTER SIX

THE GENRE, THE EPIC AND THE SAGA

"Having now finished the work assigned me, I retire from the great theatre of action; and bidding an affectionate farewell to this august body under whose orders I have so long acted, I here offer my Commission, and take my leave of all the employments of public life." [34]

The core question that the American people face every Presidential election cycle is not economic or even ethical, it is theological: Do we want a God or do we want a human? And largely our answer is 'We want a God please," though we will settle for a hero. Even if it means we are going to risk major disappointment when the candidate shows the same human flaws and frailties that all human flesh is prone to, we hope we never have to deal with that, and almost expect the powers that be to protect our innocence. Our "Audacity to Hope" is the story of us voters more than any candidate.

It's the same Faustian bargain we make when we want somebody to be both likeable and competent, and if we have to choose, we want someone to be likeable most of all. It's amazing how many years the long-suffering nation can endure incompetence. So long as you are a decent enough guy, we understand you are doing your darndest. Aw Shucks! We wouldn't want an incompetent pilot flying our plane to London, but we will tolerate an incompetent pilot flying the nation into a perilous future.

Herein are the in-built contradictions in the Presidential story-that he has to be someone we would chisel on to Mt Rushmore next to the original George W and at the same time, be Mr. Likeable whom we would gladly share a Bud and a hot dog while watching the Super bowl.

Why do we have to make these choices at all? If we were on the search team for the new President of Harvard or the new CEO of Microsoft, we would understand pretty immediately that heroes and gods are not in the search criteria, but they are a different story, belonging to a different genre. The Presidential Plot as we have discovered is its own peculiar genre, a story formula that repeats its patterns in such a way that we know exactly how to read it.

---

34   1783 George Washington as he retires his Commission

What is peculiar about the Presidential Plot as a genre is that it is a very old form, ancient in fact. It's an **epic**. This is a story for heroes, not humans. And yet, likeability is the hero factor. It's a measure of how much we like and admire the character. If we don't like you, you aren't going to be much of a hero.

"Epic" originally means a long narrative poem like Beowulf or Gilgamesh, or films like *Narnia* or *Lord of the Rings*, and they are stories about action on the grand scale, not a story about ordinary humans. Even George Washington, retiring his commission, knew he was retiring from what he called the 'great theatre of action." He knew he was on an epic stage. Presidents consort with or fight against the gods and in fact, are expected to be half-divine themselves.

But let's take a closer look. Here is one learned Professor from Carson Williams College, Dr. Wheeler, and his definition of the EPIC. Let's see if we can recognize any traits of a presidential campaign and check off those that fit.

What is an Epic?[35]

An epic in its most specific sense is a genre of classical poetry originating in Greece. The conventions of this genre are several:

> *(a) It is a long narrative about a serious or worthy traditional subject.*

The Presidential Plot as Subject matter is serious and worthy-This is a weighty story that matters- so this fits easily-CHECK

> *(b) Its diction is **elevated in style**. It employs a formal, dignified, objective tone and many figures of speech.*

The high blown rhetoric of both the McCain and Obama camps are certainly elevated, talking about love of country and the fate of the free world-CHECK-though sometimes the tone is perhaps not so elevated.

> *(c) The narrative focused on the exploits of an **epic hero** or demigod who represents the cultural values of a race, nation, or religious group.*

Absolutely! America votes for its new face, its new voice for the world-CHECK-and note the word 'demigod'.

---

35 Dr. Kip Wheeler :web.cn.edu/kwheeler/documents/Epic.pdf_ Used with permission. Emphasis mine

(d) The hero's success or failure determines the **fate of an entire people** or nation.

Absolutely! The tone of 'This is the most important election in your lifetime" blah, blah, blah, is a tell tale sign that we are in an epic story-CHECK-which doesn't mean we aren't living in historic times, though did anyone besides Frank Fukuyama not live in historic times!

(e) The action takes place in a **vast setting**; it covers a wide geographic area. The setting is frequently set some time in the remote past.

Fifty states, and Iraq and Berlin and London and Columbia- and yes- sometimes the rhetoric might make us think we are back in ancient Rome or Athens or even the Garden of Eden- CHECK

(f) The action contains superhuman feats of strength or military prowess

The marathon campaign itself is a test of superhuman strength, and previous military prowess helps prove you have lived an epic life before this your latest blockbuster -CHECK

(g) Gods or supernatural beings frequently take part in the action to affect the outcome. This **supernatural intervention** often implies two simultaneous plots.

Is that why Obama goes to see Rev. Graham and preaches at a Chicago church, and why God or maybe it's just James Dobson is mad at McCain? Or Obama? Or Hillary? And why Obama witnessed to Jesus in his heart, and McCain visited Our Lady of Guadalupe. Yes, this all makes sense, that this is a campaign about faith too. God Bless America. -CHECK

(h) The poem begins with the **invocation of a muse** to inspire the poet-- i.e., a prayer to an appropriate supernatural being. The speaker asks that this being provide him the suitable emotion, creativity, or diction to finish the poem. Often the poet states a theme or argument for the entire work.

Themes-yes, "Obama for change" or "McCain for reform" and Obama starting in Illinois, and invoking Lincoln as Muse when he says:

"And that is why, in the shadow of the Old State Capitol, where Lincoln once called on a divided house to stand together, where common hopes and common dreams still live,

69

I stand before you today to announce my candidacy for President of the United States of America." [36]

Does that sound epic enough? CHECK

> *(i) The narrative starts **in medias res**, in the middle of the action. Subsequently, the earlier events leading up to the start of the poem will be recounted in the characters' narratives or in flashbacks.*

All those beginning stories, "A child in Kansas," "My father in the Navy." Yes-though McCain needs to beware of having too many flashbacks for fear that he seems time-challenged- CHECK

> *(j) The epic contains long **catalogs** of heroes or important characters, focusing on highborn kings and great warriors rather than peasants and commoners.*

We have and will hear about the occasional "commoner" with a sob story, the choice between health care and food, etc, but mostly, we will hear about Reagan and JFK and Martin Luther King Jnr. and all the obligatory heroes that this potential hero wants to claim his blood line from- CHECK

> *(k) The epic employs extended similes... at appropriate spots of the story, and a traditional scene of extended description in which the hero arms himself.*

I guess the traditional scene of arming oneself is the Convention, and extended similes, "Audacity of hope" "Bringing people together," "The Land of Promise," "Reforming Washington," etc is all there- with all the other campaign slogans -CHECK

> *(l) Often, the main protagonist undergoes a terrifying journey-- sometimes a **descent into the underworld**--i.e., into hell or the realm of the dead.*

Yes, ask Al Gore, and John Kerry and Bob Dole and Hillary, and for Bobby Kennedy, tragically too true. CHECK

It's not hard to see why the epic form does the job. This is not simply the selection of a CEO. This is the selection of a person whose personal biography will enter the hagiography of the nation, who will be the head of state, the face and the voice of America. If he sneezes, America catches a cold. If he chokes on a pretzel, Washington coughs and splutters.

---

36 Barack Obama "Obama declares his Candidacy" ABC News Jake Tapper Kate Hinman Feb 10,2007

It all makes eminent sense as you read back through history because a nation that is born from a myth about the heroic struggle for freedom needs to keep its precious epic alive and elect a character to fit that story, to be the next President.

It has narrative logic and proportion because major endings can't be produced by minor players in minor plots. Martin Luther King Jnr. or JFK can't simply be murdered by random madmen. They at least deserve a conspiracy, even if we can't prove it. The high drama of the consequence demands it. So if Kings and Queens need royal stories of succession, Presidents need presidential stories of election. And in theological terms, election means the hand of God as in pre-destination. Who knew it but God is a super-delegate too!

And let's face it; the epic form is the most compelling story in our cultural memory. The stories of Homer and Beowulf and Gilgamesh and Moses are originally all oral traditions that at some later date, come to be written down, but they only survive through history because they are memorable, and they are not short stories. They grab their readers and invade their imaginations.

Such is the power of the epic story and why it is still compelling viewing when it comes to the Presidential Plot. However, there are consequences. *"Potential presidents,"* an advisor to Nixon wrote,*"are measured against an ideal that's a combination of leading man, God, father, hero, pope, king, with maybe just a touch of the avenging Furies thrown in." (McGinniss, 26)* Maybe nowadays it's a little more than just a touch of the Furies.

The Presidential Plot has no time for ordinary heroes, or heroes that are flawed, that cry too publicly, that have any history of mental illness, or who have hired an illegal worker to cook for them. At least now you can be a draft dodger, a recovering alcoholic and a former drug user, and these might even add to your heroism. But you have to have achieved BIG or fallen BIG because, like our steaks, we like them 14 oz, and so long as the order of events conforms to the redemptive arc, you get to reprise your boozy youth or your business incompetence as prelude to the main event.

As the candidates send out their Vice President vetting teams-(a curious term-'vetting') they know they are recruiting for the role of best supporting hero, trying to find a Robin for Batman, the Lois for Superman, a Vanna for Pat. Forget about the ticket in terms of winning Iowa or the South, or the Hispanic vote. Most political experts will tell you the VP can only hurt you some. It won't help you much. But all the same, there must be a fit for this heroic team portrait at least before the game begins. Remember they don't do statues of VPs on the Mall. Do they do them anywhere? In the Senate, I am told, but it's a state secret because they don't want kids to have nightmares of Dick Cheney and Richard Nixon and Dan Quayle and Spiro Agnew. What a house of horrors; perhaps Madame Tussaud's, newly opened in Washington, would be more appropriate.

Physicist Freeman Dyson[37] maintains that there are two basic stories in our cultural memory and they predate the bible. They are epics of course, and they are from Homer-*The Iliad* and the *Odyssey*. Even if you haven't read them, you still know them. They are basically the story of the warrior's journey through war and the veteran's journey home to peace. The stories are happening every day in Iraq and Afghanistan.

Since we know that the Presidential plot is an epic, and since we know that stories get their meanings and their depth from the intersections of stories with stories, let's explore what resonances there might be between the Presidential campaign and these core epics of our culture.

The *Iliad* is about the young hero battling at Troy to win back the beautiful Helen who has been carried off by the enemy. The young hero is *Achilles*, an Obama figure, with the adventure all ahead of him.

The *Odyssey* is the journey home, the great war-weary warrior *Ulysses*, who recounts the story of the Trojan Horse and other heroic tales from his time of battle, and who finally brings his crew through the Furies and the Straits and comes home to reclaim Penelope, his wife, and reclaim his kingdom. He is blind and comes in disguise, but his faithful dogs recognize him.

In as much as Obama and McCain can craft their stories as the *Iliad* and the *Odyssey*, they will be mapping stories that are the secret underworld of our language, stories that undergird all our stories, and are the spine of meaning for our western narrative.

We have read or been influenced by Virgil's *Aeneid* or Milton or James Joyce or Shakespeare's versions, because these are the people who re-invented the language by re-telling Homer's tale.[38]

---

[37] Freeman Dyson "Tragedy is not our Business" <u>Weapons and Hope</u>. Perennial NY 1984 Page 296

[38] See Alberto Manguel   <u>Homer's the Iliad and the Odyssey-a Biography</u> Atlantic 2007

Our language is a living museum of the stories it remembers even if we don't. We call a long journey an 'odyssey' even if we have never heard of Homer. We might have seen the *'Poseidon Adventure'* or read it without knowing that Poseidon is the Sea God that made Ulysses' return journey so scary. If the computer I am using to write this has a virus, I am looking to find the Trojan, and this time, it's not a horse, but every day, anyone working on a computer is channeling Homer. Words have stories that once gave them life and can even now resuscitate them. Take the preamble to the UN Charter. A Storywise colleague is working to help renew the UN by asking Ambassadors to tell stories that revivify those inspired words.[39]

Every word has a story that gave it oxygen in the beginning, and stories continue to be a word's life-support supplying contemporary meaning and context. Though meanings change as the stories change, powerful words like "Freedom" and "Democracy" still retain their original power that made them a key part of our language and our identity. President Bush and his speechwriters who coined "Operation Iraqi Freedom" knew this well. Originally, it was known as 'Shock and Awe' which sounds more like a parents' reaction to a teenage bedroom than a military campaign! Certain language fits certain stories, just as particular characters fit a particular plot, and names evoke stories, or invite stories.

INSIDE EVERY NAME IS A STORY.

In our workshops, we invite people to get curious about names and why they got the name they did because every name is a story. Obama's middle name being Hussein is an unfortunate accident of history because, as Rev. Wright explained before he was "blacked out," people only have to sound the name and we are in another story altogether. Then there is the rhyme of Obama and Osama. For people who will not read the papers and not tune in to the news, (and Washington hardly believes such people exist) just the sound of someone called Hussein and Obama will trigger a reaction that places the candidate into a story that will disqualify him, rightly or wrongly. One instance of that already is the controversial *New Yorker* cover that pretended to be satire but which could as well serve as a McCain recruiting poster![40]

---

39 Madelyn Blair at www. pelerei.com

40 *The New Yorker* July 21 2008

Recognizing the genre of The Presidential Plot as epic means we understand the need for an aesthetic fit between language and story and character that not only must gel with the political and historical story that is in place, but also the story hidden, yet remembered, inside the language. That is why having a literate and literary presidential voice is such an advantage. Oh for the days of a Bobby Kennedy quoting Aeschylus.

The epic fit is that Obama is Achilles, and McCain is Ulysses. They need to keep that straight and not blur the lines. If Obama were to try and play a Ulysses, by pretending to have more experience and wisdom than his years and his young face will validate, or McCain to try and remake himself into an Achilles, by offering change and the future and a new America, that again will not align with his image that best echoes the Homeric myth. Of course, if Obama picks a Ulysses and McCain picks an Achilles, (or an Amazon) as their running mate, it might make even Homer smile and blur the lines as a tactic, to make us think to vote youth, we vote McCain and to vote experience, we vote Obama.

Whatever the VP sweepstakes, the Candidates are meant to be the contending heroes, and if they step outside of their age-appropriate epic roles, our deep seated story map will register some disconnect, that this does not fit the submerged story that underpins language and is its implied structure of meaning making.

Because our words remember the stories they belong to, even if we don't, Homer Simpson and Homer the original Greek poet and Winslow Homer are all in there somewhere defining the boundaries and possibilities of our sense-making.

YET THESE GODS HAVE TO BE HUMAN

Epics are full of gods and humans and sometimes it's hard to tell which from which, and so too in the Presidential Plot. It seems such a crazy contradiction, the candidate who has to be both Mt Rushmore and the Brady Bunch. Yet as anyone can see, McCain has the scars to prove he is human. He is Ulysses come home from the battle. It's Obama that has to be careful of being divinized out of the race. (And the human race for that matter.)

THE DIVINIZATION OF OBAMA

The adulation, or to use the word Nixon's tricksters used, "aura" will make Obama fit for heaven rather than fit to govern a country at risk. When he can gather 70,000 fans just to hear his stump speech in Portland, or 200,000 Germans at the Brandenburg Gate, or when he has to change the venue of his acceptance speech in Denver to the more spacious football ground, we know we have a serious celebrity candidate on our hands. The campaign knows that and they can milk it, pump it up, and sell all the T-shirts they want, but this is no pop star.

In the end, the voters want more than a show. They want a human being underneath it all. So, you can see the Obama campaign using smaller intimate settings and bringing in Michelle, his wife and the kids. At a 4th of July speech, there they were standing as disconnected appendages. And if Barack hasn't bought that dog for the kids yet, he'd better go out and get an adorable puppy, and he seen playing with it. Or get him back to bowling where at least most others who have bowled less than seriously know they can at least beat his score of 43.

THE HUMANIZING OF JOHN McCAIN

In the humanizing of candidate John McCain, the Senator has done a great job without even trying. In this campaign and even more in the earlier attempts with his Straight Talking Express, his jokey camaraderie at the back of the bus proves that he can be as crude and as cynical or off hand as the press are. Perhaps John McCain has to work at the hero thing a bit more, especially when his opponents can pull the Swift Boat tactic on him or repeat the Max Cleland libel so effective in defeating another hero of Vietnam.

We know in the world of genre that if someone writes a best seller called The Tipping Point,[41] then you know that the next 50 new books will try to capitalize on it, because one book makes way for another, as one story carves a path for a another one, sounding the same. So, the disparagement of a Vietnam hero, who is a hero in a largely discredited war, seeking to lead the country out of what appears to be another discredited war, is fair game. And the genre is tried and true and tested-just like "scare the hell out of them" with Communists (1950's) or Terrorists, (2000's) or Crime (1970's) or Illegal Aliens. (2000's)

So Campaigns need to anticipate such story attacks. The drama for us to watch is how McCain holds on to his hero status, and how Obama holds on to his human status. John Kerry and Jesus might have some good advice.

---

[41] Malcolm Gladwell The Tipping Point Little Brown 2002

POSTSCRIPT

EPICS THAT ARE WRITTEN ON THE MALL

I was on the Mall in Washington recently showing a group of South African interns the Lincoln Memorial and one of them, Udo, couldn't reconcile the size of the monument to the size of the man. He was disturbed at the worship that the memorial forces on you. As you peer up at this brooding Buddha figure, it reduces you in size, and Abraham is looking out at the vista, not at you. He is looking at his America.

I try to explain that with all the monuments, this one and the Jefferson and the Washington Monument itself, these are the pantheon of the gods for a young nation that did not want ordinary heroes. It wanted greatness. It saw that as its destiny. This city of Washington was to be the place where that epic is written in stone and marble. That was its designer, Pierre L'Enfant's dream. So, a President has to compete and live up to these myths in stone.

My intern was struck by how well America does the "re-inspiring thing." I tell him that if he listened to the numerous school tours, and the tourists and all the Trolley Bus commentaries, he would hear how, every day in DC, the stories of the nation are told and re-told and how, every day, the nation of America is being made up again, being re-constituted in those tellings.

What happens around a structure in marble is a mythologizing and a license for poetry and for lyric, and for the epics and the sagas where memory is based on myth more than historical truth. These stories like the Presidential Plot itself fit the sensibility and the aspirational reach of America, its sense of itself. It is a city, after all, named after a war hero who invented the presidency when he could have easily allowed himself to be crowned King George I.

"What about the ordinary heroes?" Udo asks. "We think of Mandela as great and yet ordinary." And I explain that we only do ordinary heroes when a policeman or fireman is killed in the line of duty, or a soldier. On the national stage, we have to have epic in campaigns and myths carved in stone on the National Mall.

It is this city and into these pathways and among these pantheons that a new presidential contender has to show he is ready to enter, which he will do literally on the day of his inauguration.

He will be sworn in within the panoramic gaze of the seated Lincoln a mile away. Anyone who is too human, anyone who cries too much or plays the victim or who does not wear the mantle of greatness with the dignity and the reverence that the story demands is simply not going to be voted President. The president has to fit this story, one he does not make or invent. It is the song America is singing before any President lifts his voice to take the oath of office. As Walt Whitman wrote "I hear America singing, the varied carols I hear," so too the successful candidate will have heard the songs and sighs of the people who crave for epic elections, and the ultimate coronation of one heroic Candidate.

Mark Shields and others often say that the candidate has to pass the Commander-in-Chief test, but I always feel it is more the passing of the epic test. Can this person become a legend? Can we build him a memorial with his words chiseled in stone accompanied by an eternal flame or waterfalls of living water to mark the memory and keep it fresh? Can this person command a kingdom in our imaginations, where it counts, at least to get him elected?

Our election is fought and won in the imagination. A battle of ideas yes, but more a battle of who can bring to the national stage, a personal image that is full of an enlivening passion for America's story, and for why it is still so compelling. And that truly is an epic undertaking in every sense of the word.

MAPPING THE NARRATIVE LANDSCAPE

"Being part of government in a time of distrust like this is like walking across terrain where there are camouflaged pits with sharpened poles at the bottom, where at any moment you might fall through and be impaled. So you govern tactically, by the latest poll. You never pull back and try to figure out the bigger narrative where the story is going and where it ought to go."[1]

"I wonder what sort of tale we've fallen into" Lord of the Rings

Let me give you a quick plot summary: The Presidential Plot is derivative and it exists prior to any campaign. It exists as a time tested genre. It can be mapped temporally across beginnings, middles and endings and it belongs to that ancient species of story called Epic. Now that we have that out of the way, (Phew!) we are now ready to go outside and play. But wait a minute! Do we even know what is out there in the narrative landscape?

CAUTION-ENTERING A NARRATIVE JUNGLE!

We could be Teddy Roosevelt exploring the Amazon Basin, or Steve Irwin entering a crocodile infested lagoon, but either way, we know like them that our survival depends on how well we respect and read the signs of our environment. Whether we come as the tourist or the invader or the trader, we know that the land is populated with stories, some of which are wild and dangerous. And we also know that the stories we hear will only be a random sample of the proliferation of life and story-forms in all the habitats we traverse.

Our candidates know this. When they tour New Mexico or California, the stories of that story-scape are a different breed to the stories of New Hampshire or Massachusetts. Presumably the candidate knows the story he wants to tell the nation, but what he doesn't know is how it will play in the hearts and minds of the electorate, how his story will relate to or connect with voters in all their diversity? He will only know that if he can learn what are they living through and what gives specificity to their experience.

WHAT IS MISSING?

What our Candidate needs to be especially aware of is what is not there, what story is missing, and what gaps his story might speak

---

1 Bill Bradley-Democratic Candidate 2000

to? It's not just practical matters of lack of jobs, or failing schools. There is a broken story in these towns, a story that is not working, the story of hope, the story of active citizenry, the story that a government can actually respond to a local need in a local way, a story that corporations do care about their workers. Something is missing.

The system is broken, as Obama and McCain and their predecessors proclaim at every whistle stop, but what they need to understand is, it's broken because a story is broken. People do not merely cling to their guns or their religion; they cling to their core stories to wring from them some sense in times when lots of things don't make much sense.

Guns speak to my citizen rights, my freedom to defend myself especially if it feels like no one else will protect me. Religion speaks to the human realities deeper than the pocket and the check book, especially when no one else dares to address the real human story that spans life and pain and death. We have to make sense of things. That's what we humans do.

For many, the story of citizenship no longer seems to work. And so, for the candidate, the key question is, what stories are broken and how can my story as a candidate heal or inspire or feed the hunger for a story of national government that works, that expresses the people's voice? That's the candidate's mission in narrative terms.

FIELDS OF BROKEN TRUST

The narrative landscape of American politics at the moment is largely a field of broken trust. The story of power has become so corrupted that voters express a deep cynicism toward Washington. They give up on government as a force for good and retreat to their family and their faith as their only way of defending themselves against political spin and media manipulation.

If Obama or McCain offer more of the same, they will be infesting the landscape with more of the same junk, the cheap grace, the narrative pollution of easy promises and pandering that will poison the hope that after years of broken promises, people once more dare to harbor. When it comes to an election, voters have the audacity to hope that this time, it might be different.

Revolutions happen not simply because people are poor or oppressed but because their hopes, once raised, are dashed, and yet, they decide that they cannot go back to the old story. So the stories of hope that McCain and Obama and Hillary are peddling to the heartlands, are not just campaign messages. They either add to the toxic wasteland of empty rhetoric and broken promises, or they offer something different, something that is not illusion, something that has the ring of the real about it, neither lies nor ideology. Public words and promises make or break our meaning making capacity, testing our belief that words actually have any living relationship to action, to what is real.

A SHIFT IN THE WAY THE STORY IS TOLD

To think about what story field the candidate is entering rather than what story the electorate is hearing from the candidate is a major shift in the way we think about elections. Candidates naturally think the election is about them. The media hit us with the candidates as celebrities, 24/7, so it's only natural to think the campaign is essentially about Obama versus McCain, as if this is some heavy weight fight between their stories. That is the drama for which the media can easily provide us ringside seats, through debates and dueling commentators left and right, until election night itself.

However, that is where a narrative analyst will beg to differ, because one of the key questions we ask is, "Whose story is this?" and "Whose power is being exercised in the telling of it?" If the answer to the first question is different to the answer to the second, viz- if the story of who becomes the next President belongs to the people but the power to tell it belongs only to the media and the candidates, then, there is a major disconnect. Houston, we have a problem!

IT'S THE PEOPLES' STORY

"It's not about you," we want to keep reminding our candidates. And if they forget that, they will fail. There is a prior landscape littered with a wasteland of lies and failed campaigns that each of the candidates is trying to enter, a storyscape that pre-exists their campaigns that we call the Narrative Landscape. Unless they legitimately win entry into that field of stories, it doesn't matter what story they come up with, they will become the victim of the stories already out there.

A smart Candidate will remember often to stop obsessing about his own story, his own issues, or resist ramping up the stump speech to even loftier tones and realize that he has to model being the Listener in Chief before being Teller in Chief. He will want to demonstrate that leadership is about learning and remind his campaign that it remains a study tour where, instead of the candidate trying to convince the voter, it is the opportunity for the citizen to convince the candidate that government has to take on board the real stories from the real lives of its people.

Whether the candidate heeds this warning or no, the narrative landscape will show no mercy. It ultimately decides the presidency even if it's a story that no one quite knows how to tell. The media can only cover the short story, can only tolerate about a three minute span of human interest, but there is a novel buried out there in the heartland.

What little glimpses we get of this novel come to us through the ubiquitous techniques of polling or focus groups. But they are usually at the service of the campaigns or the media. They are not really about surfacing the people's stories as they would want to tell them. Pollsters are hired by campaigns and media to ask all the questions and market test some of their ideas or work out if a candidate is making progress in getting audience share.

WE ARE NOT GETTING THE REAL STORY

What would it look like if the election story was told as a People's Thing, a "Res Publica," and it began as the Constitution begins, "*We the People*." We would have McCain not stumping in New Orleans for a night but working in New Orleans for a week cleaning out houses in the Lower 9th Ward, so we see how he learns about disaster relief, breathes in the air in Miss Latisha's formaldehyde infected trailer, and watches helplessly as schools dump thousands of new text books because the Charter schools moving in don't want them, while impoverished kids in St. Bernard's parish crave storybooks and picture books.

What if we have Obama spending a few days in rural Pennsylvania and sharing the life of those he said cling to their guns and gods, and then, we watch how Obama learns about the real concerns of working people who, with no health insurance and failing job prospects, feel that they are being written out of the story of the Democratic party.

The election is not some media deal between Obama and McCain. The deal that must be sealed is between each of them and the people. This is not a pop concert.

Senator Obama, you know about community organizing. You know you don't come in with the answers before you even ask the questions.

And Senator McCain, you know about leadership, you know about the honor code and how to level with your people, if you want to lead them anywhere.

THE CANDIDATE EXPERIENCING THE PEOPLES STORIES

Candidates must know that you have to explore the narrative landscape; you have to hear the people, like an Eleanor Roosevelt or a Bobby Kennedy did. Then they would realize that you have to do more than give some 10 second sound bite naming someone who has a sob story. It may sound nice to be invited to pity Jo and Mary who have lost their house, but it is tokenism at best and exploitative and paternalistic at worst. It's a technique that should go the way of typewriters and VHS. A Narrative ethic says you never appropriate other people's stories for your own gain. If you want to tell their story, make it yours by telling us what you did about it. Taking action makes it your story too. But bearing witness for the sake of winning displaced sympathy votes is cheap and melodramatic.

WHOSE CHOICE IS IT?

Elections are all about choice but the media and the candidates make it out to be about their choice to run, and that becomes the drama of decision that the media drive. It starts with speculation piled on speculation, as in, "Will Obama run?" A candidate has to deny it at least three times before the media know for sure that he is a serious contender. Last month, we were in the middle of the "Drama of Decision" with Candidate's pick for Vice President. And since then, it has become 'What will the McCain campaign do to counter this charge of being Bush's third term?' and "What will Obama do to defuse the accusation of being elitist?' It gives the whole presidential plot a distorted look and feel because it puts them at the center and their choices as the most privileged.

Yet it is also a case of narrative necessity because the real story, the story that the people are in right now, the storyscape that the candidate's story must enter, is much harder to express. It is the story of 300 million Americans for starters. It is fragmented across the nation, clustered around local issues and concerns. So the media's best attempt to get at it is through polls and focus groups. It is much more dramatic to map the narrative landscape surrounding the candidate. But while that is compelling and full of human interest, it is largely irrelevant to the election result because most people aren't watching it or reading about it.

For most voters, elections are about their story, and deciding what candidate offers the best fit for the story that I, and my neighbors want for America. Though we won't see our story on television, it remains the decisive story. It reminds me of my favorite Nasrudin stories. He is this mischievous Turkish Sufi storyteller and he says he has lost the key to his house one dark night and he is outside cursing to himself and searching on the ground out the front near a street lantern. His neighbors come and help him, but after a while, when they have no luck, they ask the obvious question, "Where did you lose it?" and Nasrudin answers, "Out the back." And the neighbors stop and scratch their heads and ask, "Then why are you looking for it out the front when you lost it out the back?" And he answers, "The only place where there is light to see is out the front."

You tell the story you have, and from where you have it, with whatever light and from whatever angle. It might not be that important or where the real story is happening, but no matter. Go where you can get a shot, or a story already set up for you by the campaign, not where you can get the deeper dramas. That's often much messier, more expensive and less sound-bitable. The media are undiscriminating story hosts of opportunity. If the key is lost out back, but the light is out front, we know what story we will see. In elections, the candidates provide them with the pre-packaged story of "Why I am better than my opponent," and "Why I want to be your next president." The media invariably swallow it but the real drama is, do we the people want you?

A narrative understanding makes clear that their story is not the story that ultimately matters at all. It is the story writ large in the nation of *"We the People."* The candidate seeks to enter that story, to interpret it, to speak to it and articulate it, but their stories have to be a subset of that story already in play.

WHAT STORY HAS THE NATION FALLEN INTO?

The most critical question any candidate needs to ask before anything else, is what Story am I entering, what story is America in right now? Or to paraphrase Sam, what story am I getting myself into here? Kenneth Gergen gives us a wonderfully simple short-hand for the three types of stories that basically summarize most patterns of narrative.

America is either in

- a progressive story, things are getting better, the plot line is rising, or

- a _regressive_ story, things are getting worse, and the plot line is falling or
- a _status quo_ story, that things are pretty much staying the same.[2]

When I asked recent seminar participants which story they feel America is in right now, (and this is before gas hit four dollars,) almost everyone said they feel we are in a regressive story, that things are heading downhill, and that we are headed in the wrong direction. We don't need polls to specify what people mean. The wrong direction is "DOWN" and the preferred direction is "UP."

The two polling results that the press keep hammering into our brains is that George Bush's approval rating is lower than Nixon's during Watergate, and that 85% plus think America is headed in the wrong direction. So my seminar group was fairly typical.

If we wanted other indicators to justify their assessment, we only have to look at the gas prices that continue to rise, at the mortgage meltdown, at the car companies signaling that they are way down on their sales targets, that airlines are cutting staff and flights, that job losses are higher than ever, and global warming is a warning that we keep hearing but no one is sure what to do about it, and Congress while enjoying less than 20% approval, seems to want to delay or deny any urgency about anything and go on summer break.

It is all lining up to be a story of recession or worse, and the emotional energy of the people is being drained of hope in the future, toward a depression, toward a pessimism that dampens consumer confidence, and means that people do not trust the future to be better than the past. They are fearful for their kids and expecting the downturn to continue, for things to get worse before they get better.

This is the narrative landscape in the broadest possible terms. For sure, in certain states it will attach itself to particular issues but the mood of the country is the key barometer that a candidate needs to be measuring before he even begins to think about his own story or his party's story. Like a doctor, you diagnose before you operate. Or you take the pulse of the nation, realize it has a fever and only then, seek the right treatment.

Of course, this is all relative too. Other parts of the world would love the chance to pay four dollars for petrol. They are used to

2 Kenneth Gergen, _Realities and Relationships_ Harvard 1994 Page 196-7

paying three times that much, or other parts of the world are dealing with famine and disease and war and the US isn't in the middle of any kind of calamitous meltdown. But it's a matter of perception, not reality. There is enough evidence out there to sustain this pessimism, and we are being fed by the media who rely on the stories of the sad and the bad. It's their staple serving. And Campaigns seem compelled to assume the voice of a social worker-in-chief believing that there is electoral gain in pain.

America clearly is not in a story about maintaining the status quo. They want some changes and they want them pretty urgently. Hence, the narrative landscape is primed for a character to enter as 'The hero as change-agent.' To make things right again, a leader has to give us a new sense of the future.

WHO DO WE TURN TO WHEN THINGS ARE GOING BAD?

When things are bad, we want someone, a parent or a trusted partner to make it better. The more dependent and insecure we feel, the more we want a parental figure to reassure us that it will be alright, that we can get through this middle passage and turn it around. The more desperate, the more we will want to rely on someone who is not just offering bromides but has actually dealt with these kinds of situations before. This sounds like the worse things get, the more it might favor McCain, but let's continue the analysis before we jump too far ahead.

We have our plot; things are going downhill. Where do we want the story to go? We want to head back uphill, to have more security about the future, about the economy. We want to feel our kids will once again have the chance to own a house and get a good education and have a better life than we had. We want the curve to move back up, to go from the regressive to the progressive. That is what the Presidential campaign will boil down to in its most basic form. Restore our optimism.

Without insulting the experts or dismissing the detailed analysis by paid pundits who have to tell stories to keep viewers interested, we propose that the Presidential Plot in narrative terms is never as complicated as they make out. It is basic at the core. It's about the primary need for meaning that in times of trouble and stress trumps the need for means.

In the recent Australian elections, the new Prime Minister Kevin Rudd's campaign was inspired by the Maslow pyramid of needs, where Maslow says basic needs like food and shelter come first before the higher needs for self-fulfillment. In politics, it means you offer voters tax cuts, incentives, and other takeaways, not pipe dreams. But the irony is that Maslow realized late in his life that he had the pyramid the wrong way round.[3] The higher needs normally come first. We can put up with enormous deprivation and hardship if we have a story that makes sense of it all. As Victor Frankl said, quoting Nietzsche, "Give a man a why and he can endure any how."

Even if Rudd's team got Maslow wrong, they got the election right, and he was elected Prime Minister over an opponent who had delivered ten years of unparalleled economic growth and prosperity. Rudd's campaign realized that Australia wanted a bigger story for their future than business as usual and that meaning trumped means.

If things are booming, then we can vote for the candidate with the better sounding voice, or the more fashionable tie, but when the chips are down, people cut to the chase. They are not fools, and they want someone who can sort the mess out and bring back some of the things that America used to take for granted.

People assess their lives the way they assess their country. There isn't some special political brain that they turn on and off at election time, though some sell books telling us that. Citizens know if their kids' schools are in good shape or not, and whether the teachers are professional and committed. And they know if their aging parent is getting good healthcare of not. No PR campaign can finally fool people all the time if they are attentive to what their kids are saying, or are engaged with the normal needs of work and family life. More than that, people read morale. If morale is high, no one worries about morals except those busybodies who have nothing better to worry about. The best thing to happen for gay activists is the depressed economy. People don't worry about bedrooms when they have to worry about the kitchen table. Big problems require bigger stories.

A NARRATIVE ACCOUNT OF PAST ELECTIONS

If this way of viewing elections has some validity, let's test its explanatory power for some past elections. When we cast your mind back to the Gore campaign, we recall a candidate whose promise was to make a fairer America and reform education, energy and health-care. He offered a program of change when the mood of the country wasn't that hungry for reform. That was the note that Bush and his party focused on; not economic but moral reform. Gore misread the narrative landscape, thinking that the

---

[3] Danah Zohar, Spiritual Capital Berrett-Keehler 2004, p.19

nation was into his big story, whereas, Gore didn't story himself sufficiently into the national story of his time. He was global and we were still complacently local.

When the general population is content, when the mood towards the future is positive, then the electorate can afford to vote on the smaller story of moral values, to reward and punish through their vote. But had the 2000 election been held in tighter economic times, we would have seen a different response because the bigger story of Value/Meaning rather than private morals quickly becomes the issue. That is the case for 2008. This is a big story election because there is too much happening that we don't understand.

When the Republican Congress was ready to impeach Clinton for lying, the nation did not much care, much to the dismay of the media elite. "Where is the rage?" one headline screamed. Morality or immorality did not affect the people's checkbook though the Republicans knew they had little else to throw at a successful Presidency. Abortion and Gay rights can only become the new flag-burning issue when there is no other burning issue. It wasn't that Gore in the end did anything wrong, but he promised Value, (the big story) and Bush ran on values, (the small story) and values won. It is hard to see how Gore could have done anything different, because the narrative landscape was not ready for his preferred story as a candidate.

BLAMING THE VICTIM

The usual summary of a failed election campaign is to explain what the candidate did wrong, e.g., Gore was too aloof, or how the campaign was mismanaged, e.g. Hillary presumed it would all be over by February. Again, within the framework of epic, it makes for a compelling story, that our would-be hero falls from grace and ultimately becomes tragic, flawed, failed by his own hubris or the fact that the gods were against her. But narratively, it's a story told for the drama of it and not for the truth of it.

Al Gore lost or John Kerry lost because that is what the majority of the people decided. In the case of Gore, he may have won the popular vote, but if ever a candidate should have won in a landslide as a validation of the Clinton years, it was Gore. His story did not match the story and the mood of the nation. Right story, wrong time, or wrong story for that time or just plan unlucky. His stars were out of alignment.

Yet to keep interpreting the elections and their results or the primaries as to what <u>they</u> did wrong, is to perpetuate the fiction that elections are about the choices the candidates make, whereas it is ultimately the choice the people make. It is not that the candidate got it wrong so much as that the people got it right, in the very fact that they had their say. And if democracy means anything, it means that the people get to decide. What they say counts in the end more than any campaign post-mortem.

WHEN YOU DON'T READ THE NARRATIVE LANDSCAPE

If there was any fault with these candidates, it was that their attempts were doomed from the start by their failure to correctly assess the narrative landscape they were entering. As Democratic Candidate, Bill Bradley, said in 2000, it is full of "camouflaged pits with sharpened poles at the bottom." Candidates are prone to think that simply by force of their own charisma, their story will shape the election conversation but no candidate's story shapes that. Their job, if they want to win, is to join in and fit in, not attempt to take it over.

PRECEDENTS OF THOSE WHO DID SUCCEED

There are many models from the past of those who did their narrative homework. On the Republican side, take Ronald Reagan, who as an elder statesman, offered the country a sense of pride in itself again, and though some of his policies were a disaster, he elevated the national story to one of confidence and restored optimism. No wonder Obama is quoting Reagan rather than Clinton.

On the Democrat side, one might well take the play book from a JFK and his New Frontier idealism, or even better, an FDR coming to office in the midst of the depression and immediately setting the tone, "We have nothing to fear but fear itself." Morale may not be an economic policy or measured by GDP, but its power to harness the energy of a nation is incalculable and indispensable. Output follows tone. The president has to be an entrepreneur of the nation's emotional economy because the basic source of human energy is emotion, and perhaps that is the real energy crisis of America at this moment in its history.

The candidates need to read the plot, the storyline, which is 'America wants change.' To win, the candidate has to audition to be that hero who will bring that change. You can cut this a number of ways. A new star on the stage can promise to bring a whole new era of open government, more attuned to the people's needs and a new sense of bi-partisanship, and if he is young and adventurous, he might fit the story at large and he may get the part.

On the other hand, an equally compelling change story could be to change back, to restore America to her greatness abroad and to prosperity at home, and to bring back fiscal responsibility coupled with a new sense of the environment and the need for sustainability. But here, the hero says, what I can offer is regaining what we have lost, that is the change we need, not chasing after some windy city utopia, some radical new vision of government.

But "change" becomes the story that they have to fit themselves into. This is what we mean by reading the narrative landscape. It is also an awareness of what the schemers knew back in 1968, that the power to make meaning lies ultimately with the audience, and that the teller is not the sole agent and deliverer of meaning. That means that Obama and McCain are not in control of their message or even the interpretation of their message. They at the mercy of first <u>how</u> people think the country is going, and second, <u>where</u> they think the country is headed.

AS THEY SAY IN INDONESIA- APA KABAH?

In Java, where Obama spent part of his growing up, the local greeting between people is 'Apa Kabah' which means 'How are you," but literally translates into "Where are you going?' since to the Javanese, your current state of being is related to where you are going. And they are right.

The geography of meaning by which we navigate our world is simple. We are going forward or back; we are moving up or down, and we feel we are at the beginning or the middle or the end of something. These are the compass points of our narrative GPS, or the basic compass points of life by which to take a bearing and make our decisions. These are also the co-ordinates of the national story and the national mood. This is what each candidate is stepping into here, or as Heidegger would call it, *dasein*, what they are thrown into, the story that's already sprung, and they are going to be part of it. You either work out rules of engagement to ensure it works for you, or it will work against you.

The work of a campaign, regardless of all the bells and whistles, is where and how they join up, how they add to this momentum, this sense of direction in the already-happening story. They are asking permission to join a story they did not shape, but which America, through its history, and language and memory, is already moving ahead with. The candidate has to work out how to jump on to that moving train and not trip up or end up under the wheels.

EVEN DATA AND POLLS NEED STORIES

The narrative landscape in the end is more than the sum of the polls-which mainly demonstrate what sense the people are making of the Candidates, not what sense the candidates are making of the people. All that pundits and the economic indicators and focus groups provide is data, and data is good for analysis, measurement, tracking the trends and calling the horse race. But people don't live out of data which is the detritus of their lives, they live out of stories. Data is dead at the point of being captured. Stories are fluid, capturing the ebb and flow of life. Even the pollster needs a story for his data to make any sense. The narrative landscape is tricky territory but a narrative analysis of the presidential elections will claim that it's the story that counts even if it is not told. If we are to find a better story, one whose hero is the people, then it's critical we find a better way to tell it.

CHAPTER EIGHT

THE FOUR BIG STORIES

"It is through stories revolving around others and around ourselves that we articulate and shape our temporality...narrative identity takes part in the mobility of the story, in its dialectic of order and disorder...Thus the story of my life is a segment of the story of your life, of the story of my parents, of my friends, of my enemies, and of countless strangers. We are literally entangled in stories" [4]

Stories come wrapped in stories that come wrapped in stories. Hence a narrative analysis proceeds like a series of unwrappings. But let's recap. We began our analysis trying to sort out the species of the story, identifying the genre as epic and understanding the inner dynamics of beginnings, middle and ends.

Then we moved out into the narrative landscape, first as intrepid explorers before we realized we needed to become ethnographers, hearing the stories by which people map their lives and ensuring that whatever tactics a campaign may adopt, the people must remain the hero of the story. Election means choice and that choice belongs to them.

Now we need to take the next step and become cartographers and surveyors, reading and hearing the stories behind the stories, trying to distinguish the identifying features of this dramatic landscape. To read the lie of the land is a great asset for any politician, to know the terrain both literally and narratively. It perhaps is not co-incidental that at least three great Presidents were trained as surveyors.

George Washington believed the Potomac River to be the life-line to the inland and wanted the nation's capital beside it. Jefferson's father was a surveyor and under Washington, Thomas himself became Surveyor General. Abraham Lincoln worked as a surveyor before he won his first Senate seat in the Illinois Senate. We are going to argue that any successful Presidential candidate needs to resurrect that kind of skill.

Just as we discovered predictable specimens of stories that power the Presidential plot, we will also find predictable patterns in the narrative landscape. A candidate is not going to find 300 million uniquely different stories because most will cluster together like

---

4 Richard Kearney <u>Paul Ricoeur The Hermeneutics of Action</u> Sage 1996

families, gathered around certain core themes that echo the dominant stories stored away in the archive of our national memory.

In mapping the nation, a candidate realizes that there is indeed an American story, and that citizenship is not so much based on a shared set of timeless ideals as a shared set of living stories. Whatever our Candidate's story, it must resonate deeply with this vibrant American story. When the issue arises in an election cycle about whether a candidate is "American enough," we get a sense of how critical this matching of stories is in the minds of most voters.

THE FOUR STORIES

But what are these key stories, the signature narratives by which we might recognize what is quintessentially American? Robert Reich, former Secretary of Labor in the Clinton administration offered a useful summation in 2005 when he wrote about four key stories that he thought his Democrats needed to reclaim if they wanted to win back government.[5]

Regardless of Reich's partisan agenda, his list is instructive. In summary, here is my version of his four core stories:

- The Heroic Individual
- The Beloved Community
- The Enemy at the Gate
- The Rot at the Top

Before we dissect each of them, a cursory glance will already reveal a pattern, in that two of them are positive, and two are negative. They map fear and hope, possibility and paranoia.

Reich doesn't discuss his theory at a meta level but his narrative compass reveals some of the more basic co-ordinates of our lives, the relationship of boundaries to belonging and the critical balance between who is inside and who is outside, and the relationship of hierarchy to power, of who is at the top and who is at the bottom. One set of stories is measuring movement on the horizontal plane that we could mark as identity (the axis of Individual and Community) and one on the vertical plane that we could mark as power (the axis of Top to Bottom.) The core stories of America are

---

5 Robert Reich, "The Lost Art of Democratic Narrative" *The New Republic*, March 21, 2005. Reich calls them the Triumphant Individual, the Benevolent Community, the Mob at the Gates and Rot at the Top.

about identity and power, and that perfectly fits our election agenda.

They all speak to identity with two speaking for what we are for, and two speak about counter-identity based on who we are not, or who stands against us. Two have the citizen as agent, creating his own life and meaning, (1 and 2) and two are about the citizen as victim, as the one who has to react to enemies without and corruption within. (3 and 4) Already as a species of stories, we can predict what outcomes each will produce or what imbalances will occur if for instance the Enemy at the Gates dominates over the Heroic Individual. They are all in play.

Let's keep all this in mind as we describe each set of stories because the skill is to see the narrative terrain as patterns and repeatable features rather than be sucked too deeply into the content. The role of the Surveyor is not to climb every mountain but to draw up the plan that marks the recognizable features that allow us to plot our course around them.

STORY ONE-THE HEROIC INDIVIDUAL

America treasures a core set of stories, the first of which I call the **Heroic Individual**. It is the Horatio Alger story, the Emersonian self-made man, the triumph of the individual, that says emphatically that anyone can make it here, that anyone can re-invent themselves, and that I can better myself. These stories are central even now to the American dream and they are so self-re-enforcing that it is said that 80% of the American population believe they are in the top 20% as far as class and success. It is the informing myth that keeps cropping up in the background of countless policies and promises of the Presidential Plot and of the Presidency itself.

For instance, take Obama's sermon on Father's day calling for men to demonstrate individual responsibility, or McCain and his tax policy reprising the nostrum that the individual and not the State is best able to decide how to spend our tax dollars. From owning guns to a woman's right to choose, all of these are appeals to the individualist ethic. And in case we think this is just a Republican issue, it is not. The Hillary-Obama debate on health care boiled down to who would allow the individual to opt in or out.

When such a story is projected on to the world stage as foreign policy, it becomes unilateralism and exceptionalism. We become the indispensable nation, the heroic republic, the last best hope on earth. To any outsider, we must sound like a nation of messianic narcissists but this is the inner story, the family saga, the one we keep telling each other to remind ourselves that we are all so special, and that we can do anything we set our minds to. As a work of the imagination, it has to be one of the more enduring and enchanting tales in all our Magic Kingdom.

Knowing that this story is so much the inner structure of our language and our national psyche, the candidate will seek to cast his own biography in the same vein. McCain waging his individual war against his captors in Hanoi, his *dering do* as a lone fighter pilot, his maverick status in the Senate; here is the man who lives the American Dream in defiance of anything that would diminish the human spirit, or deny freedom and honor to a valiant warrior. McCain fits the formula well, along with John Wayne and Clint Eastwood.

Obama in his debut speech at the 2004 Convention was smart enough to cast his life as the fulfillment of this American Dream, son of foreign student and absent father, raised alone by mother, strives to become Editor of the Harvard Law Review after years as a community organizer, and finally wins public office. When we applaud his achievements, we are applauding America, congratulating ourselves, that this is what we believe is possible for every one of us. Obama is a walking talking self-help book and no wonder Oprah endorsed him as her living and breathing Book of the Month.

This set of stories taps a deeper ongoing conversation about what story of the individual does America want to live inside of? We enter into the territory of our secular theology once again, though only theologians would recognize or dare admit that.

In an increasingly networked world, this classical American story might seem at times dangerously out of touch. It means if the individual can be anything he or she wants, then failure is your own fault. Welfare and pensions become dangerous props that emasculate human endeavor. We must enthusiastically punish failure as the incentive to help turn whiners into winners. The story's inner logic is solipsistic and irresistible and also cruel.

A narrative analyst dares ask the question of whether a core story like this is still working for us, or whether it's time for a better story? But that is probably another book and another election. This story is still too deeply resonant of our own sense of ourselves even if at times it works against us.

96

The Heroic individual is enhanced by the second set of stories that I call **the Beloved Community.** The farmer needs a new barn so, on Saturday, the whole community gathers and erects it for him, or the harvest is ready, and the entire village works together till it is brought in. This rural vision of a Jeffersonian America that sounds like an Amish community proposes this ideal of a convergence of self interest with altruism. It's the Boy Scouts and Mister Rogers and the School Board and the Soccer and Hockey Moms' view of America, "e pluribus Unum."

The story of the commons is also deeply ingrained in the narrative landscape, that we as citizens pool together for the common good. The 'Common Good,' is a term rarely heard these days, because the election will ask us "Are YOU better off?" not "Are WE better off?" Yet in the smaller communities that make up the heartland of America, it is the PTA and the churches and schools, and the police and the youth clubs that embody America at its best. It is what so struck de Tocqueville on his visit, this civic virtue.

Here again, an election poses a fundamental question of what story of community does the nation adhere to? Sociology is warning us of disturbing trends like "Bowling Alone"[6] and the deterioration of social capital, and more recently, the economic segregation of our cities. These are all compelling stories, but going way back to preacher John Winthrop, we love to hear periodic sermons about the demise of our social fabric. These are the sorts of confessional rituals that we find cathartic and remind us that we still must have it if people think we are losing it. When no one notices or cares is going to be the time to worry.

A candidate in the attempt to run a campaign has to not only adopt the rhetoric of bringing people together, he must actually form a dedicated team to get himself elected. If his campaign falls apart, then he has disqualified himself from leading the Beloved Community. But if he can gather the faithful, he will be bound to preach the cliché that "He is a Uniter and not a divider," that he can reach across the aisle, whatever aisle that might be. And though this sounds so predictable and obvious, it is only in America.

The spectacle of the recent Olympic Games in China demonstrates what a nation with a different defining story of community might look like, with thousands of dancers all in mechanical unison, and

---

[6] Robert Putman <u>Bowling Alone</u> Simon and Schuster 2000

no room for the single celebrity performance. Once the made-in-China Olympics moves on, we will once again take the world stage with our Conventions, made for prime time shows, where the news even now is whether Hillary will speak on Night Two (She did memorably) or Mark Warner Night Three, (He did forgettably) and whether Hillary's name is entered on the ballot? (It was but she moved the winning Obama motion) It was all about individuals. What happened to the synchronized Democratic chanting? The celebrity Conventions are the academy awards for individual star politicians with delegates there as props along with the balloons.

It is obvious that the story of individual and the community, of the one and the many, are and should be two chapters of one identity story, but recent experience seems to have disturbed the balance between individual and community rights and made it one of the new political battlegrounds that the Candidate has to enter and stake out a position, if he dares.

STORY THREE-THE ENEMY AT THE GATES

Since 9-11, we live every day reminded of another set of stories that tell us that the **Enemy is at the Gates**-OR more latterly, the enemy is inside the gates: And the enemy list is extensive: Terrorists, and illegal immigrants and sexual predators and drug fiends and radical Muslims and we might add liberals and gays and feminists and evangelicals, depending on our tastes in paranoia. Our media-incited fear about immigrants is barely assuaged by building our own Berlin Wall on the border. With Mexico, mind you, not Canada. This fear has the familiar stamp of an old fear, of marauding Indians and treacherous Redcoats and rebellious slaves. Muslim terrorists take the modern place of the foreigner, the outsider, once reserved for the Jew, the Catholic, women, gays, the Irish, the Japanese, the Chinese. It is the shell of a story waiting to be filled with the new foreigner, the new scapegoat, and all that comes from outside that appears to threaten the inside because it doesn't fit, or doesn't fit the prevailing story and therefore doesn't make sense.

Anyone who has flown overseas since 9-11 experiences the real effects of this story which translates into the daily airport drama of the "Enemy at the check-in counter." We suspect that it is pure theatre played out only to reassure us that terrorists won't get through next time. But when you have to watch helplessly as security guards vigorously body search a frail 80 year old white haired lady who has had a hip replacement that sets the scanner off, you realize how ridiculous this story has become. I guess you never know what those crazy grannies can get up to, especially when they can hardly walk.

"Enemy at the Gates" has become the touchstone story of an entire administration, not only influencing immigration policy but prompting the biggest public service reform in history with the creation of the megalithic Department of Homeland Security, plus the policy of pre-emption, and scary defense budgets and security, and intelligence and surveillance, all targeting terrorists. What hasn't it influenced?

Yet as a story, it keeps the citizen as reactive victim and makes the government the hero. Any story that deposes the people as the hero of the democracy story is one that you know is inherently anti-democratic. And a story built on fear is high maintenance, because it has to keep ratcheting up the intensity to stay alive, or else, you breed complacency and cynicism, the very opposite of the vigilance a nation needs to defend itself. If you want to observe the signs of this story fatigue, look at the faces of the line next time you are going through security at the airport, or hear the Public Address tell us solemnly that the department of Homeland Security has declared a code Orange alert. It feels like one is hearing an advertisement for an alarm system and no one believes it anymore.

A nation at risk better have stories that help it work out who is my enemy, and what are the real as against the phony threats. If the nation is not at risk, this is the story that we can best leave to our military and get on with our lives. If the nation gets obsessed with it in a time of comparative peace, it surely indicates the militarization of the citizenry whether they realize it or not. Eisenhower warned us of the military industrial complex but even he would have been stunned to realize that the industry teaming with the military to threaten our way of life was not steel-making but story-manufacturing. We are back in the Cold War where stories of fear are the weapon of choice of enemy and friend alike.

America used to be the melting pot defining itself by who could come in to create wealth and seize the new opportunities. Now, America wants to define herself by who she does not want to bring in. Someone will need to chisel a caveat to the message on Lady Liberty's "Give me your tired, your poor, your huddles masses" in Manhattan Harbor to say "So long as you pay your fine, and wait in line." Meanwhile, Europe old and new, works on one passport, one currency, and the walls between old enemies, nations a thousand years older than the USA, are being torn down. War has taught Europe that perpetual defensiveness is the climate which breeds wars, and that integration of peoples and economy will eventually make war an anachronism.

A nation whose sense of identity was forged on the battlegrounds of Yorktown and Antietam is never going to be a country too far removed from the fear that national identity can be threatened again. It is why we honor our military heroes above most others, but the Candidate has to negotiate carefully in this area because stirring fear is a short term strategy, valuable in emergencies, but not for sustaining longer term goals. Fear will paralyze a nation from embracing a broader future that it could be building. Fear closes down, narrows the aperture of attention to see only that which you fear. It releases one of the most primal stories available to us, but perpetual war is a contradiction as far as a story goes because of the law of beginnings middles and ends. If the end is not in sight, it is no longer a story. The energy will drain away along with any sense of purpose or meaning. Iraq is the perfect example of not only a failed war, but a failed story.

"USA AS ONE"-"WORLD AS MANY"-FOREIGN RELATIONS

The relationship between the one and the many within the State finds its mirror here in the relation of this one nation to the many nations of the world. It is more than just foreign policy. What is our stance towards the world? McCain and Obama are thrust into that story by the recent actions of a resurgent Russia in the Caucuses. A speech moment in Berlin near the Brandenburg Gate makes a good event to signal to the world that Obama will renew America's connection to the world but he knows he has no connection to that place or time. He is inserting himself into the scene, some would say rather pretentiously, though it was a good photo op.

Meanwhile, McCain can live off the days of the American GI being greeted as the Liberator, as his Dad and his Granddad surely were, though his own experience of Vietnam or Iraq might give the lie to such nostalgia. Yet he could stand in the Potsdamer Platz and speak of a family that sacrificed so much for a united Germany. Ironically, he had more rights to that story than Obama did but he was never going to get 200,000 adoring fans.

Disregarding these PR stunts, which is all they seemed to be, the issue remains: do we want to embrace the world, and does the world want to embrace us? And do we want to spread freedom and democracy to the world? Is that still part of our manifest destiny? And are we, as President Bush proclaims, the lead actor in the march of liberty thru history?

STORY FOUR-THE ROT AT THE TOP

The final story is the standard line for budding politicians who, like Mr. Smith in the movies, want to come to Washington to fix the mess, because there is a **Rot at the Top.** The rulers are corrupt and have been ever since George III. Unrepentant reformers all, we always want to get rid of the ruler, or make it impossible for any form of tyranny to seize power.

Translate that into the Presidential Plot and it becomes "Washington is broken." But it refers not only to government, or the corruption in Congress, but to business leaders creaming off the profits before they abandon enterprises that, through their malfeasance, they have bankrupted. It is also the media in the hip pocket of power, repeating lies like lap dogs and conspiring to make the first amendment into the first apology. Washington is broken, and so was the Garden of Eden, and there will always be evidence to prove it so long as human beings are given access to power.

THE GOVERNMENT AND THE PEOPLE

This last set of stories maps out the field of the relationship between the governed and the government, a core set of stories that are not only set down in the Constitution but cover the exercise of power at every level of life, from the town sheriff, the planning board to the Federal Reserve. Reich might be a little too cynical here but he raises another key question; What role is government to play? That is central to the agenda of any election. When we have been treated to what some have called the Imperial Presidency expressed in claims to unprecedented protection behind secrecy and executive privilege, the candidates need to come clean on their view of the power they will wield. Are we voting for an Emperor or a President? Are we voting for torture and wiretaps and signing statements that act as undisclosed line item vetoes?

It also applies to the economy and corporate power. Obama wants to impose a windfall profit tax on big oil, and tax the rich to help the poor, a la Robin Hood economics. McCain wants to cut taxes to the rich so that they can continue to make more money, and create more jobs for the poor etc, an Ayn Rand economics. Their policies are reactions to their sense of this field of stories that maps the area between top and bottom, and a growing sense that power has been privatized by the wealthy who can buy access while leaving the average hard working citizen a smaller and smaller share of this national prosperity.

FOUR FIELDS OF NARRATIVE ENERGY

With these four sets of stories as laid out by Reich, we could almost chart a campaign platform because whatever the policy, it will find its roots in assumptions made within these four fields of stories. And instead of thinking of them as four separate stories, it is more useful to think of them as the four fields of narrative energy that any candidate has to traverse and fit his various policy positions into, as well as fit his own biography.

They also help us stay focused on the deeper narrative landscape. The danger of an election year is that we all get so caught up in the side issues, the high dramas that actually conceal or distract us from the core issues that will shape the future of the country.

Republicans traditionally have championed the Heroic Individual and the Enemy at the Gates, and the Democrats are usually more eloquent on the Beloved Community and the Rot at the Top. When the Enemy is literally at the Gates, such as 9-11, it makes sense that this story will strongly inform the meaning of our threatened lives and Republicans have a record delivering on that, but they think they have a monopoly on it.

When the country has to endure an ineffective Presidency and a do-nothing Congress, the story that will gain most traction is Rot at the Top, the 'Washington is Broken' stories and normally, the party of reform is the Democrats. They talk as if they own that narrative territory. However, if this becomes the clear battleground, as it appears to be becoming, the Republicans need to raid Democrat territory and convince voters that they too can clean out Washington. If they pull it off, it will be an escape act to rival Houdini's given that they have been in charge of Washington these last eight years, but no matter. If in 1968, the campaign team could convince voters that Nixon was Mother Teresa in a suit and tie, they can certainly suck the nation into a new story of those scourge-of-lobbyists and anti-Big Business Republicans, the party of reform!!!

TIME FOR A CHANGE IN THE NARRATIVE LANDSCAPE

The prospect of an election throws all these story fields into play, in that if there is a chance for change, there must be room for a renegotiation of the balance between them. For instance, will the new president roll back some of the Patriot Act's encroachments on the 'Heroic Individual' and his freedoms? If so, it would mean re-describing the 'Enemy at the Gate' story. Who is the real enemy? Terrorists or our foreign policy or our energy dependence?

Will he change the 'Rot at the Top' story and instead of government prying on the privacy of the normal citizen, will Congress bring back more oversight and regulation of those in the corporate and media world, and move to protect the citizen from predatory practices in finance and communications and media?

The state of the economy means that the top to bottom ratio is out of balance, that people feel progress and power have been privatized and available only to the top. The immigration and security issues mean the relations between the inside and outside is out of balance, because we seem to be talking ourselves into a state of xenophobic siege. And when people talk of poverty, they seem oblivious to figures that show the poorest are the immigrants, legal and illegal, who cannot afford health insurance and who are our vital pool of domestic, semi-skilled labor.

To offer a message of hope, the Candidate needs stories that re-describe what America's position is going to be on these four main axes of anxiety or opportunity, paranoia and possibility.

OUR BIGGER STORY IN THE WORLD

It is unusual for a Candidate to go campaigning in a country that doesn't have a vote, but Obama's overseas trip and his triumphant speech in Berlin reminds us at least that the Presidential Plot is played out in the global context and that the four stories that Reich lays out as core to the American sense of identity are wrapped inside an increasingly powerful global story. The American story cannot go it alone, it has to live inside the universal story, involving global warming and environmental degradation and energy depletion and Muslim religious radicalism. And when most of the national debt is held by China, and our oil comes from the Middle East and South America, the illusion that America can ever again vote for a go-it-alone candidate "maverick" like George Bush is dangerous.

A good surveyor reads the land, and a good presidential candidate needs to read the lay of the world *realpolitik*, where, as Robert Kagan has recently reminded us before world events did, history has suddenly come back to haunt us.[7] Our claim to be the last surviving super-power is looking decidedly thin in the face of a resurgent Russia and a booming China, not to speak of India.

There is a wake-up call hidden in the way the world will unravel in the next few months before and after the election and it threatens

7 Robert Kagan The Return of History and the End of Dreams Knopf 2008

to make our obsession about terrorism and Al Qaeda look like a fetish. While we were frisking harmless little old ladies in airports, China and Russia were back in play, and our economy was being gambled like a load of chips at a Las Vegas Casino.

Though we have made it into the defining event of the era, what if 9-11 ultimately looks like an aberration, a detour, an isolated tragedy that thankfully never recurred? If the candidates are only reading their polling results, we will get more of the same lame pandering to popularity, but if the Candidate dares to read the landscape of the nation and the lie of the land in the world he will be inheriting, then the promise of change that he will bring will be nothing compared to the change that will be forced upon us, whether we want it or not, around energy, around economy and debt, and around International law.

OUR STORY TO SAVE THE WORLD AND THE WORLD'S STORY TO SAVE US

If a presidential candidate has to read the narrative landscape of the nation, he must also invite the nation to read the narrative landscape of the world. It might appear to be too complex to defy any valid generalization, but the world is made of stories too, and the human being is the *homo narrans*, a storytelling primate. Why make it more complicated than it has to be? As Sting sings in his poignant song, "Russians still love their children too."

A writer on modern spirituality, Margaret Silf, [8] has the notion that we are growing inside a story that is universal. She writes:

> *There is a story growing inside you...Inside of you, and inside of every other one of us, there is a story gestating that is as big as the universe, and as mysterious, and mind-blowing and as beautiful. And the amazing thing is that when we even begin to explore the narrative of this great story, we find that we are growing inside the story. So there is a story growing inside you and you are growing inside a story.* [9]

Evolution and the survival of the species have somehow encoded a narrative deep inside the genes that we had best start to be aware of, and listen to. These are the deeper stories that can sustain the human experiment. The ones who tell it best are perhaps poets like

---

8 Margaret Silf <u>Roots and Wings</u> Darton Longman Todd 2006 p. xi

9 *Op.Cit.*

Wendell Berry and Leslie Marmon Silko. If we want to leave a world fit for our grandkids, we need to vote not just for the best story for America, but what is the best story and the best candidate for the world. The planet might be depending on it.

CHAPTER NINE

AUDIENCES THAT MAKE OR BREAK THE STORY

If there is no audience, there is no story, and if there is no story, there is no audience.

If there is one area of expertise that continues to dazzle anyone following the Presidential election, it is the depth of knowledge campaigns and their operatives have about audience. Like the media industry's knowledge of ratings, campaigns use similar tools to measure who is watching their show and when. Candidates hope to translate the winning of an audience into the winning of a voter or a donor.

Polls become the drama, and pure numbers are never so sexy as when they form part of the Times Poll or Zogby or Peter Hart. Though it can be about as exciting as watching a thermometer, it allows the interpreters to weave a story around the numbers. We get the pollsters telling us the ebb and flow of preferences, and which States will be battleground States. If McCain wins Michigan, he wins the election and so on.

CAMPAIGNS KNOW THE AUDIENCE, BUT NOT THEIR STORY

Even if it is measuring whether people like McCain's hairstyle, polls trigger stories for media consumption which then become contributive or contradictory to the candidates' narrative. And either way, they are compelling viewing for us election addicts. They rarely produce results that are determinative or even correct, but why they matter is that they produce stories. It is the alchemy of statistics to make numbers add up to a narrative. Figures only make sense through the stories they trigger. And when we know that any figure can mean anything, we need to be more skeptical of this whole process perhaps, or at least 22% on an adjusted scale more skeptical.

A DIFFERENT TAKE ON AUDIENCE

When a narrative analyst is speaking about audience, he is not going to pretend to the level of expertise of the pundits or pollsters. Rather our sense of audience comes from a more internal understanding of how a story works and what the Presidential Plot demonstrates as an audience driven phenomenon. If there is no audience, there is no story, and if there is no story, there is no audience. The two are mutually inclusive. Yet the story of the audience is another of those hidden stories that the Candidate and the voter dare not take for granted.

THE POWER IS WITH THE LISTENER

We teach in our narrative workshops that within every story, there is a secret power that shapes the story so powerfully and yet so subtlety that it is hardly ever heard or spoken about, and that is the story of the listening.[10] In other words, when we tell a story, we do so without realizing that the shaping power is as much in the listening as in the telling. And there are two key listeners, the external one that is out there in front of us on the receiving end in the exterior world, and there is the secret listener, of us hearing ourselves within the hidden world of our own interiority.

HOW STORIES GAIN POWER

The most powerful stories are those that after each telling, accumulate the power of the listening so that every inflection, every mood, and every tone that was re-enforced the last time is incorporated into the next time. There is a built-in evolution of higher functionality in the act of telling and retelling. Go to an Alcohol Anonymous meeting and hear an ex-addict's "Drunkalogue" of his life before he gave up drinking. They are some of the most compelling stories around because they have been told and retold to perfection.

This is why oral tradition is such a powerful means of transmission. If only books could improve with every reader, but alas, books only reproduce the same dead letter that we have to make alive again in our imaginations. But the living word is different. We all know if we tell a favorite joke, it gets better and better as we incorporate feedback next time on when and how to deliver the punch-line.

Like the transmission of culture that Richard Dawkins calls "the transfer of memes"[11], stories pick up adaptive changes and nuances that most enhance their chance for replication. Darwin could have written 'The Origin of the Story' as well as the 'Origin of the Species' because funnily enough, stories that survive seem to work in similar ways. It is survival of the wittiest, those stories that are the best audience adaptors.

---

10 see www.storywise.com/new_page_1.htm article "Story as the Shape of our Listening"

11 Richard Dawkins <u>The Selfish Gene</u> Oxford 1989

WHO IS LISTENING?

If listeners shape stories, how does that work in the Presidential Plot? What is the listening that most shapes the story the Candidate is telling us? It sounds like a polling question but we mean it as a narrative inquiry. How much of the story is accumulating the power of the listeners?

The winning Candidate is one who tells the story in which the listener hears not only the candidate's voice but his or her own voice as well. If in genuinely telling me your story, you are also telling me my story, I will vote for you because your story reflects that you have heard me, that my story has shaped yours, and that your story has incorporated the power of my story. Stories in this way become powerful tools of enrolling people to your cause.

THE AUDIENCE PHENOMENON THAT IS ALL OBAMA

The Obama phenomenon is an audience phenomenon like no other in modern campaigns, and this is what distinguishes it. It is not content or character but the size and power of his audience. His story seems to gain more momentum with every planned and over-produced appearance. What is going on?

Obama is a great speaker to begin with, and he knows how to milk a line for maximum effect, even if it is the cliché of "change" or "Washington is broken." Like a preacher, he draws the congregation inexorably into the emotional drama of his delivery. The chat of "Preach it, Preach it" that we might hear in a Baptist Church any Sunday is replaced by "Yes we can" "Yes we can." Audiences are expected to take part as chorus and choir.

But there is a subtle danger for Obama here, if he thinks that because audiences like him and flock to his speeches that it means that they will vote for him. Crowds might also be coming to see this rare feat of a good old time orator who can cast a spell on a crowd. I would go miles to hear Mario Cuomo speak because he is such a great speaker, and that doesn't mean I would vote for him. Whether good oratory is what in the end people feel qualifies someone to be President is another matter altogether. The lack of it certainly didn't hamper either Bush, 41 or 43 getting elected. William Jennings Bryant was known as one of the most powerful orators of the last century and he ran for President more times than he would want us to remember, and never got the votes even though he always got the crowds.

If Obama can convert his oratorical popularity into votes, then good for him, but the more presumptuous he appears that he already has, he will undermine himself in a disastrous way. He needs to remember the underdog always has the narrative advantage.

On the other hand, the McCain candidacy is characterized by a spectacular lack of audience, and if the danger for Obama is to overly play to the crowds, the danger for McCain is that he will continue to shoot from the hip, regardless of who is listening because he has not developed an ear for big crowds at all, and has never had to. [12]

He has smart speech writers who must want the ground to swallow him and them when their Candidate mumbles their punch lines and elevates his irreverent asides into newly invented themes that his team has never heard before. Yet McCain knows that if it depended on oratory, he would not have even been the candidate. Huckabee was funnier, Romney was more polished, and Giuliani had more charisma.

CAMPAIGNS AS POLITICAL THEATRE

If there is danger in the candidates becoming too audience obsessed, it's hardly their fault because modern campaigns consist of events and performances that are staged down to the last detail. Audiences are well selected and primed to be ready for the main speaker. With some theme song like "Nothing's Going to Stop us Now" blaring from the speakers, the Candidate makes a Rocky-like entrance into what's more like a revival meeting where the warm up act, an Oprah or Chuck Norris, officially hands over the stage to the up and coming messiah. It makes great political theatre, or used to until its become so clichéd that one begins to ask what it actually contributes to the art of politics. The people get to hear their candidate. True. And the campaign gets a headline. But has anything actually happened?

If the crowds are hand-picked to be mostly enthusiastic supporters and if the emphasis is on the show, then we know there is no real exchange going on. That was not the point. We know that there are no hard questions going to get asked because the audience is already signed on, so the story the Candidate learns to tell becomes

---

[12] With the rise of the Palin Factor, McCain's VP pick of Governor Sarah Palin, he is finally getting energized crowds but to watch the replays, it appears to be the Conventions Speech Road Show. If Governor Palin repeats her "Bridge to Nowhere" line a few more times, it might be a bridge too far, given that the media have decided to turn the People's Hero into a Tragic Anti-Feminist because they have not forgiven McCain for picking her without allowing the media to vet her properly.

a tissue of clichés, like preaching to the choir all the time, saying the things they want to hear, the things that will get the loudest cheers, and stir the emotions of the moment. Any invitation to pause, or to invite people to a deeper reflection and dialogue about the issues doesn't look good on the video. But getting people to cheer about the future or change doesn't necessarily change anything about the future. All it does is make for great television.

If the entertainment industry has taken over the election campaign, and the focus is on showing a winning audience in the same shot rather than showcasing the Candidate's persuasive skills of winning over a skeptical audience, then it contains no drama, no surprise, and for all the hoopla of the moment, it is ultimately vapid, too full of scripted spontaneity and pretended sincerity. Will Obama and Michelle kiss? Will McCain embrace the Iraq veterans in their wheelchairs? Will Bill and Hillary give Obama that fist to fist buddy rap?

Once you see the production behind the product, you see how the whole narrative process is being degraded in the process. We have a manufactured story served for prime time consumption and sadly, even if the Candidate didn't want that, he has little choice. This is how campaigns have to run as media circuses.

Back in 1968, Roger Ailes knew what made for more dramatic television. He loved to bring on to the TV panels people to question Nixon, people whom he knew were antagonistic, and in this way, he could show his candidate handling the tough contests and even disarming his critics. Of course, Nixon's campaign also vetted the questions and most of the time, viewers questions were ignored for the questions the campaign wanted Nixon to answer. Today, apart from one You-Tube event, the media run all the debates. They ask the questions to get the ratings and the headline, as in Stephanopolous' stirring moment probing Candidate Obama's patriotism in the infamous "Why don't you wear a flag pin?" Why and how did we delegate the media to be our official Inquisitors, unless we too recognize that it's primarily a show?

NO REAL AUDIENCES MEANS NO REAL STORIES

But here is the problem: If the audiences aren't real, then the stories aren't real. If the audiences don't reflect the diversity of America and the contrary views of an electorate divided about their future, then a candidate story is being shaped into a pep-rally kind of rhetoric. He never has to learn the art of real debate, or how to absorb a criticism or to parry and thrust back with wit and humor. How often does humor come in to our current debates? Or

111

memorable moments of wit? Our Candidates are over-rehearsed and under prepared for trusting their own spontaneity. Hence a Candidate's story does not pick up the audience-adaptive changes that could enhance it and grow its power.

We need to see Obama on Fox[13] as we saw Hillary, or on Hannity, and we have already seen McCain on DeGeneres. Mix it up guys. Make it real. Get some real audiences again. McCain surprisingly wanted Town Meetings with Obama, unscripted and small, and guess who turned him down?

If one watches the tapes of JFK and the White House Press corps, one sees a President who is at the top of his game and enjoying the contest, and answering with both wit and respect. If our candidates are so controlled by campaigns that they can't afford to expose themselves to unscripted town meetings, or dare have them speak before real audiences that are less than 100% enthusiastic, then we are seeing a constructed pageant of celebrity pretending to be a Presidential Campaign.

Ultimately, all we are seeing is ourselves, audience, mirroring audience, with the Candidate merely rehearsing lines that we gave him. There is no sense that this is an edgy, organic, spontaneous, dynamic storytelling circle where stories shape stories and can change hearts and minds. There is no sparkle and no surprise. As a story, it's lifeless and forgettable.

THE STUMP SPEECH AS PERFORMANCE ART

When you hear the stump speech from McCain or Obama or Hillary and it does not change one iota whether it's Kansas or Alaska, you know then that the audience are an appendage. The candidate displays no interest in the localized knowledge that should inform his story, or if he does, it is the last minute briefing to make it sound like this guy knows at least that he is in Ohio and not Idaho. A script is something written in a play that you rehearse without deviation, but a speech is a living dynamic thing, it is an engagement with that audience living in that moment, and feeds off that energy. Why do we never see that? I have seen *Mama Mia* in London and Broadway and it's the same fun show. But if McCain

---

[13] He has since allowed himself to be interviewed on the O'Reilly Factor and Bill did a 'great' job of bullying and baiting him. Such a contrast to how mild and gentlemanly he was with Hillary Clinton. Senator Obama appears to lack confidence when it comes to playing the media game to his advantage when he is on enemy territory. Roger Ailes advice to Nixon was "Always come in under the questioner's tone" not try and speak over that or else, it appears on TV as an argument and not a discussion, or too hot for a cool medium.

or Obama take the trouble to visit the 50 States, staging everywhere from kindergartens to sports stadiums, audiences attending want to meet a real person, not simply watch a Broadway production.

THE CONVENTION SPEECHES

As we watch in the next few weeks the big speeches at the Convention, we need to ask ourselves whether we are hearing a story or an audience playback machine? Is this guy speaking so commandingly to be heard, or is he only speaking what he thinks we are hopeful of hearing?

If it is the latter, a speech informed by the latest polling data and the dictates of party orthodoxy, then we realize that the campaign process has robbed the candidate of any authenticity, because it has robbed him of any interiority. If it is ALL about audience, he is not listening to his own story. He is listening to us listening to his story, and that is what feeds his totally audience-centered words. If he wants to convey any sense that he is a real leader, he has to speak from some deeper inner core of what he believes and dance to the drumbeat he hears in his own heart,[14] regardless of what the adoring masses are clamoring for. The forgotten audience he needs to hear again is himself.[15]

THE LOSS OF INTERIORITY

The whole campaign as an audience creating process builds on exteriority over any interiority. The candidate gets constructed from outside in, not from inside out and politics is reduced to a performance art.

The 1968 book "The Selling the President" makes it clear that elections rarely hinge on the inner reality of Candidates. The Nixon whom Roger Ailes knew up close and personal was a vain and flawed giant, but the campaign's purpose was to build an image for the audience, like building a set for a play or a drama. One advisor compared it to building an Astrodome.[16]

---

[14] McCain's acceptance speech used the "drumbeat line" as if he was reading over our shoulders

15 Both speeches were composed for prime time, covering traditional themes and uttering the compulsory clichés. Interestingly enough, McCain's was more interesting for its almost total lack of policy promises and its repudiation of the recent Republican record. And Obama the orator went for personal attack and policy. The Obama of the 2004 Convention rarely appeared in the Acropolis.

16 Ibid, McGinniss, p.39

The sense of inner story one gets when it's all about the audience is the same sense one gets in a performer. The stand-up comic is only reading his inner story to tell him, 'Is the audience laughing, are they getting the jokes? Am I a success, and do they like me?' So too with the election by media and by contrived event, it is the creation and marketing of an image that is audience-centric and it might have some connection to the inner actualities of the candidate but not necessarily much.

We can re-package and remake Al Gore to be a rural kid who grew up on the tobacco farms of Tennessee when in fact he grew up in a Hotel in Washington. Or a George Bush can be repackaged to have the ranch, even though you will never see a picture of cowboy George on a horse because apparently he knows how to ride a bike but doesn't like or know how to ride a horse.

If the story is totally driven by the outer audience, then it is hollowed out and will change and morph into whatever we think the crowd want it to be. In the election cycle, pollsters tell the candidates as to where they need to move: win the primaries on the far left or the far right and win the elections in the center, or so goes the adage.

But our narrative intelligence kicks in when we sense that someone is only trying to tell us what they think we want to hear. You can almost hear the gears changing, as they stammer and stutter and listen for the lines that we give them. We know because we did it as bratty kids coming late from school: "Why are you home late?' Was the bus late?' "Yes the bus late?" "But I saw it pass me; did the route change?" 'Yes the route changed." It is a case of *narrative interruptus,* and it has come to characterize the campaigns.

Obama says the Israeli's must never give up Jerusalem and then, hears the outcry and says, "Oh, I misspoke." If it were a cartoon with a speech balloon, you might have Obama thinking, "I will win the pro-Israeli lobby by being Moses and re-promising the Promised Land," and then hearing, 'No, that is not really what they wanted to hear'. So he tells it to them again and this time, it's what they wanted to hear. It certainly doesn't help if the candidate wants to also portray himself as a man of principle.

Or more recently, McCain reassures us that the economy is sound, and when Lehman Brothers and AIG and Merrill Lynch all collapse or are sold off, he says, "I meant the workers were sound-the economy is now in crisis but wait- I will be your Rescuer."

A man of principle is someone who has an inner audience, or a developed interiority, a conscience, someone who has the inner story as well as the outer story. It is one thing to be telling the crowd something you know will please them and it is quite another to be telling yourself that this is not what you really believe. If the media election spends enormous amounts building an exteriority, what chance has interiority surviving intact? What chance is there of the story of conscience and principle surviving the scrutiny of a celebrity campaign? The country rightly deserves a leader of principle but campaigns and media create a leader of expediency. It doesn't work because you can't keep treating citizens as viewers first and voters second. Soon we realize there is no "there" there.

EXTERIORITY OVER INTERIORITY-THE MUFFLING OF CONSCIENCE

After two years of campaigning, the election process cannot but help create a Candidate as some kind of monster who stands for nothing and falls for anything. It is inevitably a poll driven candidate who drives the Straight Talking Express with his eyes fixed firmly on the rear-vision looking for the ripples of impact behind and not the road ahead. For someone who is supposed to be a leader by virtue of his vision and his passion for the future, we are left with the image of a leader going forward backwards because to get elected, he has to be more concerned with following public opinion than shaping it.

If we look at Clinton and the reputation of her handlers or of Karl Rove as the campaign commando for Bush, they all seem to inhabit a shady Machiavellian world, where the object is to win at all costs and the prescribed means is to work out what the people want to hear and make sure you keep telling them that. Their argument is that if you don't win power, you can't do anything, but the means they use to win power cripples any prospect of its authentic and honest use.

LESSONS FROM THE BUSH PRESIDENCY

One startling characteristic of the Bush years has been his professed disdain of the polls and the boast that he listens to his inner sense of what is right and then does it. He trusts history and not the polls for his vindication. He said he was right on Iraq and he will not change his mind, even if the only people who agree are Laura and the dog. [17] This is usually ascribed to his arrogance, but

---

17 Dogs and Breeders reported that even the President's dog Tuffey has registered as a Democrat this year!

President Bush might know a few things about audience worth our taking a second look.

He has an inner compass even if it is of misguided certainty. Pretty clearly it comes from a deep sense of interiority that he has formed through his faith and his recovery from alcohol addiction. He is known to read a daily devotional <u>My Utmost for his Highest</u>, a famous Methodist manual which consists of sermons preached between 1914 and 1917 by a British chaplain who was eventually killed in World War One. If he was reading it during the days that he took the nation to war in Iraq, his daily devotional was telling him that the public self is worth nothing, and that it is the private self, where one meets God in the sacred space of one's conscience, that matters most because only God can judge a man's heart.

It also reminds him that part of the price of doing the right thing as against the popular thing is that the world will hate you. On March 19th, the day the invasion of Iraq was launched, Bush's devotional prepares him for a testing of faith: It is titled *"The Way of Abraham in Faith"* and it tells the devotee:

> *"In the Old Testament, personal relationship with God showed itself in separation ...from his country and his kin....it is the life of faith, not of intellect and reason,... The final stage in the life of faith is the attainment of character.... The life of faith is not a life of mounting up with wings but a life of walking and not fainting....faith that has been tried and proved and has stood the test."* (Chambers, 134) [18]

Bush has a story to deal with his plummeting ratings. It fits his inner story, and the cognitive dissonance is solved by making his unpopularity into a sign of his being persecuted for righteousness. This is the test of his faith more than a test of his policy for the nation. He believes and that is all that matters.[19]

In President Bush, we note a well marked border between the inner-outer territory and even if critics accuse him of being disconnected from the consequences of his decisions, he is a leader who at least displays both a public and a private zone of discretion. He might not appear to be the smartest President alive, but he is smart as a character, complex enough to defy the pundits and

---

18 Oswald Chambers <u>My Utmost for His Highest</u> Fleming Revell Company New Jersey 1935 pp. 131, 134

19 Ben Macintyre "Bush fights the good fight with a righteous quotation" *The Times* London March 8th 2003

surprise us. His is a compelling story, regardless of whether we like him or not. Just look at the number of books on the Bush Presidency, and it's not even over.

FAITH PROVIDES A CRITICAL INTERIOR AUDIENCE

How do we restore a sense of authenticity to the electoral process and ensure we get the best out of the best candidates? As a narrative intervention, it means restoring and respecting that interiority, and ensuring that candidates can recruit that inner audience to keep them grounded and anchored amidst the media circus. One interior audience comes from faith and family, and even old friends and rivals who offer to listen to the candidate in that inner realm.

Culturally the territory of the inner realm is shrinking, with the advent of the Internet 'Show and Tell' sites like MySpace and Facebook which augur poorly for the election of an inner-directed leader and a man of conscience. Candidates of the future must beware of what they put up on their MySpace site now because it will endure to haunt them. The media's oversized hunger for a story pays no respect to interiority because it wants it all to hang out. In this campaign, we have seen the collapse of the once protected realm of private audience. Elections demand everything to be public.

For instance, when Obama is speaking to an insider group in California, someone is there taping his infamous "Cling to" speech. Or Hillary and Obama are meeting with funders and it's a closed meeting at the Mayflower Hotel in DC but straight after, we have someone who taped it and someone who sent pictures over the cell phone. It was supposed to be private. Or think about the 'Makakka' incident that doomed Senator George Allen, a Virginian Senator or Bill Clinton's angry throwaway lines that a blogger had taped in his comment on an unflattering article in *Vanity Fair*. Now we are sending reporters to tape the Candidate's pastor and his latest sermon. When are we going to sneak a camera into the bedroom or bathroom?

What is the future of the interior audience of a leader's conscience? The collapse of private space into public space, or the Drudge-ification of Candidate privacy signals a disturbing trend of a surveillance and voyeur culture, where you post your break-up with the girlfriend before you tell her or your friends, and every private space becomes a potential YouTube studio.

117

THE DISAPPEARANCE OF INTERIORITY

The secret in the great stories of our literature and drama is that the hero has an inner story, one that he seeks to accommodate to the outer world. The compelling drama is about that engagement and that clash of inner conscience or desire with outer realities. The beauty of a novel and of all great fiction is that it can take us inside a character's heart as well as outside to the world of appearances. When the media is all surface, we need to bring back the novel approach to stories, if we want better stories to shape the mind and heart of the Republic and give our future Presidents the chance to dwell in a better and bigger story about their own humanity. We need to revive the story of conscience.

THE INNER DRAMAS OF HISTORY

Think back to our great Presidential stories. Lincoln wants to end slavery and the voters just want the country put back together again. How does he accommodate both conscience and constituents? Or LBJ wants to grant civil rights and the people want an end to the Vietnam War and in the end, he surrenders power rather than tear the nation apart the way his own soul was being torn apart. If the test of character is crisis and the quality of character is inner conviction, then modern campaigns creates caricatures compared to those Presidents of old, who dwelt in a larger human story than we will allow to our modern Candidates and Presidents.

LISTENING TO ALTERNATE STORIES

Sometimes, a President is better off reading Dickens than reading the *New York Times* or the latest polling data. We get locked into the urgencies of the moment, and create no space for other voices and other imaginations. JFK in the Cuban crisis should have been reading the military reports on Russian troops amassing in Cuba, but he also chose to listen to The Guns of August, the great book by historian Barbara Tuchman. It was a story that gave him a way to counter the military hawks who wanted to nuke the hell out of Cuba and ask questions later. Tuchman's tale of World War One described how, once decisions about the use of force were made, they were irrevocable and they set off a chain of events that leaders could not call back.

Perhaps if George Bush had been reading the annals of the British Empire in Iraq and Churchill's games with the map of the Middle East, instead of reading his bible that called for righteous revenge or thinking he was Dirty Harry, "Bring it on," Iraq might never have happened. Better stories make for smarter policies. But in the narrative view of the world, to listen is to give your power away and be vulnerable to having another story shape your story. Perhaps we should be asking our Presidential Candidates what they are reading and what stories are they inviting to help shape their imaginations for America?

SUPREME COURT-AUDIENCE SMART!

If we follow this narrative analysis on audience, it will turn up some other counter-intuitive results. No one thinks that the Supreme Court is innovative on anything. Stacked with a majority of conservative judges, its decisions seem to be rolling back the broader reading of the Constitution that the country got used to with the Warren Court. And as far as relating to the media, they are seen as antediluvian in not allowing cameras into the courtroom and not sending out press releases before decisions. They make everyone wait. Yet, as far as narrative and audience go, it is the smartest institution in town. Let me tell you why.

They are adamant in preserving their interiority and making sure that they work within structures where their prime purpose is to listen to the case and its advocates, and then listen to the Constitution and the history of its interpretation. They take all that into their closed chambers to quietly consult and negotiate. To listen to the polls, or to what the people's mood is, is to risk corrupting their roles. They know once they allow a wider audience, their role and their story will inevitably change. One only has to think back to the OJ Simpson trial and how poorly it served Judge Ito, who may have been a great judge normally, but he was clearly an amateur actor in front of the cameras and in the company of all those celebrity lawyers.

As Chief Justice Roberts told a group of my Irish interns a year ago, every case is a story, so he knows a few things about stories. Most lawyers who are successful do, and many of them go on to become successful lobbyists, and it's not only their skill with the law that ensures their success, I hazard to guess, but their skills in telling persuasive stories, their narrative IQ.

MAKING ROOM FOR SILENCE IN A STORY

The media is made for instantaneity and spontaneity. They offer us the surface of NOW with no time for any depth of history, and meaning thereby suffers. Meaning is layered in language's internal memory. It is laced within words woven with the textures of other times and the echoes of alternate histories. They come from other

119

places besides the here and now. To stay in the now is to stay on the surface. It is to root ideas in a very thin soil, meaning issues will have pretty thin levels of meaning and little chance to grow any deeper understanding. A good story displays a deep respect for silence, for in that silence the drama between inner meaning and outer interpretation can be heard and can play out.

Adlai Stevenson who ran for President a few times, wisely said:

> *"Sometimes in the deafening clamor of political statesmanship, I've thought that the people might be better served if a party purchase a half hour of radio and television silence during which the audience would be asked to think quietly for themselves."*

Imagine a headline, "There was no news today and so we are going to show scenes from The Grand Canyon to the score of the Grand Canyon Suite which we hope you all enjoy."

When we sacrifice interiority for exteriority or demand that of our Candidates, we inflict on the Republic a caricature of the Presidency in place of what should have all the drama and depth of a great novel. As any writer or performer knows, the more discerning the audience, the better the act and so, perhaps its time we stop accepting the pulp fiction fed to us in the name of campaigns. When all the hoopla dies down, we have to appreciate that elections are about finding the best human beings to lead us. If they have to sacrifice their humanity to fit the straitjacket of party, and betray their consciences to feed the censorial sensationalism of media, then we need to find a better story so humanity can make a belated comeback to the Presidential Plot.

AN OCCASIONAL COLUMN

THIS ADMINISTRATION MUST THINK WE ARE AN AUDIENCE OF SUCKERS

Someone smarter than me said that we should never overestimate what the people know and never underestimate what the people understand. When the White House Press Officer, Dana Perino, tells us on the fifth anniversary of the day the now notorious "Mission Accomplished" hit the news, that the only mistake was that it should have been more specific to the actual mission of the ship, she is clearly presuming that we, the masses, are total idiots. We must look totally clueless, totally undiscerning in sorting white lies, where truth is impolite, from outright lies told to deceive, from plausible lies where at least some attempt has been made to lie credibly. This one does not even give that backhanded compliment to truth. Perhaps we can rally to her in support and suggest other excuses that work better: such as:

"It was the end of the Chaplain's revival on board and the Reverend Fire and Brimstone just finished preaching conversion and even the Captain had come to Jesus, so Mission Accomplished and they forgot to add- "Praise the Lord.""

Or the White House asked the Navy to delay the ship's arrival into San Diego and all the crew's families had to wait, and it was cruising too fast for the Presidentially flown plane to land properly, so they had to slow down, and the angle of the sun was wrong for that iconic Independence Day photo op in the flight jacket, so 'Could the guys on the bridge turn the 50,000 tonne carrier around so the sun was setting over the presidential shoulder, as it were, rather than the lights of San Diego a few miles off?' And the officers were so amazed at what a ship of state was being asked to do by its Commander in Chief to not only win the war on terror but also win the war of images on the 6 o'clock news. So they put that banner up, out of their own frustration, and a signal to the White House, "Don't go asking us to harpoon a White Whale. We've done all we are gonna do, Mr. President."

Sure the mission preacher isn't quite a fit because we know all the evangelists are in the Air Force, and to accuse the harassed crew of being guilty of Mission Accomplished-Gate is unfair because they probably loved the attention, but unlike the White House Press office, I did at least make an effort.

All we have left is believing the banner, according to the official excuse, should have read "Mission Accomplished by the crew of the USS Carrier *Abraham Lincoln* on their 30 day surveillance mission in the Persian Gulf between co-ordinates 30 degrees NE by NW and 20 degrees SE by S at the average speed of 18.3 knots." The banner would have been so large that in a strong wind, the carrier might have gained an extra knot or two. But I guess we believed this White House about WMD's and "No Torture" etc so they have come to presume we'll let them get away with anything, and at least that's a mission they have accomplished until now.

CHAPTER TEN

CAST OF CHARACTERS-DRAMATIS PERSONAE

"People think that stories are shaped by people. In fact, it's the other way around. Stories exist independently of their players. If you know that, the knowledge is power." Terry Pratchett

If we know the plot, that the country is going in the wrong direction because over 85% in continuous polling say that, and we know we need a hero to put it aright, then the next question is about casting. What is the cast of characters that usually play in this kind of story? And who gets the lead?

POPULATING OUR PLOT-SEARCHING FOR A HERO

Who will be our hero? Brad Pitt? Matt Damon? Heroes are usually young and daring and beautiful and the kinds of people that we support because in the movies, the odds are stacked against them. They challenge the powers that be and come close to being destroyed, but in that final scene, they pull it off, and we leave the theatre feeling that all is right with the moral universe we like to imagine we inhabit. So we have a good idea of who fits the part in our movie universe.

Unlike the challenge facing a Hollywood casting agent, the Presidential Plot doesn't require us auditioning thousands of aspirants. The primary process has whittled them down to just two. We know the story, and we know the setting, and we know the result. We even know there will be unpredictable moments of stress and strain. So, all that remains is deciding who gets the part?

Obama and McCain are auditioning for the role of *"A Hero Saving the Nation."* One is a younger man and one an older man which means we have some predictable and parallel plot lines to explore. How does a young man become the hero? Can we spin out that story? And how does an older man become the hero? Can we tell that one just to see how it might work?

We have already heard them do their preliminary readings of all those scripts of past elections like "Washington is broken," or "Time for a change," or "This is the most important election in a lifetime." They are all great lines that we know have worked before and they worked for them in convincing their respective party delegates and voters that they fit their Party's requirements. But now the big audition is whether these lines will work for the national audience? And what other story lines might work? A narrative perspective invites us to play with the different characters in this story and imagine alternate scenarios.

PLAYING WITH A VARIED CAST OF CHARACTERS

The old Shakespearean text books from High School days used to always have among the title pages, a Dramatic Personae, outlining who is who in the story. Hamlet is the young Prince of Denmark; Ophelia is his crazy girlfriend, Claudius is the evil King etc. Story exploration means we do the same thing for the Presidential Plot. We can start moving characters in and out of the plot as an experiment to see what kinds of stories might or might not work. It's like finding people for our Big Brother House.

We know already that this is an epic, and that it must follow the law of beginnings, middle and ends, and we know that the story is for heroes. We know the four dominant stories that define America's narrative landscape into which they must venture. The hero story must also have healthy villains, along with characters who play for and against the lead, as patrons and spoilers and prophets, while others intrude to give us comic relief. Every decent plot needs some sub-plots too and plenty of extras. This one has a role for potentially 300 million extras.

POPULATE YOUR PLOT

In a workshop earlier this year, I asked people to draw up a list of potential characters who would be invited to play some role in the story of *"The Hero who turned America around."* So long as the two Candidates themselves are in your list, you could make up your own. Below are out suggestions of the kinds of people we are looking for to make the Presidential Plot work at its dramatic best.

THROW IN SOME HEADS OF STATE

The Presidential story is about Heads of State and so we need Kings and Queens and Presidents and Prime Ministers. We might add Vladimir Putin these days or President Clinton or the President of Georgia or the new President of Pakistan. We are creating a world stage. So, what world leaders do you want?

WE NEED SOME RELIGIOUS LEADERS

The religious dimension requires either a Pope, or a Reverend Billy Graham or Reverend Wright or more lately, a Rick Warren to be part of the mix. For a country that prides itself on the strict separation of Church and State, a visitor from Mars would certainly be confused to see the role that the religious right and other faith communities play in selecting a President. But it wouldn't be an epic without gods in there somewhere. So, pick a religious person, a Rabbi or even a Mullah.

WE NEED SOME RELIABLE ENEMIES

Osama Bin Laden, Muslim Terrorists, Kim Il Sung, Saddam Hussein? Saddam has quit the show though his ghostly presence still hangs over the theatre of war. Osama Bin Laden has made a recent comeback as Public Enemy Number One but since no one knows where he is, he won't sell too many tickets. Our current campaign lacks for a good reliable enemy. The Democrats or Party out of power suffer most from this absence because the role of enemy most easily goes to the incumbent President. He doesn't even have to audition. Bush is smart enough not to entertain any ambitions of influencing the elections directly. In his absence, the Democrats have to dress up McCain as the enemy, as Bush Number 3 "more of the same" or else find some other appropriate enemy like Washington corruption or Wall Street greed to drive their story. But a villain is essential, because otherwise, there is nothing for the hero to overcome. So, be sure you pick an axis of evil, or the Evil Empire, or some such character. In this capacity, Obama is badly missing his Hillary and has his work cut out to thoroughly demonize Senator McCain.

McCain will steal the Giuliani play and hark back to 9-11 and remind us that the terrorists are still waiting to attack, that the Enemies are at the Gate, and when asked about evil, he will eschew theology to immediately swear to chase and capture Osama Bin Laden even if he has to go to the "Gates of Hell" and back. He has already cast himself in Dante's epic. And he was quicker off the mark than even the President to denounce Vladimir Putin and company, because there is no enemy like an old enemy. "Russia as Enemy" is an old friend, a tried and tested narrative, and one that a Ronald Reagan is reputedly to have won in an earlier match-up. Obama is not a warrior and he is not an accomplished hater either so, finding a convincing villain, someone we can see who actually enrages our calm and cool reasoning Obama is one of his challenges.

But every successful Candidate needs to be blessed with the gift of a good reliable enemy and it's where the Republicans usually have an advantage over the Democrats. The Liberals work themselves into a lather of conscience about going negative, when narrative intelligence says, it is not going negative at all but learning how to craft a better story, because a better story needs something for your hero to fight against and overcome. What good is a story without evil? Heroes don't easily inhabit the territory of compromise. If the Democrat narrative is too full of nuance and dwells in the debatables more than the definites, it's hard for any hero to defend that territory and come off heroic. He will sound more like Don Quixote. Republicans love their enemies and they invented the tradition of enemy hit lists, and hence, they have an advantage in the story wars because they make better haters.

FROM CENTRAL CASTING

So, we have Kings and Popes and enemies in our cast. Let's make a list:

>Queen Elizabeth II of England,
>Pope Benedict XVI,
>Saddam Hussein,
>President George W Bush,
>Hamlet,
>Hillary Clinton,
>Barack Obama,
>John McCain.

This is the Dramatis Personae of our Play. Next write the description of role after each name. Here are some of the descriptors we got from our seminar participants.

Pope Benedict-	Church-religious power-Faith
Queen Elizabeth-	Head of state-tradition-inheritance,
Hillary Clinton-	Witch, Fairy God-mother, Lady Macbeth,
Saddam Hussein-	Ghost of the evil past-Scrooge, scapegoat
Hamlet	The quintessential flip-flopper,
President Bush-	The old tyrant, misunderstood hero seeking vindication, torturer
John McCain-	Old Veteran and Warrior, Ulysses
Barack Obama-	Untried Prince, ambition, pride, hope, Achilles

People now move into story production groups to work on storyboarding the play by imagining the characters were all dolls in a play house, or puppets in a show, and exploring what happens when you let them interact. What stories can you come up with that allow Obama or McCain to win, using as many of the characters as you can? You can give this game to your family and friends at home, and after 30 minutes in their groups, and a few beers, bring them together to tell their stories and ask everyone to listen for the commonality of roles the characters are plotted to play. How did Obama win using the Queen and Hillary? How did

McCain win using the Pope and Saddam? Any number and variety of characters can be made to all serve the one plot.

But things won't go totally according to plan if we are to have a successful story. There also has to be some late, unexpected detours, and just before the Teams announce their winning scenarios, you can mix it up by announcing a late breaking development, the October surprise.

LAST MINUTE DISTRACTIONS AND DETOURS

Life will always manage to intervene to upset the best laid plans. Someone will die, a plane will crash, hurricanes will threaten, or some former running mate and Candidate will be outed as being gay or having an affair, or owing back taxes. We could imagine all this as a sort of board game where this is the pile of Wild Card Entries to spice up the story, except that you have to determine whether it is a distraction or potentially destructive. For this contest, we already have Wild Card Entries for

- Rev Wright's sermon on "God Damn America"
- Senator John Edwards affair with his staffer
- Lobbyists on your campaign lobbying against lobbying
- Associating with assorted convicted criminals-Resko, Ayers
- Saying voters "cling" to their gods and guns
- Bill Clinton's outbursts at the press
- Wall Street panic and company sell-offs
- Campaign wishes for terrorist attack to help their vote
- One of your strongest supporters gets very ill-Senator Kennedy
- Senator McCain forgets how many houses he has
- Pigs, Hockey Moms and Lipstick and VPs all get mixed up

Added to these will be Candidate gaffes as defined by the media, when McCain forgets that the Korean War ended in a draw, or when Obama's attempted joke about Chicago hamburgers back fires and the Meat Packers Union disown him. And these are all the predictable surprises.

LET'S PLAY

Put the cast into action, knowing that the plot demands conflict, enemies, alliances, betrayals, and an arc of redemption whereby what was once lost is at last saved. And have one team of friends develop the scenario of an Obama Hero and another team develop the McCain Hero scenario. Quickly we will fall into predictable patterns of conflict that we know well because we know how stories work. And before we know it, we have characters forming conspiracies, and eliminating or neutralizing rivals. People will think we have studied Machiavelli but we have seen *West Wing* instead.

RELIGION TRIES TO DOMINATE THE ELECTION

One story scenario from our cast of characters might see Religion trying to influence the outcome, as in the Pope declaring a Candidate cursed, or the Evangelical Right warming to the born-again McCain who once described them as agents of intolerance. Or Evangelicals energizing the vote to protect the conservative majority on the Supreme Court. We can be pretty sure that a McCain winning scenario is going to involve energized religion.

On the other side, we have the Candidate seeking to overthrow the power of the Church. JFK had to prove his Presidency was not some Papist plot, and John Kerry had to battle a few Bishops who wanted to deny him the sacraments, and we recently witnessed the spectacle of Obama defending Rev Wright before dumping him. He started a fashion causing McCain to dump Rev. Hagee. Religion has a key role in American elections, unlike most other secular countries, and Candidates have to have God on their side.

WHO ARE THE RIGHTFUL HEIRS TO POWER?

Parties and Presidents anoint heirs just like Kings do. So if we make the story turn on inheritance, we can invent all kinds of internal strife where the former King- Bill Clinton anoints his wife Hillary to be his heir apparent, but the old warrior McCain returning from war after beating the Axis of Evil in the Holy Land, thinks that he deserves the throne as his reward. Ever since Caesar, we seem to think successfully killing people is a great qualification for a future leader! Another classic match is the Hillary-Obama fight for the right of succession. One could write a play about that. Where is Eugene O'Neill when you need him?

Or try on a young Hamlet-Obama haunted by the ghost of his absent Father and opposed by the ugly and ambitious Queen Hillary, seeks to avenge or find his Father and reclaim the throne. There is always at least one Hamlet in any Presidential Plot.

It all sounds like a cross between *"Lion King"* and the *"Lion in Winter"* and these are only a small selection of imaginative episodes, but it helps warm us up for the genre game of the Presidential Plot. What is remarkable is how easily we can fit the potential plots of this election back into the history of Kings and

Tyrants and Popes and Pretenders plotting their predictable paths to power. Shakespeare would find as much inspiration in Washington in 2008 as he did in Elizabethan England. Perhaps even more!

THE YOUNG MAN-OLD MAN AS HERO

When you have crafted the stories of McCain or Obama as Hero, you soon realize that one fits better than the other. The Obama character is made for the part because in all our fairy tales and the film culture that feeds off it, the young hero is the rule rather than the exception. We worship at the altar of youthfulness. Obama fills that role more easily because it's a part made for young, handsome, charismatic Errol Flynn types with beautiful women at their side.

The McCain campaign obviously has much more work to do to flesh out a story line where the older character returns to save the kingdom. Age is one of our last prejudices, even in stories. And yet, it also works as a story and could even play more powerfully in that it is unusual, a new twist to an old tale. But like any other aging actor, Senator McCain has to face up to the reality that we aren't as used to seeing an elderly actor playing lead 007 roles or Terminator II or the star of The Bourne Ultimatum. Heroes are young and vibrant, not old and wise, or they come back as Harrison Ford does one last time, to show he still has one Indiana Jones sequel left in him.

We will wait for a later chapter to flesh out the fuller implications of this plotting technique. (CH:14-15) But even now, we are demonstrating how the candidate has to work within the narrative logic of the Presidential Plot, and that internal cohesion within the narrative matters as much as adjusting to the external pressures of the unpredictable voting patterns of the electorate.

One can crash test the model in the laboratory of literature and the imagination before you road test it in New Hampshire and Iowa. And of course, you have to keep adjusting the characterization to make sure that no one issue distracts from or distorts the character identity you are custom designing for media consumption. A campaign needs to pre-determine their narrative strategy and then maintain a strict discipline to keep it on track.

Narrative knowledge and planning is essential. Ignore that and your campaign can be doomed even before you enter the realm of swing voters or what the independents in Ohio think about energy politics. Issues are also important but they too must be carefully woven into the story. Issues need to manifest and express the deeper character of the hero and his genuine desire for change and more than that, show his capacity to bring change about. Issues alone will not save a doomed candidacy, nor will a smart exploitation of the burning issues assure victory. The Candidate has to own certain issues, not just be scripted to reel them off a teleprompter list.

There has to be a narrative logic to it all because therein lies the underlying and unifying key to its meaning. It has to make sense. Does it make sense for Obama to be passionate about energy? Does it make sense for McCain to press for tax reform? Issues either enhance the emplotment or they undermine it. But the campaign that fails is the campaign whose story breaks apart or becomes the victim of a counterplot.

RECRUITED INTO ROLES YOU DON'T SEEK

If someone has to be hero, then someone has to be villain and someone has to be a spoiler, but beware of the role that is vacant. Nature abhors a vacuum and so does drama. No villain means no hero! The unsuspecting Candidate will find himself recruited into the missing role whether he wants it or not. Stories don't care who plays what part so long as someone is there to keep driving the drama forward. And this epic only accommodates one hero, not two. As the science fiction writer, Terry Pratchett writes: *"People think that stories are shaped by people. In fact, it's the other way around."*

Later, his narrator in <u>Witches Abroad</u> tells us

> *"Stories don't care who takes part in them. All that matters is that the story gets told, that the story repeats. Or if you prefer to think of it like this: stories are a parasitical life form, warping lives in the service of only the story itself. It takes a special kind of person to fight back,"* [20]

Hillary and Obama can't inhabit the same plot as heroes. Once Obama emerges as the contender, Hillary Clinton gets recruited into the remaining role of the wicked witch, as the obstacle or enemy our hero has to overcome. And every time Hillary's campaign pull some underhanded trick or allow some action to be so characterized, they fall into the story trap of conforming to the role the plot now requires of them. And Obama can re-enforce it by swinging his campaign into a full court press on Hillary as this

---

20 Terry Pratchett <u>Witches Abroad</u> Corgi 1999 page 8-9

unscrupulous politician. The story needed a hero and a villain. The more Obama emerged as Hero, the more Hilary fell into the vacant villain trap. The story shaped her role and sealed her fate.

For Hillary, not all is lost, because she can still play the Spoiler, exacting the revenge of inflated recognition at the Convention that serves as a pyrrhic victory. It might damage Obama but it keeps her in the story, front and center. Or she can play the King-maker, becoming the young King's Fairy God-Mother, adopting this son as heir to what she herself would have achieved. Or she can wait for the wheel of fortune to turn again.

The story Hillary wanted to be in was the plot of the great New Zealand film, *Whale Rider* where the young girl is clearly the leader, but Maori tradition does not have a story about women chiefs. The drama of a Hillary challenge was the newness of her gender. Everything else about her was old news.

If Hillary had read the landscape and listened less to her pollsters and read a little more Hans Christian Andersen or Grimm's Fairy Tales, she would have known that her task was less about winning the blue collar workers in Pennsylvania, which she did, and more about how to avoid being tagged as the wicked witch, the cruel step-mother, the all devouring Mother figure, the Lady Macbeth. She called it misogyny but it was worse than that. It's the narrative landscape that is still hostile to women as leaders. She had to hack a new path through an unforgiving forest. But once Obama emerged, she became the victim of the counter-plot that didn't care who it victimized. The story needed her as Villain and the media have always loved her in that role, from the days of Whitewater and Travelgate. Whatever the facts, the fictional Hillary required by the media factory served her up as the wicked and ruthless Queen who is ultimately vanquished.

FEED THE STORY MACHINE

I once spent a summer working in a sausage factory and whatever was fed in at one end, the result at the other end was always the same, the recognizable shape of the pork sausage. I like to think of story culture as a similar machine. It doesn't care what you feed it; it can't discriminate between immigration or Iran or nuclear weapons, or Hillary's laugh or Obama's tie color because it's all meat for the grinder to be ground down and delivered as a story. So long as it has some real meat, some drama and conflict, some crisis and suspense, a story will use anything it can to keep the plot moving.

The characters function as agents of the plot and plot advancement, as it inexorably moves towards its denouement. Here we are basically taking an Aristotelian view of narrative, that plot is dominant and characters are its pawns. It makes the story feel over-determined, but let' face it, this is an over-determined story. We can't escape it, nor can the Candidates.

THE DRAMA TRIANGLE GAME-BLAME, DEFENSE AND RESCUE

The plot requires a cast of compulsory characters; a goodie and a baddie and a rescuer and someone who makes it worse and someone who is the comic relief, and someone who is the red herring, and someone who can be the hero, and someone who can redeem his life, and all the rest.

In Transactional Analysis, a method of therapy, they speak of the Drama Triangle where there are always three roles in any one hero story, the Victim, the Persecutor, and the Rescuer. Their titles explain their roles and once you play one part, you get to play the others too, because as the plot unfolds, roles become interchangeable. It all sounds a little complicated but if you remember when your big sister hit you as a kid, and you screamed to your Mom, but your sister blamed you, and your Mom told you, "Wait till your Father comes home," and made a Federal case about it ; that is the Drama Triangle! Let's trace out the three acts.

Act One-the Rescuer moves to save the Victim from the Persecutor, just as recently Georgia (Rescuer) moved in to 'save' South Ossetia (Victim) from Russia. (Persecutor).

Act Two-the Persecutor attacks the Rescuer just as Russia (Persecutor) attacked Georgia back. (Rescuer).

Act Three-the Rescuer (Georgia) becomes the Victim and appeals for a Rescuer to save them and beat up on the Persecutor, (Russia). Georgia now becomes the Victim of Russia and Senator McCain wants to play the part of the Rescuer of Georgia.

Finally there is an Act Four where the original Persecutor (Russia) gets beaten up in the press and now claims to be the Victim. Russia-The Persecutor, claiming to be Rescuer is now Victim, appeals to the world that Georgia-the Rescuer who became Victim of Russia is now Persecuting Russia, so Russia and Georgia dance through all three roles in the space of a week. Like your big sister, the aggressor gains Victim status and you, the Victim, become the hapless Persecutor.

It's ingenious and it seems to work in every country plagued with enduring violence and war. It explains Northern Ireland and Reconstruction USA and Bosnia. Prolonged conflict creates a nation of victims all fighting for the 'Victim as Hero' role. Characters become products of plots, and plots work in dramatic cycles. In family therapy and addiction treatments, the Drama Triangle is a recognizable pattern of dysfunction that one needs to avoid, though it doesn't seem to stop nations on the world stage getting tricked into the same melodrama. The trap is for characters to think they are controlling the plot when, in their story role, the plot is controlling them and they will eventually become its victim.

This same drama triangle plays out in the election cycle. Here is how in Transactional Analysis, the roles are described:

- Victims are helpless and hopeless. They deny responsibility for their negative circumstances, and deny possession of the power to change them. They attract Rescuers and both need someone to blame

- Rescuers are constantly applying short-term repairs to a Victim's problems, and they need a Victim to feel worthwhile in their role as Rescuer.

- Persecutors blame the Victims and criticize the enabling behavior of Rescuers, and they always find their victims[21]

Let's map that on to the election drama. The Drama Triangle for the Democrats looks like this:

The **Rescuer**-Obama beats Hillary for the role of Rescuer in Chief and Hillary assumes the mantle of Victim and her supporters seek to be Rescuers to save her from Obama who proves he is still a Persecutor by refusing to make her his VP choice. Obama's has no long pedigree of Rescuing, save for his time working as a community organizer in Chicago, but he can rescue the Democratic Party from irrelevance, and the nation from international scorn.

The **Victim** is the American people, beaten down by the failing economy and job losses, and war and terrorists and no health care and this prompts the Candidate as Rescuer script first originated

---

21 http://hans.wyrdweb.eu/how-us-could-move-out-drama-triangle-about-games-people-play

in its modern form by Al Gore, then echoed by John Edwards and Hillary, and finally perfected by Obama, the "I will fight for you every day," to show he qualifies as Rescuer in Chief.

The **Persecutor** is President George Bush and his Government and Washington and Bush-McCain and Bush-Cheney as Victimizers in Chief and let's add lobbyists and partisanship and Wall Street and the Middle East oil empires and Russia and all Republicans

The Drama Triangle for the Republicans sounds like this:

The **Rescuer** is Senator McCain who is going to save America from terrorists and from those tax and spend Democrat liberals because he has done that before, and because he is the *Uber* Victim of Vietnam who therefore qualifies to become the Chief Rescuer of Victims because he knows their pain first hand.

The **Victim** is once again the American people, jobless, clueless, hopeless, and doubting themselves and add small businesses and the middle classes. The Candidate is going to take on the vested interests and the parties to cut spending and cut taxes.

The **Persecutor** is Obama and those of his liberal ilk because he has no experience and he is no Reformer or rescuer, and all Democrats who want to stack the Supreme Court and ruin the country and murder babies, and the media who are always being unfair to Republicans and women. Also, McCain has tried to obliterate the memory of the Bush years, naming Bush as the enemy and betrayer of Republic ideals, who with his big spending, torturing and lobby loving, had wrecked government for the people.

Interestingly, the American people stay firmly in the Victim role regardless of party, and Victims by definition have no agency in a story. Ironically, when it comes to the vote, they will finally shed their victim status and become the Deciders and one day, heroes of the story by voting for the Candidate who perhaps showed the most victim empathy. What the drama triangle does is allow everyone to dodge responsibility, or as one site defines it:

> *"The Drama Triangle is a seductive, high energy blame game which serves to redirect the focus of attention, energy and dialogue from personal accountability to the engaging interactions of blame, defense and rescue."* [22]

---

22 http://www.dramatriangle.info/

Doesn't that sound like an election campaign at its worst, or a Wall Street Bailout? Other characteristics of the Drama Triangle also sound vaguely familiar.

- *The greater the intensity of the drama the more distracted from the truth the players will be*

- *Most drama players prefer the excitement and adrenalin of drama over the perceived boredom of the truth*[23]

When the media or the campaigns start to sound like Drama Queens on steroids, or when there is stiff competition for the Victim role because McCain has "gone too far" attacking Obama or Obama has "Swift boated" Governor Palin, or the Media are accused of being bullies, you know that the drama triangle has taken over. But not without a cost.

The longer one plays a Victim in the story, the more one is likely to be a victim <u>of</u> the story because victims have no agency. They are story set-ups for Rescuers. To portray the people as hapless and helpless is to give the lie to their power to choose and it narratively inflates the power of the Candidate as Rescuer. People don't always get the government they deserve, but most of the time, they get the government they voted for, and if they are victims, they are victims of their own bad choices. But imagine any Candidate daring to say that!

RECRUITED INTO ROLES THAT SERVE THE PLOT

The Drama Triangle can lull any of us into this trance of serving the dramatic needs of the plot rather than the needs of reality. If we don't have a villain or a victim, we recruit someone whether they are villains or victims or not, and as Pratchett says presciently, we will even change a country to fit a story.[24] After 9-11, Saddam Hussein got caught in this dramatic Bermuda triangle, because we were victims, we needed to hit back at a Persecutor and Iraq was handier than Saudi Arabia (though most of the terrorists were Saudis and none from Iraq) and hence we restored our role as Rescuers to escape this horrible and unprecedented feeling of being Victim, being nationally vulnerable. And once the President realized that war enhanced his role as Rescuer in Chief, he knew he could declare wars on terror and wars on drugs and wars on all sorts of things because war means he gets to play top

---

23 <u>Op.Cit</u>

24 Terry Pratchett <u>Witches Abroad</u> Page 82 "Changing a whole country just to make a story work!" is Iraq as a narrative strategy in a nutshell.

dog as Commander in Chief. But don't blame Bush, because it was FDR's idea and every President since.

MEDIA MANUFACTURING CHARACTERS

When you know the presidential plot needs all these bit players in the cast, where do we get them from? That's easy. The media itself is one large story factory and given that enemies are a core ingredient of a good story, it gives a livelihood to people like Rush Limbaugh and Bill O'Reilly and Scarborough and Hannity and Colmes and Olbermann, who all act as our permanent Villain casting agencies, with their 'Pinheads and Patriots' or 'Ten worst persons of the week' awards. We have never had so much fun mocking people, and viewers can also sign up for the "Get your nightly outrage' club and the 'Church of righteous indignation.' It is oddly moronic and vaguely sermonic and the American writer Hawthorne would be fascinated to learn his story "The Scarlet Letter" is now a nighttime obsession, the sport of marking people with the mark of Cain, the mark of shame. It is not to reform them but to keep us viewers feeling both moral and entertained as if we were hearing a sermon at church.

Obama and his coterie and McCain and his band of brothers are fed nightly into this story 'heroes and villains' machine to add some melodrama to the 'election by media' process.

The media want stories, and the Candidates want to get elected and the people want the truth. The people only count for the media if they are potential viewers, and people only count for Candidates if they are potential voters and consequently, nowhere in the Presidential Plot do people count as people. Given that the media is the broker, the go-between for people to meet and judge the Candidates, the dictates of story increasingly rule the whole process. If the truth is dramatic and sexy, we will hear it, but otherwise, what we get is stories, and drama triangles and soap operas until one Candidate wins the votes and gets elected, one media outlet wins the ratings wars and attracts more sponsorship, and the people, feeling unsure if they won or lost, go back to watching *Survivor*. Candidates have had to become characters and voters have had to become viewers and the 'people as people' aren't in the story anywhere.

THE CRUCIBLE OF CONFLICT–CHARACTERS TESTED IN FIRE

Cast of characters is one thing, and we know where to get all our extra villains and heroes, and we know the hero aspires to become *the Hero who saves America,* but we need one last ingredient to make a cake out of this potent story mix. We need heat! We need fire! We need the incendiary conflict. So once you pick your characters, your last task is to pick your fight. The story and the characters will shape themselves around what is at stake. If the story involves Senator Obama and Senator McCain and a fight over Abortion, that creates quite a different story than if their fight is over global warming. The wise counsel of "Pick your fights carefully" applies to constructing a good story, because some things are worth fighting for and some are not. What if the defining conflict of the story was one of the following:

> World Peace
> The survival of the Planet
> Having an extra week of holidays
> Inner peace and harmony
> The restoration of America's power in the world
> Getting elected President
> One's salvation
> Having cheaper gas
> The future prosperity of the nation
> Better Jobs and houses and education
> Enough Food and clean water
> To not have to die of starvation
> To get a good education
> To be free from fear to say what you think
> To have your family covered by health insurance

Just as we did with the cast of characters, we can swap around the various defining conflicts of the story, and imagine what is at stake if the hero wins or loses.

THE NEED TO ELEVATE THE CONFLICT

Sometimes a story gets stuck or frozen because the conflict is too small or too entrenched and then, the battle is wasted over things that used to matter but don't really matter anymore. If conflict persists, you can assume it is disguising the real battle over the things that really do matter. In Northern Ireland people are said to be fighting over religion and become stuck in intractable positions. By elevating the conflict to fighting for the future of their kids, the communities have come to some resolution because the cause of religion, perhaps appropriate to the times of Cromwell and William of Orange, is no longer what is at stake. It is much more than that.

Traditional mediation looks for common ground and calling a truce, whereas in a narrative mode, the key often is to elevate the conflict to the level where all combatants have more to lose, even if

137

they win and much more to win if they win together. Raise the stakes and intensify the urgency by giving the story a not-negotiable take-it-or-leave-it ending. Senator George Mitchell was the master of this in leading the negotiations that led to the Good Friday Agreement in Northern Ireland.

The importance of raising the stakes and making sure everyone knows what they are fighting for is demonstrated by Lincoln and Douglas in the Civil War. The civil war, begun to preserve the Union, became the war to end slavery. Campaigns talk about change or fixing Washington but they remain vague and narratively uncompelling until the voters or the Candidates can dramatically demonstrate what is at stake, what is worth fighting for? Sometimes, the world or the economy intervenes with events to clarify what is actually at stake.

When the stakes are higher, such as the fate of the world with global warming, which was the case that Al Gore made so passionately at the recent Convention, it makes our national quarrel sound rather self-indulgent. Candidates fighting simply to be elected President are not fighting a big enough battle. That is too much about them. They have to elevate the conflict to a larger moral cause, if they want to build a bigger story. It is one of the key questions of a campaign, deciding what issues to fight your opponent on, but it is also a narrative question, because once you pick your fight, you have picked the kind of story you can build and the kinds of qualities your characters can display. The conflict creates the fiery crucible to test and mould the hero. An anti-terrorist warrior might look like a John McCain but a global warrior or energy warrior might look like an Al Gore. We know Obama is fighting but do we know what he is fighting for? Does he? To revive the American Dream, to renew the Promise, to change the way things are done in Washington?

As a hero, you can only be as big and delineated as the enemy you want to overcome. Saint George could slay the Dragon and look the part, but what Obama and McCain will slay is still uncertain as they audition to replace our current Saint George. Meanwhile, the world keeps providing more dragons than either candidate knows what to do with. Russia, Wall Street, Recession, Energy Crisis, Racism, Natural Disasters.

CONCLUSION

When they say that Presidential elections are all about character, they mean it morally and not narratively, but in our analysis, they are right twice over. Success depends on how well the character fits the story and the story fits the character. Candidates have to conform to the Presidential Plot, and play off the obligatory cast of villains and clowns and sponsors, and deal with upsets and surprises and personal attacks. The defining conflict must serve to sufficiently heroize the Candidate character and elevate the contest to a moral urgency that makes it clear that <u>my</u> future is also at stake. The Candidate will face enormous criticism from opponents and from a villain-creating media, but he must avoid at all costs the traps of the drama triangle which is the Bermuda triangle for many a campaign that simply disappeared without trace. Maybe campaigns ask these questions already, but if they don't, they might have a better story if they did and the narrative of electing a President might rise to the level of great literature, which it surely deserves. Great heroes deserve great stories. That's where they live.

CHAPTER ELEVEN

HOW BIOGRAPHY MAPS POLICY

"The president we get is the country we get. With each new president the nation is conformed spiritually. He is the artificer of our malleable national soul. He proposes not only the laws but the kinds of lawlessness that govern our lives and involve our responses. The people he appoints are cast in his image. The trouble they get into and get us into, is his characteristic trouble. Finally, the media amplify his character into our moral weather report. He becomes the face of our sky, the conditions that prevail". [25]

Over the last ten years, I have conducted hundreds of interviews to find suitable applicants for a leadership program that I used to run. The key to our success was in the selection process that was based on the principle that potential could be predicated on life-story, that when you get a sense of the turning points and crucibles even in young lives, you have a better grasp of whether they are going to fit into the mission of a program that is about service and leadership. [26]

This is an idea that is increasingly coming to inform practices in Leadership Development, [27] because practitioners who study the lives of successful leaders have come to understand how mission grows out of vision and vision grows out of values and values grow out of what kinds of life-shaping experiences you have had on your leadership journey. If we make this same assumption about the Presidential Plot, then biography becomes a more critical tool in informing the selection process of the next President.

George Bush didn't write a biography before the 2000 election and cynics might ask what could he have written if he had? We can surely expect the memoirs to flow in his retirement years, but it's hard to realize we didn't have the same opportunities back then that we have this year with multiple autobiographies by both candidates. It is almost a requirement of any modern campaign to get your life story out there well in advance of any campaign as a way to market test your story.

---

25 E.L.Doctorow "The Character of Presidents" <u>Poets and Presidents Selected Essays 1977-1992</u> Papermac 1993 Page 92

26 See wiprogram.org "The Washington Ireland Program for Service and Leadership"

27 Bill George <u>True North</u> Jossey Bass 2007

Let's take our narrative tools to the two life-stories, viz. _Dreams from My Father_[28] and _Faith of My Fathers_[29] to see what they reveal about the candidates. We are not simply analyzing content. We want to pay as much attention to form, to what kinds of stories candidates translate their own experiences into. We all have our habitual patterns of meaning-making that we reveal most easily when we tell the story of our lives. We get to play author, the leading character and the narrator, and we can't help but disclose how we interpret ourselves and the world in the relationship of meaningful action. Boris Cyrulnik calls it our "preferential perception of the world."[30]

If our mission was to become the next President of the United States and restore the nation to a sense of pride and progress, how could we show this mission as growing out of our story? And from the way we tell it today, what is tomorrow's chapter of being Commander in Chief going to sound like? 'What tales have we fallen into?', as Sam in _Lord of the Rings_ asks, and thereby, what stories will the nation find itself falling into if they elect us?

THE LIFE STORIES OF TWO SURPRISE CANDIDATES

Perhaps it should be said at the outset that both candidates wrote their books a while back, so both never expected to be here in 2008 as their party's nominee. McCain's campaign was broke and on the ropes only 12 months ago, and Obama was always the rank outsider. They both waged a David and Goliath contest against the favorites and their early narrative surge was due in no small way to the energy of the underdog, the little guy taking on the invincible powers and turning the tables. In as much as they even got to this stage of opportunity, they epitomize the American "Can Do" spirit, a species of that Heroic Individual story that defines the narrative landscape of America. (See Chapter 8)

GETTING INTRODUCED-THE NOVICE VERSUS THE MAVERICK

Obama is 47 years old, a young Dad in the prime of life, seeking to build a new dynasty of Democrats from his new and rising generation born after 1960. He is forging a new alliance with the young, and presenting a totally new face for America, giving it a fresh start, a new story. He has never run before, and even in his four years in Washington, most of his time has been taken up with getting ready to campaign and campaigning, so he has barely had a

---

28 Barack Obama Dreams from My Father Three Rivers Press 2004

29 John McCain with Mark Salter Faith of My Fathers Random House 1999

30 Boris Cyrulnik Talking of Love on the Edge of a Precipice Allen Lane 2007 Page 124

chance to know where the Senate bathroom is. As a young African American nominee, we have no way to measure him against previous campaigns. He is opening a new frontier, breaking open a new story, and hence, he will appear at best a little strange, and at worst, more than bizarre.

Elections are full of surprises but his candidacy is unprecedented. He presents a totally new type of candidate and this becomes a challenge to our habitual models of meaning making. We have to file him somewhere to have his story make any sense and therein lies both the danger and the opportunity of the Obama candidacy.

McCain is 72 years old, a Grandfatherly figure, visibly bearing the scars of war and torture, with over 25 years in the House and Senate, from which he bears other scars of former electoral battles. A self-described maverick, he is a last resort for his party, their potential restoration candidate. If he is offering change, it is a change back to an older style of leadership, with a face and a CV not unlike a John Kerry or a JFK or even a latter day Eisenhower or Teddy Roosevelt; all war heroes turned leader.

He is not new as a type, and therefore, the stories stored in the memory of our political language easily recognizes a candidacy like his, unlike his opponent. McCain has a long history and a host of enemies with memories and scores to settle, and he has comrades in arms ready for one last battle, because this old soldier refuses to die or fade away. The fact that he fits a "tried and true" story of presidential aspirant is also his danger and his opportunity. If the country wants change, what does he have to offer that is new? We've been here before.

STORIES TOLD IN THE SHADOWS OF THEIR FATHERS

The titles of their respective autobiographies-McCain's <u>Faith of My Fathers</u> and Obama's <u>Dreams from My Father</u> reveal a common thread of paternity with both stories told under the prevailing shadow of a father figure, who dominates through both his presence and absence.

All of us grow up being recruited into stories about our faith and our family, or our nation and our future. Both of these candidates were recruited into their father's story in the very act of their being named after them. Both are juniors; John McCain Jnr. the Third and Barack Obama Jnr. It is not surprising that they have chosen to anchor their narratives in the form of a 'Quest for a lost Father' that either comes in the form of dreams "<u>From</u>" my Father in Obama's case, or is contained in the faith "<u>of</u>" my fathers in

143

McCain's tale of him, his father and his grandfather. McCain's title echoes the opening line of a famous militant Christian Hymn that speaks of believers battling for their faith *"in spite of dungeon, fire and sword"* and enduring to the end, *"We will be true to thee to death."*

Semantic differences aside, we read shared tales of sons becoming fathers and in the process, having to deal with the legacy of their own father who, when he was a younger son, was trying to deal with his own father. These are intergenerational stories of lost sons and lost fathers.

If either candidate for the Presidency has been recruited into a father story, does that mean that electing him means we are buying into a father story also? It surely does. And if the Candidates have formed their own life story as a reaction to the Father story they inherited or felt forced to inhabit, how then did they come to find their own story, if indeed they have? Hopefully they have.

Or will the nation have to endure another President lost in a middle age funk while he tries to seduce every beautiful woman he sees in between running the country. You think I mean Clinton but I mean JFK, another son overwhelmed by the story of the Father who reputedly bought the votes that got him to the top. Or a President who is intent on showing his Dad that he can do a better job by being tougher and more independent? You think I mean Bush Jnr. but no, I mean Lincoln, another lost son who didn't even go to his estranged father's funeral.

A President, as E.L. Doctorow says, becomes our moral weather report, his issues become our issues, his shadows and light become our day and our night. So it pays to spend some time seeing if we can identify what might become our issues locked inside their autobiographies.

DISTANT FATHERS AND VICTIM SONS

Both Candidates portray themselves as victims of absent fathers, each in their own way, but both unsure if their father really loved them, or approved of them. Every son craves a Dad's approval and so as readers, we are drawn into the drama of how each Candidate publicly negotiates a reconciliation with the past, to find a new story of their father that they can embrace as adults in ways they could not embrace as kids.

McCain goes to great pains to rationalize why his Father never so much as sent a letter when he was in prison, and Obama has to build the 1000 piece jig-saw puzzle of his father's life from a dozen skimpy and romanticized memories of their only month together when he was 10 and the stories his mother could share, until he makes his own journey to visit his father's grave years later.

Their life stories are a reconstruction of a childhood reality experienced as painful then but transformed in the writing to become a usable past, or something that can inspire and give continuity to the kinds of lives each has created as an adult.

REPAIRING AND REDEEMING THE FAMILY STORY

What do we learn? We know we are in the hands of confident narrators who can creatively reinterpret their characters, and resurrect and redeem the figures of their fathers. They can also relocate their lives within the family re-imagined in a way they never seemed to be able to do when they were children or troublesome adolescents. "Where did I fit in?" seemed to be the guiding question of their adolescence, and "What must I do to gain acceptance?" Goof off, be the tough guy, play basketball, do drugs, invent pranks.

They each tell stories of their own redemption, and their drama is that they realize that they have to redeem their respective fathers if they are to find some sort of redemption themselves. Their stories are about intergenerational repair, and in the case of Obama, intercultural reconnection for what the narrator experiences as a bi-furcated identity.

FATHER FIGURES AND HOW FATHER FIGURES

If one were to put each Candidate on the therapist's couch, one would hone in on what seems to be a craving for parental approval, for authority figures to sit up and take notice and finally acknowledge that they have arrived, that they have achieved. Imaginatively, it is not hard to get inside that kind of story because most of us know the feeling. Sons of emotionally absent fathers feed on that long imagined scene where they can say to their parent, "See Dad, I told you so," or "See how wrong you were." It could even be more Oedipal as in, "See Dad how I got over you by getting beyond you." The story is traditionally about the son having something to prove to the father to make him change his mind, or to bring him back into his life. And the energy of the plot is about healing the family wound caused by that lack of affection and recognition. "The search for the missing father," writes author

David Ray, another abandoned son, "is a lifelong ache."[31] Somewhere from these depths arises the quest for the Presidency.

SIGNS OF A DEEPER MOTIVATION

Why does anyone want to be President? The Candidates get asked this a lot and they have to develop an answer as part of their stump speech. One imagines their having to tap a deeper source of motivation than us normal mortals, to aspire to be the Leader of the Free World. Perhaps the Father-Son axis of resentment (or competition) provides a sufficiently fertile soil for such epic human striving to grow and flourish in adult life. Getting to be President must prove something, and if life inflicts upon you an absent father, this is surely a convincing way to silence his skeptical voice that might have said, "Son, you won't amount to much," or "You were never as good as me," or for the son to be able to spit back, "See, I never needed you anyway!" We all know that nothing creates energy like revenge, and the desire for vindication, the "I'll show them" attitude. If it can start world wars, it can certainly power Candidates to presidencies.

We aren't making this up, nor are we turning into amateur Freudians. Both Candidates have given us a story, and so probing character and motive is part and parcel of any literary analysis. If the faith and dreams of their fathers are good enough to encapsulate the dominant theme of their written life stories, then, we are justified in assuming it also has something to do with why they are running for President.

The corollary is that we hope they understand their inner motivation too, and that if revenge or vindication is part of the motive that gets them there, they might also discover richer motives that would guide their style of governance. One only has to think back to the Nixon years to see how destructive "revenge politics" can become, or how the paranoid style of the last eight years has made even Kafka's stories sound reasonable. Kafka invents absurd tales about anti-heroes waking up in prison facing secret charges that no one will tell them about, and with no way to defend themselves. They used to be read as examples of the horror genre, but today, they read like a movie script about Guantanamo.[32]

---

31 David Ray About Men 'The Endless Search' *The New York Times Magazine* August 28 1994 P.32

32 See <u>Kafka Comes to America</u> by Steven T Wax, See also Richard Hofstadter "The Paranoid Style of American Politics" in Harpers November 1964

WHAT OF THE MOTHERS WHO WEREN'T MISSING?

It would certainly be a different story if their titles were "Faith of my Mothers" or "Dreams from my Grandmother." And yet, indirectly, that is also what their stories are about because who raises the sons of missing or absent fathers but their mothers, and grandmothers. John and Barack both come from families where the one constant was Mom/Grandmother. She is certainly included in their stories but she is not what is missing. Both ambition and a good story feed off what is not there. As we have said before, there is no drama in stability. It may be the absolute bedrock of our lives but we struggle to make that story sound as sexy as the story of how "You done me wrong." The richer narrative dividend always comes from dysfunction and struggle and abandonment and failure so long as its ends with the hero's humble victory, as each of these books do.

Another piece of their story that seems to be missing is the childhood dream of avocation, that one wants to become a pop star or a famous scientist or a Hollywood actor. Neither confesses to any dream detached from solving the family quest and even more strange, neither dreams that one day, "I want to be President of the United States." Perhaps they will wait to be elected before that gets redacted back into the text, as assuredly it will.

All their hopes and dreams as expressed in these books of their lives are contained within the field of relationships and family, not about any dreams of achievement much beyond that. (Their later books are more concerned with their budding political ambitions.) The father is the hero who has gone missing from their story, and it's as if the young boy cannot dare to build any dream beyond that until he has this primary family drama sorted out.

McCain should grow up dreaming of becoming an Admiral but the way he tells it, he seems to end up in the Naval Academy in Annapolis more out of habit than choice. Likewise, Obama finishes his degree and ends up as a Community Organizer in Chicago. We are never sure why he goes there, and never sure why he leaves, and its not that we aren't told so much as this narrator doesn't seem to know, or if he dares to settle on any one answer, he tortures it to death with endless "if's and "buts' and "maybe's." If McCain's story is the history of his Faith, Obama's is the history of his doubt. He is an unreliable narrator (as every first person story is) trading on his unreliability as his literary persona. "I am not sure and I am still working it out" is the tone of the Obama tome. But remember this is how they choose to tell their story and why their stories work so well as literature.

McCAIN AS REBEL-IN-CHIEF

This character 'John McCain' finds a compelling need to escape or rebel against the dominance of the father story, because his dad "John Number Two" is but a chapter in his grandfather "John Number One's" story and he, John Jnr. or Number Three is expected to be a chapter in his father John II's story. They do sound like a dynasty. Granddad, a Four Star Admiral was there with Admiral Halsey on the *USS Missouri* when General MacArthur took the surrender from the Japanese in 1945. And the Senator's own Dad saved his crew from peril to become a submariner of renown before making the rank of Four Star Admiral in charge of the Asian Pacific Fleet during the Vietnam war.

From generation to generation, the son witnesses to the glories of the Fathers rather than the Father glorying in the achievements of the Son, unless of course, the Son finally outdoes all the fathers that have gone before him. His Dad struggled long and hard to achieve the rank of Four Star like his Dad. So what is John Jnr. to do? The story is sprung for a final chapter, where posterity can be put in reverse. When the new McCain as Commander in Chief takes the salute from his paternal ancestors, it will be the Fathers singing the praises of the son. And the story still continues with one of McCain's sons serving in Iraq and another at the Naval Academy in Annapolis, a fourth generation to carry on the warrior tradition.

OBAMA'S LOST HORIZONS AND NEW FRONTIERS

With the character of Obama, there is hardly any family history. We start and end with a sense of dislocation and constant movement, Hawaii, Java, Kansas, LA, Chicago. In fact the story works because it is told by a narrator who is both a son in search of a lost father, and a teller in search of a lost story. The tone is constantly questioning, speculating, turning over every fact for what it might mean. Towards the end, the narrator goes to Africa and finally meets his father's family and hears the stories of the son-His dad-whom they lost to America, and who then returned only to run afoul of the ruling junta and whose life and talent seemed to drain away and get lost before it tragically ended in a car crash. The return of the lost son Barack Jnr. revives the dreams of family for the father, also called Barack. And it is in this recovery of the memory of the father that the son can finally find a place for his life and move on.

TESTED? McCAIN LEARNS FREEDOM IN CAPTIVITY

We have two wonderfully contrasting stories, not only in the characters but in the way they chose to tell them. One candidate is trapped inside a family tradition, like father like son. As another harassed son expressed it, "I feel so much of my Dad alive in me that there isn't even room for me." [33]

When he ends up in prison, he finds a central metaphor for his life, and even though his Father's authority in the military forces the Vietnamese to offer him early release, he rejects the power and influence of his father and chooses instead the honor code and his mates.

He is also choosing to center his own authority in his sheer will to endure. In Hanoi, McCain becomes the father of his own life. And somehow, if one was writing the great novel, the prison and the torture are less the symbol of inhumanity than they are of the inner freedom that this character McCain is slowly winning. Like classic stories of inner liberation through imprisonment, e.g. Thomas Moore, Eldridge Cleaver, etc. McCain has a classic story, and a wonderful platform from which to inspire the nation about what the struggle for freedom costs. His is a true hero story, the kid who went to war and come back a man, and despite the five years of torture, he expresses a surprising optimism because he considers what he had lost as nothing compared to what he had gained. He knows how to re-story adversity as triumph.

Vietnam becomes the signature story of the McCain narrative, teaching him how to endure, how to reclaim freedom and how to be his own man. McCain is the rebel, trapped inside his family tradition and seeking ways to find his own way out, and then, trapped inside the Naval tradition, where his rebellion almost cost him his place, as he delights in telling us.

In Hanoi, his rebellious spirit almost cost him his life and certainly cost him his health, and he still carries in his body the living reminder of that resistance like a badge of courage. But his rebellion saved him, and inspired his mates. People call him a maverick because of his lack of party loyalty, but flying solo plays a much bigger character role than that. McCain has always had to dig deep to find an inner strength to counter the oppression without. If rebellion is about overthrowing one rule of law for another, McCain's life as a rebel seems to tap into a deeper law

---

[33] We Feel Fine project Jonathan Harris TED talk John Harris TED tape www.ted.com

which is his trust in his gut instinct, if only because it once saved his life.

And through all his years in Congress, he has been Rebel in Chief,[34] taking unpopular stances on electoral reform, on torture, on overspending. It is almost the only way he knows how to do it because freedom resides in pushing back. His stance on the war in Iraq likewise is informed by an insider's knowledge of war and a parent's anxiety for a child serving in Iraq, not to mention the memory of how incredibly stupid and misguided the US Military were in their policy in Vietnam. When you lose one war, you don't want to lose any more.

When he returns to civilian life, our hero can get angry and be immature and irresolute and all the rest because he knows the system will endure his wrath and he will not be tortured. The hero in <u>Faith of My Fathers</u> will come to realize that the military gave form to his patriotism, that structure and discipline and the code words of 'Honor' and 'Service' are real, and the foundation of both his personal and national life. He looks back rather embarrassed at his adolescent rebellions, owning that only later did he learn the wisdom within the tradition, a tradition that to a young, impetuous guy full of himself, seemed so restrictive and out of touch.

He may accommodate the political deals in order to win back his Republican base but this is not a character who panders to anyone. He has survived by going inside, and there he found an enduring inner strength and compass. Only after Vietnam can he willingly connect his struggle to the heroic tradition that links him now like an umbilical chord to his father and grandfather.

In seeking the presidency, he lives out their ambition and destiny which was always to have their own command. His Grandfather captained a carrier fleet in the Pacific fleet and his father captained a submarine. McCain left the Navy before achieving a command rank equal to a four star Admiral, but he still has a chance, not to command a fleet of carriers or a submarine but the ultimate command, to be Commander in Chief.

He would not only fulfill his father's and his grandfather's dreams, but he would fulfill the narrative law of three's, that goes from good to better to best. A President McCain would show that the son has proved worthy of the father and not only won the Oedipal conflict but also become the apex of a military story of service through three generations of McCain's. It is also a story that can even reach

---

[34] see Clotaire Rapaille <u>The Culture Code</u> Broadway 2006 Ch.11

back to an ancestor serving in Washington's army in the War of Independence. From founding father through a chain of fathers, to being the newly elected father of the nation is a story of paternity that's hard to top. You can already see the TV series on PBS-"The Fighting McCains-The American Experience."

OBAMA-TRYING TO FIND A PLACE TO BELONG

In contrast, the Obama hero story is almost anti-epic, anti-heroic in that the narrator never even wants to place himself in the center of the story. He is the witness more then he is the actor. We hear what others say more than what Obama says, and his voice has the tortured brooding tone of the Thinker, trying to work it all out. He is a Hamlet figure so full of questions. As readers, we want to know what being a community organizer working at the grassroots of Chicago does to shape your view of engagement with the world? But we never really find out. Obama gives an account of everyone else but himself.

As someone who never had the father influence to help shape him or to push up against in the act of defining himself, his is a more modern sounding tale, rootless, tentative, with its only dramatic movement coming from searching and finding and searching again. In contrast to the McCain story, Obama is unsure of both the limits and boundaries of his life and of the vaguely sensed horizons of opportunity. The family keeps moving, the parent figures keep changing. There is no anchor to his early identity. And there is no great epiphany in the end, so much as a quiet resolution of the past and a resolve for the future.

His rebellion is a sort of existential revolt against life but he seems too unfocused for it to be aimed at anything in particular. His character is never solidly enough inside of anything or any one story to push back or want to get out. It's rather an identity search for something to get inside of and feel a part of. As an amorphous chameleon, the character in the biography seeks to find a way of belonging to the black American story, which in a way is the story of his Father even if only tangentially. Hence the visits to Africa, and later, the community organizing in the Black communities in Chicago and the constant references to the black heroes his white mother is constantly referring him to.

But this Obama character is not a direct descendant of slaves and not a natural inheritor of the slave story save by the color of his skin and his own choice to want to make that story his own. His black story on his father's side is one that goes back to Colonial Africa and before that, to a proud African tribal tradition. If McCain is trying to escape a dominant story or find room for his place within it, Obama is a narrator in search of a story to get inside of and to live out of.

If this is the biography projected on to the public arena as an Obama Presidency, one can predict that the story is going to be more open, more exploratory, much more formless as a story. This candidate even as President is going to struggle to have deep convictions that are specific, because unlike McCain, there has never been one defining and wounding battle that has shaped him, according to his telling of the story.

OBAMA-HIS ELECTION WILL MAKE HIM A HERO

He is still a relatively young man so his election itself will be the high water mark of his life. It will make him the hero rather than his being the former hero who is elected. His defining battle is this election. It has already made him, regardless of his winning or losing. This is his Vietnam, his Hanoi Hilton moment. We are watching a candidate in the very act of defining his life and that is our ringside seat to history.

If Rep. John Lewis or Jesse Jackson were running, clearly their election would cap off a life of fighting for civil rights and equality, but Obama cannot and does not pretend to that depth of experience or longevity of service. This Candidate is asking the nation to join him in the urgency and immediacy of his quest now, and the exciting and the defining part of his story lies ahead, not behind. That is what makes it so inspiring in prospect and also, so risky in terms of picking a beginner to lead the nation's new beginning.

Though lacking the dramatic sequence of father trumping father evident in the McCain epic, Obama's odyssey, should it end in the Oval Office, will have its own power in the fact that the son who grew up without a Dad and who had a lost adolescence searching for approval is finally chosen to be the father of the nation, and in so doing, he fulfils the dreams of greatness that his Dad once had and lost. Being elected President of the United States is not a normal way to heal the wounds of lost fathers and lost sons but it sure is a stunning ending to an uncertain beginning.

LEADERS ARE LEARNERS-HOW DO THEY LEARN?

A mantra we use in teaching leadership is that leaders are learners and learners are leaders. We know what McCain has learnt, and we can predict his leadership style from his learning style because we

152

have seen it these last 20 years. He leads from the gut, he is impulsive, not given to details but sees the big picture and he has little patience with nuance and subtlety. He is a man of action, and someone who has the authority of his own life and the tradition of service to back up his convictions.

He is also a fighter and someone with resilience and perseverance. He is not a quitter and his stubbornness will both enhance and hinder his chances of being an effective leader. The advantage with McCain is that all this is out there, on the record, and just to watch him operate, we sense we know who this guy is. Whether we like him or not, we get him, and that is crucial in any election.

What we need to know about Obama is how he learns? How will he cope with the pressures of international crises, Russia threatening to nuke Poland, and economic meltdowns, more Banks collapsing, and Congressional scandals and all the rest?

We simply don't know and more to the point, Obama is untested at this level so he doesn't know. But can we predict the sort of story he will find himself in when they do occur? Can we anticipate his habitual patterns of meaning making that will allow him to graft these next thrilling chapters on to the already existing and already told chapters of the life he has lived up till now? Narrative analysis says we can.

Obama leads from the head rather than the gut. If the narrative voice of the autobiography becomes the voice of the nation, it will be suspicious of the "leading from the gut" style. This is a leader who doesn't display gut feelings about most things, and he simply doesn't come at the world that way. In contrast, he will assume that every issue has to be seen from every angle and that the best way to make a decision is to dialogue and parse and weigh up and deliberate and if possible, seek a middle ground. He is a Law Professor specializing in Constitutional Law, in case we forgot.

To watch him in the debates facing Hillary, we see someone whose passion is conveyed by the way he thinks, rather than by the way he feels. He is apt to take a question about health insurance as a problem to be solved rather than a person to be reassured. He has yet to master a more emotive style of engagement with the voters or to fully employ his biography as an authority on the deeper values of life, as McCain is apt to do. McCain meets each question or issue as a chance for his listeners to engage with his story while Obama treats issues and questions as a chance for listeners to engage with his mind. He has not consistently been able to translate "What do you think about...?" into "What do you feel about...?" which is what

153

it has to become if he is to join with the questioner, and share his story. People are not going to be swayed by what he says; they are going to be swayed by whose speaking.

CASE STUDY-THE SADDLEBACK CIVIL FORUM ON RELIGION

One of the best and most recent examples of these two very different styles of leadership that demonstrate some of our conclusions was the recent Saddleback Civil Forum that both candidates had with Rick Warren, of "Living Life on Purpose" fame.

When asked about faith, or about abortion or evil, McCain, whether he had some heads up on the questions or not, dives right in, no hesitation, no stutter, no clearing of the throat that might allow him a second to take it in and think of the implications. No, evil exists and it must be defeated, and life begins at conception. He answers with a conviction that is both reassuring and frightening, because certainty is no longer such an asset in an increasingly uncertain world. Or maybe it is, but even now I sound like Obama. But the voice and the tone of answer on the campaign trail is the voice and the tone of the biography, speaking from the gut. It is laced with humor and a cheek and an ability to be self-mocking that blunts the impression that this is one stubborn old dogmatic Senator. He knows where he stands, and we know too.

Obama on the other hand takes the question and parses the concept, lays it out before his own mind first to have a closer look before he offers an opinion which is nuanced and balanced. "When life begins can be seen from a theological point of view and from a...and that is way above my pay scale." He is eager always to admit that the answer is not univocal, nor certain, but that the best way to approach any issue is exploratory and dialogic, with the assumption that the answer will come out of collaboration rather than from the gut of the leader himself. Even if you haven't read "Dreams From my Father, you could still hear its voice at this Forum.

There is an attractive modesty about him and a gentle humor but also a deep earnestness that belies the impression that he is equivocating or weighing up every answer so as not to say the wrong thing. It is a very cautious style, which stands in contrast to the story of being the candidate who is going to be this dynamic agent of change. One can see that he will change the way decisions might be made, but hard to see what radical changes he is going to make in the body politic. There is clearly a thirst for conceptual clarity but no communicable passion for an all embracing vision of what could be different. The character Obama doesn't do "all-embracing" anything because his life has been and still is about this fragmented journey of exploration. He cannot promise a promised land he hasn't found himself. Whether the voters will accept that story as the new Presidential Plot remains to be seen, but the challenge of McCain's story and style is going to be more formidable than Obama or anyone expected.

WHAT IS THEIR STORY OF CHANGE?

We all live under the authority of our own experience. We cannot escape it, even if we aren't aware of it. And the more decisive it has been in shaping our lives, the more definitive it is likely to be in shaping our futures. When a Candidate presents a platform of change to the nation, we rightly inquire as to the specifics and issues-taxes and energy and health care but underlying that is the story of change that they have experienced in their own lives and what they mean by change from the inside. Do they mean change as rescue, reform, renewal, restoration, or is it something more radical, a revolution, a reinvention?

McCAIN- CHANGE AS VALUE BASED

Strange as it may seem, the person who can speak with the most personal authority about change is McCain. He has seen more of it, been the victim and the agent of more of it, and experienced it from the inside in the most traumatic way possible. Change for him means values, it means faithfulness to timeless traditions and preserving a Constitution that he sees as this unchanging bedrock of laws. Change is measured against that which does not change, and he conveys a sense that the failure in America is not its principles but the way people corrupt them, or contradict with their lives the very values that they espouse with their lips. We have not lived up to our greatness.

Coming from a family that prizes tradition through many generations, and being a veteran of the oldest and most tradition-bound arm of the armed forces, the Navy, and having been educated in the Temple of the Plebs at Annapolis, and then, being an elder statesman of the most history conscious house of the US Congress, the Senate, we have a Candidate who has tradition and conservativism written all over him. He will measure change by what does not change, and he will initiate change when he feels deeply convicted that his code of honor and service is violated, that we needed electoral reform or torture is wrong or we need a more compassionate stand on immigration. McCain will echo many predecessors by stating his reason as, "Because it's the right thing to do." And in the world that formed McCain, one could presume everyone knew what that was. That is no longer the world in which, if elected, he will have to govern.

OBAMA-CHANGE AS PRACTICE BASED

On the other hand, if McCain has an inside expertise about change, Obama can also lay claim to knowing change as the reality of his life because what he lacked was any sense of rootedness in one place and one tradition or history, quite the opposite of McCain.

Change is not any big deal in the Obama story. It's life. And when he speaks of change, one can still hear the pragmatism of a community organizer in the Chicago tradition of the Saul Olinksy method which views change as connected to the situation, to what are the pressing needs of this particular community, and change measured to match their resources and their desire to act to improve their lot. It is not change from on high or change arising from any sense of timeless truths.

Obama is of a different generation to McCain, a generation where one does not presume to know "the right thing to do" but rather one works with people to empower them to claim their own wisdom and insight. So change for Obama is not any "conversion" or epiphany so much as a sense that things are not working, and that there must be a better way if we can search together.

He is committed to change the tone of doing politics in Washington and echoes the promise of Bush, to work across the party divide, but part of Obama's appeal and his vulnerability is that he talks in high rhetoric, exciting his base for major reform, but when it comes to the hot button issues of the moment, he retreats back to the safety of a cautious, calculating politician. As Mario Cuomo said, "We campaign in poetry only to govern in prose."

Obama is no idealog, nor is he a big thinker of the big thoughts. His later book "Audacity of Hope" has plenty of hope and much less audacity because there are no big new ideas, no New Deal or Contract with America except perhaps an appeal for A Grand Consensus. In his youth, he was never captured by any one big idea, and he remains a realist and a pragmatist. His challenge is to package that as a New Deal for Washington which has suffered the neo-cons and the loss of the good old fashioned politics of the possible and the practical. Even George Bush has reverted to that default position in this final year of his term. Obama wants to institutionalize it, but the promise of pragmatism is not going to win it alone as a story. Pragmatism is seen as the default position of a failed idealism. It is not epic enough and it suggests a minimalism that contradicts the "audacity of hope." Obama has yet to lay out a compelling vision of what difference he thinks he can make. Naming the problem without a vivid sense of the solution only increases our sense of helplessness.

CONCLUSION

Andrew Sullivan succinctly sums up the genre of Presidential wannabe's memoirs:

> *The memoir of every presidential candidate must describe a Political Time of Testing, some point at which, if the narrative arc is to prove satisfying, the hero encounters criticism, most of it unjust, but then rallies, overcomes hardship and misfortune and the petty, self-serving attacks of enemies, and emerges chastened but wise-and come to think of it, more qualified to lead the greatest nation on earth.* [35]

A Candidate, as we have said earlier, needs a good sense of what story of change America is in right now before they measure and calibrate the story of change they are going to promise to get them elected. We have already heard "the change you can count on," or "the change we have been waiting for," and even, "the change you most fear."

Having explored the changes they have lived through as described in their memoirs, and the changes they have been agents or victims of, we now have a better sense of what they mean by the term. And knowing that "change" is the emptiest cliché of the Presidential Plot, the candidate who can give it content beyond the cliché, and flesh it out with the authority of his own life will end up having the best chance of winning voters. A Candidate has, to paraphrase Gandhi, model the change by which he hopes to inspire the nation and that means we have to not just hear you think it but we must feel how you are living it. In Autobiography then, we find the promise and the foretaste of policy.

President Bush didn't set the world on fire by running a sports team, nor by running an Oil company, and the current report card on his Presidency will say that he has not fulfilled the promises of being compassionate or conservative. If we had read his autobiography before 2000, had he written one, what would be in it

---

35 Andrew Ferguson Read, Weep, and Vote A bookshelf of "writing" from the presidential candidates.
The Weekly Standard by 2/03/2007, Volume 013, Issue 12

that would lead us to even realistically expect he could run a country? Or run it any better than he ran his Team and his Oil Company? Surely we need the same inquiry in 2008.

CHAPTER TWELVE

THE GREEK CHORUS-THE ROLE OF THE MEDIA

"Journalists or reporters...are very much like the ancient Greek chorus, constantly interrupting the narrative of Potomac life to draw attention to themselves. Further, each party in Potomac Land has its own chorus, which will sing praises about its partisan protagonists and moan constantly about the failings of the other side." [36]

Twelve chapters into a book about the Presidential elections and only now do we take the time to consider the role of the media. It's not as if it didn't deserve a higher billing, but placing it here is to insist that the narrative analyst prefers to view media as a function of story rather than stories being mere subjects of the empire of media. We have to understand stories first, the laws of beginnings and ends, the genre, the casting, the crucibles and drama triangles and then, use those insights to understand the story factory that media has become, and its dramatic effect on the Presidential Plot.

Before we get to November 4th 2008, we need to clear away a fog of misconceptions about the media, and the propaganda that the media put out about themselves. A narrative analysis of the media needs to challenge the story they have of their role in the polis. Many of the problems we have with elections have little to do with politics but rather with the media and the unholy alliance of TV/PR with the GOP/DNC.

We saw this develop as far back as 1968 so it's not new, but clearly the campaigns keep using the same Nixonian tricks to get their man elected, and hence, we as the unsuspecting public, the public that is a sucker for a good story, needs to be reminded again and again of what are the necessary and the unnecessary deceptions of media when they come to cover a Presidential election. And not just elections.

WHY THE MEDIA MATTER MORE THAN WE THINK

An expert on Al Qaeda recently described the goal of terrorism as "To kill one in order to scare a million." Murder is a crime we struggle to prevent anyway, but the terrorists won't scare anyone other than those at the scene of the crime, without our willing co-operation in carrying the terrorist's story to the wider world. While 9-11 was such a tragedy in itself, the power of the television images

---

36 Dana Milbank Homo Politicus the Strange and Barbaric Tribes of the Beltway Doubleday NY 2008
p. 251

of collapsing towers and the world's greatest city paralyzed with fear sent even more powerful shock waves around the world.

Terrorism is a deliberate attempt to intimidate citizens by infecting them with an irrational fear that can only be spread through the sharing of stories, images and memories provoked by the original acts of terror. As stories of fear spread, they morph into 'scary monsters,' creating so many more rumors and half-truths that turn every shadow into the boogey man, every unaccompanied backpack into a bomb, and every bearded Muslim into Osama. When the people of London courageously returned to the buses and the underground the day after the July 2005 bombings, they were disrupting the story chain and the Terrorists knew even then they had lost.

SPREADING THE VIRUS OF FEAR

Here in America, 9-11 only inspired more horror stories, anthrax attacks and hoaxes, as we closed our airports and then choked them with security checks. We fixed inane signs to our highways asking citizens to report anything suspicious, and the first thing people wanted to report was the sign! Fear spreads virally. It shuts down reason so that instinct takes over to create a pandemic of panic. The herd smells a lion! See that herd run! But most of us were nowhere near New York or Washington DC on September 11th, and most of us have never come anywhere near a murder scene let alone an act of terror, so why were we feeling so scared? It was the power of that story released into the world. In New York, it was all eerily reminiscent of the Orson Welles "War of the Worlds" radio broadcast of 1938, another time the city was in the grip of a story, prompting hordes of New Yorkers to hide or head out of town before the aliens landed.

Sadly 9-11 was not a work of fiction but if a terrorist knows that his efficacy depends on the power of those stories rippling out from his violent act to paralyze a nation, we had better get a better grip on what is ultimately a narrative strategy. Their weapon is not cardboard cutters or hi-jacked planes but stories!

If the terrorists killed but hardly anyone got to know about it, they would quickly be rendered useless as an international phenomenon. Terrorism, someone said, is merely a more violent form of PR, and the media are unwitting accomplices in helping them achieve their aim of "killing one and scaring a million." It is hard to think of alternatives because it is the way our modern world comes to us.

160

In a similar way, national elections could not happen if the media did not willingly carry the stories of the Candidates across the nation. And Governments could not mobilize the national will to go to war unless it could use the media to broadcast the news of WMD's and Saddam's house of horrors. Strange bedfellows here, Presidents and Terrorists and Candidates, but all need the media, all use the media in the same way, and all are being used by the media in turn to achieve their mutual purposes.

WHO WAS SMOKING MUSHROOMS?

The media's role in each of these transactions is largely reactive. For all the criticism they receive, they too are suckers for a good story, and with increasingly poor editorial oversight, they remain at the mercy of anyone smart or cynical enough to manipulate them, whether that be Osama or Jayson Blair, Dick Cheney or Obama/McCain. A media manipulated by the terrorists first, by the government second, and by the political campaigns third, has helped create one of the defining issues of the 2004, 2006 and 2008 elections: Terrorism, the gift that keeps on giving.

Tune in to the Convention speeches and hear how our electoral processes are still subtly infected with 9-11. The Towers are like domino's that keep falling as we go from ground zero to Cheney's folktale, (as Dana Milbank calls it) about the "smoking gun-mushroom clouds" or simply "smoking mushrooms" which spawned the "Let's invade Iraq" putsch which earned Bush a second term, and helped create a budget blow out from the war which has now put the economy at risk, and which may yet determine another Presidential election. What a catastrophic story chain! And all fed and fanned by the media like a California brush fire in the Santa Ana winds.

Osama must be laughing because as long as that story stays in circulation, the terrorists have won. And they have won because at the heart of this Republic of Stories is the media, a relentless parasitical story-machine that like us, is a sucker for a good story. Lacking any narrative ethic, the media run with stories that end up running them and they, like us and the whole nation end up being its victims. We as the citizenry are cheated of our own un-mediated experience of the world. Yet, in the case of an election, we seem to have no other choice.

ELECTIONS AS MEDIATED EXPERIENCE

This election is going to be a media experience for most of us. We don't have the time or the resources to follow a candidate around and watch his performance, and Conventions are harder to get into than Rolling Stones concerts. But we will tune the TV into Denver or St Paul or some of the debates, and we might read a few commentaries and listen to the local talk-back radio. We won't be able to avoid the Obama and the McCain ads interrupting our favorite shows. We can at least participate from the living room. And given that the majority of voters will do the same, campaigns have by necessity become media-driven.

Much of the current writing on 'Politics and the media' are agenda driven jeremiads. They accuse various outlets of liberal or conservative bias or attempt to expose the whole business as corrupt. That is not our intention here. Rather, the media are key because the Presidential Plot wouldn't work without a way for the Candidate story to spread. Media are the instrumental means for positive and negative story infection. Sure, there is bias and sure, there are some questionable practices but that is not the main problem. Bias is part of any story.

THE MEDIA AS HERO OF A STORY THAT'S NOT THEIRS

The larger issue for us as we seek to unwrap the secrets of the Presidential Plot is that the media set themselves up with a cover story that seeks to overturn a core narrative assumption. The hero of a story is the character at the center of its action, and the teller's role is to be the voice of the story, but not its star. By increasingly reversing this, our media have made the teller and the critic into the hero. Imagine Homer supplanting Ulysses, or Scott Fitzgerald displacing Gatsby. The media have degraded the quality of our reality by the unapologetic insertion of their egos into stories they claim as theirs simply by the fact that they are covering them.[37] Teddy Roosevelt would be outraged. In defense of the good old fashioned hero, he said,

> *"It is not the critic who counts: not the man who points out how the strong man stumbles or where the doer of deeds could have done better. The credit belongs to the man who is actually in the arena, whose face is marred by dust and sweat and blood, who strives valiantly, who errs and comes up short again and again, because there is no effort without error or shortcoming, but who knows the great enthusiasms, the great devotions, who spends himself for a worthy cause;*

---

[37] "In a better novel, the media would be an admirable minor character, the aw-shucks, self-effacing narrator whose keen eye for detail would enable him to explain the candidates' positions on issues...In a better novel, the media might even decide to give more air time to the contender's views than to the views of various talk show hosts and pundits." Stephen L Carter *Washington Post* May 4th 2008 B2

who, at the best, knows, in the end, the triumph of high achievement, and who, at the worst, if he fails, at least he fails while daring greatly, so that his place shall never be with those cold and timid souls who knew neither victory nor defeat."[38]

When the spectator gets the same cheers as the gladiator, you not only upset the Coliseum, you disturb the balance of story power. You come close to contradicting a basic principle of narrative ethics about 'whose story is it to tell?' Plagiarism is outlawed because you are stealing someone else's words but what is worse is stealing someone else's story and shamelessly using it for your own self-promotion. In their defense, the media will say that their role has changed from simply reporting all the news that is "fit to print" and that now, they are creating most of the content. Hence media deserves to be the hero of the stories and shows that they themselves are creating. Hail to the new heroes-O'Reilly, Blitzer, Stephanopolous, Couric, Olbermann, Hannity, Howard Stern and company.

But creating the news is a whole other game. Governments do it and we call it propaganda, and PR companies do it and we call them pseudo-events,[39] and lobbying firms and investment brokers do it and we call it disinformation or worse, graft and corruption. But now the media are doing it and calling it 'news' and in the process, turning the media into a hero factory, where they pretend to own every story. They want to be on the cover of every story they cover. Freedom of the Press was established as a founding principle of this Republic so that the propaganda, and lies and pseudo-happenings could be exposed, not featured on prime time.

Yet the Presidential Plot needs the media as much as the terrorists and the government do. David Axelrod and Rick Davis have no choice but to feed their Candidates into this ego driven madness, and they are prepared because they hire operatives who have the smarts to know how to feed the beast, and how the system works. And they know what the Government and the terrorists know, which is just how easy it is to exploit the media by feeding their vanity, their craving to be in the story.

---

38 "Citizenship in a Republic," Speech at the Sorbonne, Paris, April 23, 1910

39 See Daniel J Boorstin The Image-A Guide to Pseudo Events in America Vintage 1987

MEDIA-THE STORY FACTORY OVERCROWDED WITH HEROES AND VILLAINS

On any one night, you can watch shows that expose predators, find murderers, try criminal cases before phone-in juries, sell furniture or perfume, help you with your golf swing or how to say the rosary. You can enjoy the judges who expel and humiliate wannabe singers and dancers, or you can thrill to Doctor Phil's' "What <u>were</u> you thinking? show as he deals with the most exotic family dysfunctions you have ever heard of. Media are creating and adding another layer to the news in order to expand its narrative possibilities. And they have to, because otherwise, there isn't enough news to go around to fill a 24 hour news cycle. In Australia, Rupert Murdoch solved the content problem by simply buying the rights to all the rugby and cricket. Aussies couldn't endure all that chatter.

If the media has become a story factory and stories are dramas about heroes and villains, then is it any wonder we are a nation over-stimulated by petty dramas and overpopulated with saints and devils? If the Presidential Campaign is a media driven process, it cannot but suffer the same fate, where the complexities are always in danger of being reduced to clichés, and where each side will be sucked into the media game of heroes and villains. Going negative is not a product of the campaign, but rather a result of the feeding frenzy of the media who will provoke faux debates over flag pins and orchestrate adolescent Candidate interactions like; "What do you say to people who say they respect you but don't like you Hillary?" Or "Raise your hand if you've owned a gun?" "Raise your hand if you believe there is such a thing as a global war on terror?" and "Raise your hand if any of you want to go the bathroom?" I made up the last one, but Candidates have had to endure all this demeaning torture from the media, all in the name of public debate.[40]

VOTERS VERSUS VIEWERS

It does not serve the best interests of the nation, nor show the best side of the Candidates, but once the election process buys into the modus operandi of the media, it is serving a different master, the gods of media, the headline and the story. That's what they want, that's what wins audiences. Media care about viewers first and voters second. Keeping them entertained will always win out over keeping them informed.

---

40 Atlantic September 2008 "Rhetorical Questions" by James Fallows Page 34ff

The talking heads will tell us with all earnestness that they are there to inform people and create a conversation about the issues that really matter to the future of the nation. But you only have to watch *Meet the Press* or *Crossfire* or *The McLaughlin Group* to realize whatever conversation the nation is being asked to join, there is little chance anyone else will get a word in. Don't they ever see the absurdity of grown men and woman screaming to be heard? The story is told of a little girl who watched one of these shows and asked her Mother, "Mommy, Why are they so mad at each other?" and Mom said, "Because no one is listening to them. " The media are so inbred that they become the victims of their own story of self-importance.

The age of the celebrity journalist is upon us, and whether he is embedded in Iraq or she is swimming in a New Orleans flood, they seem to have taken up Gonzo journalism's agenda of ditching objectivity to get inside every story as a player, not an observer. What better way to cover a hurricane than being seen swept up in its 100mph fury, or to show Iraq by being able to show how close you came to being blown to bits by an IED in Baghdad? To give up your life to get a story is quite a story, but one you never get to tell, so it's even narratively absurd.

Presidential campaigns are run by PR and media professionals who come from a culture of celebrity journalism and who know how to do business with this ego-driven industry. To ensure that their Candidate stays in the news, they have to book sessions with Jon Stewart and with Bill O'Reilly and Jay Leno and all the other important newsmakers, because to just appear in these shows is to make news. Nixon did it too. But the deal is-you cannot share your story without sharing your glory. The Candidate wants Jon Stewart to make them look good, hip, funny, so people will vote for him, and Jon Stewart or Charlie Gibson wants the Candidate to make them look important, influential, and incisive, so more people will watch their show and grant them the status of a player in the political game.

It's a marriage made in heaven because political campaigns and news media are both peddling stories, and one knows how to use the other. But what does it do to the Presidential Plot? It makes the media into a powerful broker of access and meaning and it means that presidential campaigns are the product of mutual exploitation, between consenting adults of course. The campaigns use the news outlets as their echo chamber and the media, being lazy story slaves, dish up the latest tasty morsel that campaigns have served to them with garnish on a platter. Campaigns know how to keep the media both hungry and satisfied by the denial and granting of access in a manner that would have made even the Marquis de Sade proud! Remember how Obama and McCain kept the media hunting like a hound of ravenous wolves trying to find their VP picks. They had live stakeouts on four residences, and Jim Lehrer on "News Hour" had to deliver the portentous headline that "Obama's team are still getting ready to name VP." Ouch!

NEWS CYCLE AS STORY CYCLE-RISE AND FALL AND RISE

Someone once marveled how the news of the day seemed to fit exactly on to the front page of the *New York Times,* and how did they manage to do that? Surely, some days there would be too much and others too little, but every day, without fail, the daily news conforms to the size of the broadsheet.

As naïve as that sounds, the observation is not far from the truth, in that the news of the day has to fit the dimensions of what is tell-able within the time-slots allotted. There is almost a law that a good story will grow in direct proportion to the time and number of media outlets it gets to feed. The size of a story measures coverage, not necessarily significance. An election is really a one day event, so the narrative design that informs stretching it out over two years requires the broadest span of beginnings, middles and ends, and creating a cast of thousands, recruiting the compulsory heroes and villains and spoilers and clowns and witches and all the dramatic retinue that serve this epic story. It is bigger than Ben-Hur.

If you search back a year or two, you will find the rise and the fall and the rise and the fall of just about everyone on both tickets. Remember Ron Paul or Bob Barr, and whatever happened to Ralph Nader and Adlai Stevenson. Oh, sorry, Adlai was earlier.

Obama is down, Hillary is up, and then reverse that, Hillary is down and Obama is up, and then reverse that and then reverse that again and you know the odds are, you will eventually get it right. Obama wins. Whoa! Giuliani has it won, and then he hasn't, and he's gone to Florida, leaving the field to Romney who has it won because he has such a slick campaign and Edwards has tanked and McCain is in such a shambles, and then, rise and fall, rise and fall, McCain has it won. Wow! How did we miss that story? Media should create the shorthand of 'to RF it' (Rise and Fall) to mean they are stretching it out on the rack of the story cycle or coin the phrase to 'Gibbon a headline' in honor of Edmund Gibbon's famous "The Rise and Fall of the Roman Empire." He got six volumes out of that story!

166

The media call it the news cycle and the critics call it spin, but it's much more of a story cycle in that given the same facts, they can box every candidate except the winner into a mini three part opera. The Romance is the 'Rise of X' as the beginning. Then 'Will he get traction?' is the middle as a Detective Mystery and then, the 'Why s/he failed' leaving Tragedy to the end. They don't think Giuliani the candidate, they think Giuliani the comic opera. Win or lose, they get a story.

Nature abhors a vacuum and the news abhors the status quo because stories track movement. If the news of the day is too static, the media or the campaigns have to invent movement, or even the hint of movement, as in "Hillary may," or "Obama might," or "Experts predict." "Obama is getting ready to name his VP" Events like earthquakes may intervene and become the hard news of the day, but the work of a campaign is to keep the story cycle spinning and it is as predictable as going from 'a' to 'b' to 'c'. And when all else fails, just use the subjunctive because it "might" work.

If things are going too smoothly, the media will want to iron in some wrinkles so that if the news is up, they get story extension by anticipating the come down, and if the news is down, they fill countless cable hours in speculating how to get it to rise. Think of all the ink spilt and the hours of cable chat and blogging spent on the Rise and Fall of Hillary, or the Fall and the Rise of John McCain. Drama is generated internally by changing the pressure points of a story even though nothing has changed in reality, but it doesn't need to. The editor says, give us another angle on the sun rising, it's happened every day this year and people are bored with "Sun to Rise again," so why don't we try "Sun rise delayed tomorrow due to earth wobble." That should do it or "Sun's future Cloudy." Come to think of it, that's why the Sun gets its best headlines in Ireland!

TRUTH IS STATIC BUT STORY IS DYNAMIC

"Fair and Balanced," and "No Spin Zones" have become popular promotions for programs that vouch for the truth of their coverage, but they have a problem before they start. Truth used to be grounded in facts, those verifiable evidences of something that has happened and cannot be undone. If something was true today, it must be true tomorrow or else it wasn't true in the first place. Makes sense! Truth doesn't change. And when someone tells us a story, our habitual response is to ask, "Yes, but is it true?" because there is a deeply held suspicion that stories are not true. "It's only a story," we say in dismissal, or "Did you actually believe that story?" in disdain.

"The facts speak for themselves" we hear Bill O'Reilly solemnly declare, but they don't have to, because he does. Facts only speak because we speak them, and we speak them through stories. Facts only matter because we make them make sense in a larger frame of meaning. A fact is a fact but it needs a Sherlock Holmes to elevate it from its place in an anonymous infinity of data into something that might mean something, e.g., the evidence of the murderer. Stories turn the inconsequential into the consequential and therefore what gives life to a fact is its potential that it might mean something.

The media are caught in false truth claims because facts never add up to anything resembling the truth, and they don't even add up to a true story because *a true story* is essentially a contradiction. Truth is about an unchanging reality while stories track change and movement. We intuitively tell someone, "Your story was very moving," because narrative allows us to follow the world, to notice that something moved from here to there. "Do you follow me?" we say.

A changeless truth is no fit for a living story whose purpose is to map change. If anyone claims something to be a true story, he is lying, full stop, and not just James Frey. Oprah may get all scandalized but it's the nature of the beast. Truth and Story come from two different ways of representing the world. Truth means no change. Stories mean change, because they map change. So the conclusion to the syllogism is: no change-no story. It's what every news editor knows, even without having to study philosophy. Story and Truth have an ironic relationship. It's like you and your big brother. You want to be best buddies, but he says, 'You gotta be kidding me.'

It means that the media is not built to deliver moral truth or eternal laws or timeless essences. That probably explains why there is no Philosophy Channel. Eternal verities are too static for prime time, except maybe for Mother Angelica. But there is another truth that the media can and does deliver and it's aesthetical truth, existential truth or literary truth, which works in as much as it is "true to life," true to life's texture and true to the feel of experience. To campaign by media means you have to deliver an authentic candidate, not a true candidate, because stories can't deliver any other kind of truth. Authenticity is a package that has to fit what we expect "authentic/true" to look like, and sound like, and feel like. And that changes. It feels nothing like propositional truth or the first law of thermodynamics.

CREATIVE LYING

If 'true' for the media does not mean truth in the normal way we hear the word, then by definition, the media and the campaigns are in the business of creative lying to achieve a "true to life" experience. That should not shock our moral sensibilities or start us on a moral crusade for truth because this is just the way it is. Whenever someone accuses the TV of lying, the truthful answer is, "But that's what we are supposed to do. How come you don't get it?"

Alas, the old moral code of determining what is right and what is wrong based on true/false distinctions doesn't work in the media or in presidential campaigns. That is why we need a new narrative ethic which will make us Storywise about sorting which stories we buy and which ones we don't. (See Ch. 18) We have to decide which "lies" to trust, given that deception is not a deviation from the media's true purpose but rather the precise means by which they convey a "true to life" experience.

As they say, in the kingdom of legless men, the one legged man is king, and in a kingdom of liars, the person who doesn't expect the truth is the only honest one. We have to learn a new art of deciding which liars/storytellers to trust, and which ones to reject. This might startle you but I don't mean it to, nor am I being a cynic. It's the break-through we need for a new understanding of Presidential campaigns.

Think of it this way. The fact that we were lied to, or told a story about Iraq is not a reason for not going to war, because there has never been a nation that hasn't used lies/stories to start a war or to win one. Nations are lied into wars all the time. After Vietnam and Grenada and the Bay of Pigs, how come we didn't know that? The debate about truth and lies distracts from the crunch issue which was always, "What was the best action to take in the national interest?" Cheney's and Rice's media blitz, aided and abetted by the *New York Times* should have been so narratively obvious that we could have dismissed it for what it was: "On the warpath propaganda." You have to arm the stories at the same time as you arm the troops.

But we are suckers for a good story. Let's admit that so we don't have to work up a lather of righteousness about being lied to. That is beside the point. In this campaign, we are being fed stories, which is to say, being lied to and that's the game, from Obama no less than McCain. Which lie/story do we want? That is the more critical question.

We have to reclaim our inbuilt bullshit detector and use it to sift out the artful and more honest attempts to tell a story from the more self-serving, knowing that the media that presents the stories is self-serving by definition. As a wise old Bishop once told the young deacon before his ordination, "When I ordain you, son, you know you give up the right ever again to be surprised or scandalized by humanity." When the media wants drama and their secular priesthood wants goodies and baddies, the bishop is telling us that our indignation or surprise expressed in "They lied about WMD's!" reveals either our childish naïveté or our culpable ignorance, but both make us dangerously vulnerable to being deceived.

WE ARE ALL VICTIMS OF STORIES

We may sound too critical of the media but for all their pomposity, they are just as much victims of their stories as we are. Not a consoling thought I know, but if Charlie Gibson says something is true, or Dan Rather, or Cokie Roberts, and there isn't a strong tradition of editorial vigilance, or reportorial humility, what are we to believe? When these experts, our media heroes, are either fools or fooled, what chance for us amateurs? We are all victims, (and all victims are entitled to their very own drama triangle.)

OTHER MYTHS WORTH DEBUNKING- A BIAS ABOUT BIAS

Is the media biased? I hope so. Of course they are, because the power of a story is its bias, the way it bends the facts and the way it invites its listeners to lean. A straight story is dead on arrival. No one accuses Jesus of being biased against the poor Pharisees or having a thing about shepherds because he is always telling us these embarrassing folk tales about them losing sheep, or we don't accuse Shakespeare of being anti-semitic to create a Shylock as a villain. OK, some do, but what a character!

Stories work because they are not neutral, and because they carry a bias, and because they are not disinterested. There is no such thing as narrative neutrality. For a story to work, it has to get you on side by getting you inside. How else does it get you engaged? Bias is a function of narrative long before it factors into political prejudice.

I habitually turn to Fox and the O'Reilly Factor not because I agree with what he says, but because he tells the most compelling stories. I would disagree with his point of view most of the time, but O'Reilly and Roger Ailes, who created Fox News, know that bias gives you a point of view, and a passion which allows your anchor to create himself as this crusading hero persona with an obsession to expose all the bullshit and fight for the "folks" against the bad guys. These are all the ingredients for a great story in the tradition of all our superheroes, Superman, Spiderman, and now O'Reilly Man. Bill is straight out of a comic strip.

Somehow, the bias of the other side of the political divide always seems more reactive and derivative. Perhaps people like Lakoff and Westen are right, and that Democrats are narratively challenged because they are into propositions and policies and not stories. I don't think so, but it makes you wonder when you think about Gore and Kerry and Obama and try and find one story between the three of them that would stand up against one three minute oration by Ronald Reagan.

The call for more balance or for less bias in the media is a call for boring stories, and that would mean suicide from a narrative point of view. Bias and passion and taking sides is what a story is about, that's how it works, unless you want to go back to formal news in the style of an old BBC voice with its Oxbridge snobbery.

Or perhaps we want news to go back to the old fashioned weather report about isobars and squiggly lines on maps and old men in suits with pointing sticks? Even weather reports aren't weather reports anymore. El Nino is a character and tornado watches have become high drama for forecasters who have become celebrities for looking at the sky and transforming rain into Noah's Flood, or every wind into the next Katrina. And even the weather forecaster gets all excited about high pressure systems. He is not neutral because it doesn't work as a story. Media translates everything into story. This is what Roger Ailes realized back in 1968, that politics did not have to be boring. Why even Nixon could be entertaining with a little make-up, some music, an enthusiastic crowd and someone to debate.

PARTISAN POLITICS: FOR AND AGAINST

The conflict model of story works within a story, and it works with a first person antagonist like Bill O'Reilly. But commentary is another thing altogether, because it has a different purpose. It doesn't have to be a narrative duel. In fact, it gives us the chance to stand on the sidelines and work out what actually is going on. Not

171

everyone has to be in the fight between Parties when the more critical fight is the fight to understand. But when you turn on the TV and turn to pretty much any chat show on politics, you get the cross-fire model of someone from one party dueling with someone from the other side. Or if you go to C-Span and you want to contribute a comment, you have to call a Democrat line or a Republican line or an Independent line. And then, of course, as you listen, you will hear them decry the increasing partisanship and the souring of the relationships between members of both parties and how negative public debate has all become.

What they don't see is the delicious irony that they are feeding a system producing the results that they condemn. It reminds one of Northern Ireland where everyone decries the mutual distrust between the Catholic and Protestant communities but no leader will face up to the systematic segregation of their private schooling system that helps produce the result. When you don't think 'systems,' you miss the irony. We are blind to our own complicity in a result we despise but which, if we were honest, is a result of our willing co-operation in the first place.

If C-Span or other outlets were seriously aiming to open the space for conversation, why does it cater only for partisans? Once you know I am a Republican or a Democrat, you think you can predict my view and the whole element of surprise is gone, and with it, the drama that someone might actually change their mind as a result of what they hear. That used to be what serious conversation was about, not inviting the public to mimic their political leaders.

Why does it require people to identify their party loyalty before they share their ideas? I guess it's the best way to prove you are an even handed broadcaster, but imagine holding a forum on God and requiring people to identify if they are Christian or Jewish or Muslim or even atheists before they said anything. Or if we were having a phone-in on race and we asked people to identify if they are black or white? Or on aging, and people over 40, phone this number and under 20, text that number and if you have Alzheimer's, forget about it. Having worked in divided communities like Georgia and Ahkhazia, or Northern Ireland, the last thing you do is demand that people declare what side they are on, when true dialogue depends on people growing beyond such tribal loyalties. In our political media, party identity is the first thing we demand!

Cementing people into this old story is to institutionalize a narrative structure that clearly is not working. Yet the media themselves seem to be uncritical followers, slavishly replicating the same old stories in the same old way. And when it comes to critical issues where we desperately need a new story, the media are the greatest force for conservatism in the culture because they do not cultivate or nurture new stories. Do we have to think energy and gas prices as Democrats, or think mortgage rates and the Iraq war as Republicans? The story of our political Parties is a broken story. It might deliver power to those who govern but it no longer delivers for the people save a divided and competing set of loyalties and excuses. At least it gives us someone else to blame.

Inviting contesting stories of victimhood shields us from our own complicity and creates irresponsibility and inaction. Someone phones in and says,"It's the Republican's fault because..." and be answered by "See what those Democrats have done this time..." Come to think of it, they all sound like The O'Reilly Factor, or Countdown and the Obama and McCain campaigns.

The media wants us to fight each other and that gets us involved, but the surely the bigger fight is the fight against ignorance, and the fight to understand, and that is a fight we the public are losing.

THE NECESSARY SEPARATION OF STORY AND STATE

TV is about stories and stories are about drama and conflict and crises that elicit heightened emotional responses, so in a way, it makes eminent narrative sense to always deal with political issues from the point of view of contestation. It can make for reasonably engaging television without at any point having to shed any new light on an issue. Why call up an expert who actually might know something when you have a stadium full of Democrat and Republican consultants ready and waiting to parrot the party line before the cameras.

Yet, can't we see the demands of the story are not necessarily the demands of the state? Stories need contest and complication, and the state needs compromise and civility and calm, and above all clarity. No one likes prima donnas in politics, but stories and operas wouldn't survive without them. If the media is there to inflame and distort the political arena to better serve the viewer and the advertiser, the danger is that they are poisoning the well. They are continually polluting the air in which the business of government is being done.

The promise that someone will cross the aisles in getting laws passed is a claim a politician from a former time might find extraordinary, as if one was promising not to torture dogs or not to bash your wife. What has become of politics if we can get elected promising we will talk to those other guys who might think differently to us on issues? We used to have a sense of theatre that worked in public and a sense of a more private realm where, without scrutiny, we could cultivate a more collaborative working culture. You knew what you needed for prime time, and you knew what you needed to get laws passed and it was something else.

If the theatre of public action, as George Washington called it, becomes the totality of the political process because there is no longer any separation between the Story (read media) and the State, (read Party) then we have allowed a story to distort and degrade our civil discourse into a B grade melodrama. Life and politics is more than the story, just as life is more than "Once upon a time" and we all have to grow up sometime and find stories more fit for grown ups.

THE TRAGIC DEATH OF A CELEBRITY JOURNALIST

"Gotcha politics" and celebrity journalism are some of the childish stories we have to run out of town if we want to restore, and re-story the business of government. The tragic and sudden death of Tim Russert has inspired not only many fine tributes to a fine man, but also a critical reassessment of the role of *Meet the Press* and the whole industry of political journalism. Tim was universally recognized as a player, not just a reporter because he could make or break a candidate's chances. In early June, he incensed the Clinton camp when he called the primaries over and declared Obama as the winner, long before anyone else. It wasn't an opinion, but a declaration, like the umpire signaling Game Over. It was no wonder his funeral drew Presidents and Presidents-to-be to mourn with his family when God did the same thing to him.

The Obituaries were glowing. They told us that reporters like Tim used to be naturals. They could smell a story or a cover-up at 500 yards. When he worked with Senator Patrick Moynihan, he learned a dogged respect for facts and he perfected "gotcha politics" by confronting guests with what they said 30 years ago with what they said yesterday. It worked. But if success brings you access, you have to keep paying your dues to the powers that grant you the privilege, and it's hard not to get caught up in your own hero story when Presidents and Vice Presidents are courting you. But as the trial of Scooter Libby revealed, Vice President Cheney was courting Russert for a particular reason. Dana Milbank described it:

"In the 2007 trial of Cheney's former chief of staff, Scooter Libby, Cheney aide Cathie Martin testified about the vice president's belief that he "controlled" Russert." (Milbank p.83)

"Controlled" might be a bit strong, but Cheney relied on good press to get his message out and *Meet the Press* was what he considered his best venue, the one that got the most viewers and one that presumably would not subject him to too close a scrutiny. Milbank goes on:

"Cheney adored the telling of folktales and the spreading of myths. He made many of his most fantastic pronouncements on Meet the Press, the top rated Sunday politics show. That way he could beam his mythology directly to more than five million viewers. Even under the questioning of Tim Russert, perhaps the most respected interviewer in Potomac Land, Cheney found he could make his tall tales part of the folklore long before media truth squads caught up with him." (Milbank, p.83)

Russert could skewer anyone if he wanted and his encyclopedic insider knowledge of Washington was reputedly unmatched, but to watch the tapes of Tim interviewing Cheney is to see the implicit deal the media and the White House have struck in the Bush years, that if I give you access, you had better go easy. When Tim talks about Iraq, he talks in the "we" of "Will we" rather than "Will you" signaling to Cheney that he's on board, that he's a patriot too. Irish Television reporter Carole Coleman dared to ask President Bush some less friendly questions and she was never asked back.[41] Those Irish!

Tim Russert was a great reporter, and interviewer and boy, don't we miss him in election 2008, but if someone as powerful and smart as that runs a show that the administration picked as their best outlet for spreading the folktales and myths that led us to war, perhaps we need to have another look. The media thought they were chasing the story, but the administration was obviously smarter because they knew if a famous reporter buys it, the nation will too. And their playbook was pretty standard. First feed the ego of the reporter," We want to talk to YOU on the record," and then, dangle the bait of an irresistible story, an exclusive, and they will take it hook, line and sinker and thank you afterwards. They get the ratings and you get the story out. Win-Win, as they say in Negotiation school. But though Cheney and *Meet the Press* won, we

---

41 See New York Times July 4th 2004

lost! The poor public was duped again. Milbank said *"The facts didn't matter. The narrative mattered and the United States went to war on Cheney's tale." (Milbank, p.86)*

THE MEDIA WAR AGAINST MEMORY

The media have no shame because they have no memory and it's not because they are inherently amnesiac but rather their relentless pursuit of the *new* means they need us to forget what was new last month. As Peter Allen sings "Everything that's old is new again." They would have us read about a new device that allows us to talk to people in another room if they could, except that we remember phones because they are what we use. What we don't remember is what we have no reason for remembering, and news has no reason for reminding us if its aim is to recycle and repackage the drama of the new, the exotic, the latest deviance from the norm they only created yesterday.

News has a built in bias against placing the latest happening within history, or with any feel for context because that only undermines its claim of newness which IS the story. Elections seem to do the same, shamelessly exploiting our cultural Alzheimer's. How else explain the audacity to hope we don't remember that what John Edwards tried in his "Two nations" speech in 2004, was reprising the Clinton message of 2000 and there he was, trotting it out again in 2007! Or the broken *"Washington is broken"* mantra. If only we could retire that cliché with Michael Jordan's number 23 jersey? Joan Didion covered the 1988-2000 elections and wondered why the memory on our hard drive gets erased every four years. It reminded her of Sisyphus rolling the stone up the hill and forever having it roll back:

> *"Writing about politics (has) a certain Sisyphean aspect. Broad patterns could be defined, specific inconsistencies documented, but no amount of definition or documentation seemed sufficient to stop the stone that was our apprehension of politics from hurtling back downhill. The romance of New Hampshire would again be with us. The crucible event in the candidate's "character" would again be explored. Even that which seemed ineluctably clear would again vanish from collective memory, sink traceless into the stream of collapsing news and comment cycles that had become our national River Lethe."* [42]

The lessons of one election never seem to be learned, which means

---

[42] Joan Didion <u>Political Fictions</u> Borzoi 2001 p.8-9

the Presidential Plot is like a favorite recipe that can be pulled out every four years, dusted off and used pretty much the same way as it was in 1968. Didion continues to point out that even though we learned in 1988 that campaigns can use resentment politics to fracture an electorate, and even though both parties moved so much to the center that voters had no choice but to decide between the pathology of small differences, that, come 2000,

> "*Every aspect of what had been known in 1988 would again need to be rediscovered, the stone pushed up the hill one more time.*[43]

CONCLUSION

Every time we tune in to CNN or listen to a McCain/Obama speech at the Conventions, or listen to the debates, we have to give up the illusion that we are watching reporting, or that the media is the middle man between the reality happening out there and the image and sound we are receiving here in our living room. Media are playing the role that they played with 9-11, of broadcasting the infection as the undiscriminating host of opportunity, with no commitment to fairness or accuracy or truth beyond what will enhance the story, despite their protestations to the contrary. That is not to condemn them or judge them to be immoral or partisan, or prejudiced. No, they are part of an amazing manufacturing process that produces stories like cars. Campaigns have customized their product for the media to roll out their Chevrolet model Candidate-Obama, and their old Lincoln Town Car model McCain. We will all be sucked into a good story that is produced by the campaign and conveyed to us courtesy of a sophisticated story industry.

But remember that story and reality enjoy an ironic relationship. The more real it feels, the more unreal it is. When the microphone doesn't work, or the balloons fall too early, or the commentator mispronounces a name, or the teleprompter seizes up or Hillary's fans won't shut up, you will be reminded that it's only the mess-ups that are for real. They exist outside the control room's control. All the rest is intense story production.

Our decision is not to decide who is lying and who is truthful or who is deceiving you and who is not. We are entering new ethical territory here, where a narrative ethic has to come into play because both sides aren't playing the true/false game anymore.

---

43 Ibid. Freud called it 'the narcissism of small differences.'

Stories, whether fiction or non-fiction, are still fiction and not true or false, because the false ones can be made to feel truer than the true ones. We are being manipulated, but we need to get used to it and get over it. Coleridge called it the willful suspension of disbelief and that is what a good poem or an artful story intends to do. It is no accident.

In the elections, decide which story works better for you and for America. That is not simply a matter of liking or disliking, though clearly that's part of it. But liking is also a narrative indicator that the candidate has somehow heard you, and in some weird way, he is telling your story even though you see through the props and the hoopla. Media means distortion, and story means bias, and you are being deceived by Obama and you are being deceived by McCain. Ironically your decision is, whose deception are you going to believe? Whose story invites you in, whose story gives greater hospitality to your hopes and is going somewhere? Whose story is less contrived? It's not easy and yet, you know how stories work, and campaigns know how to work the stories, and if we can find some middle ground in that shared knowledge, they can offer us an authentic candidate and we can pick the better story, and hence the better president.

CHAPTER 13

NARRATIVE VULNERABILITIES

We all have a weakness in our stories and we have a weakness for a story. Not every story, mind you, but a particular sort of story.

We know about how a story works, and we know something about the media's critical role as the insatiable story factory and the indiscriminate host of opportunity for any smart storyteller, whether that be Osama or Obama, Cheney or McCain. We can start to see how this all plays out in the Presidential Plot.

Yet that is still not enough to defend against our susceptibility to stories because we always seem to fall for some of them, like buying the car we couldn't afford, or taking out that extra loan on the house, or pledging faith in a Candidate as if he was the second coming of the Messiah. After the Conventions, Candidates come to the serious end of business and campaigns know this is their best and last shot at finally seducing the whole nation into their story. Our narrative sirens should be ringing out a warning for us to get ready for a sustained story-attack. They are really out to get us this time!

In the world of terrorism, the experts know that it's not enough to guard the gates and monitor suspicious activities. They need a counter-terrorism strategy using counter-intelligence which can infiltrate the sleeper cells and understand how the terrorists think. The same strategy applies to concerted story attacks. How can we get inside the narrative mind and work out what are the soft targets for the next narrative infection that will blind us to government misconduct or a corporate con or a Candidate who shouldn't get our vote? What might a narrative counter-intelligence look like?

NARRATIVE COUNTER-INTELLIGENCE

You may think it means we have to know what the Obama War Room are planning or what is happening inside Team McCain, but of course, as ordinary citizens, how realistic is that? But we don't have to. What we have to know is what we call our narrative vulnerabilities because when you stop to think about it, some stories have no chance of converting us from our skepticism while others, well, they get us every time. Why is that? We can do a narrative SWOT analysis. What are our strengths and weaknesses, opportunities and threats when it comes to being conned?

If we have had a bad experience of religion, then the chances that the smart, young Mormon lads knocking at the door will convert us to Joseph Smith are pretty minimal. Been there, been conned, got the tee shirt, had the therapy, no thanks! Or the person who acted on the fraudulent email supposedly from the widow of Haile Selassie in Botswana and parted with 50,000 dollars to get the 6 million into their account, what are the chances we are going to open that email again?

If we can identify and claim these narrative strongholds, the places where we are impregnable, that might encourage us to explore our narrative vulnerabilities, where we are liable to get totally swept away when the smart storyteller pitches to our weakness. We all have a weakness in our stories and we all have a weakness for a story. Not every story, mind you, but a particular sort of story.

Perhaps I am struggling for money, so I am a sucker for someone who promises me an easy way to make a fortune, or offers me the credit card with zero interest for the first 30 days. But if someone wanted to scare me off meeting someone saying they were gay, that used to work but not anymore, thankfully. Or I have been unlucky in love and a romance agency promises me the perfect match for only 500 dollars, I might take it but if they were selling me snake oil to cure my cancer, I am not as likely as my ancestors to part with the hard cash. I hope!

In politics, if we are totally disillusioned with the Bush administration or all politicians and their partisan bickering, we will discover we are inoculated against falling for that story again, but we will also find ourselves vulnerable to any candidate who promises to fix Washington and to restore competence and honesty to the White House. Then, when we realize these were the very promises that Bush made eight years ago, we are forced to own our recurring vulnerability at election time. Yet, if a candidate wants to try and scare us that world war three with China is imminent and we need to bring back the draft, we aren't impressed.

Yesterday's gullibilities are today's imponderables. How could people buy tickets for Christ's Second Coming as they did in the 19th century? Our vulnerability shifts depending on the cultural credibility of the times, but what does remain constant is P.T Barnum's adage that there is sucker born every minute. Whatever century, it doesn't matter.

It is our perceived neediness that makes us easy targets. If I know the gaps, where you perceive something to be missing in your life, I can offer you a story that promises the answer, the solution, the redemption. It's only a story, but if I tell it convincingly enough, you are already vicariously enjoying the ending before we have barely got through the beginning. If we really want something to be true, it's so easy to be recruited into the story of wish-fulfillment because our imaginations do most of the work.

Candidate X as the classic Republican will tell us that relieving the tax burden is going to create so much more revenue and jobs to jump-start the stalled economy. Candidate Y, the classic Democrat will tell us that taxing windfall profits and the upper middle classes will allow some income redistribution to level the playing field for the working middle classes. The recession will be overcome.

"How exactly?" is what X or Y won't tell us, so we don't know the details, but if we feel it, we will buy it. The Presidential Plot's job is to calculate what message is going to touch that sore spot and promise relief. Note we said neediness because an election is rarely about specific needs because that's too narrow. Specific needs are named and met. We are hungry, we eat, end of story. Campaigns will rattle off a whole litany of needs, the economy, health care, jobs, trade, energy, all to knit together a story of our neediness, and thereby, our neediness for them, our vulnerability to their story pitch. Remember the Drama Triangle-(Ch.10) Victims need Rescuers, and Rescuers need Victims and both need a Persecutor, someone to blame.

We don't even have to know if X or Y has any competence to deliver their programs, so long as they can deliver the speech. And it would ruin our collective delusion were we to wake up to the realization that these Candidates are already promising way more than any President can deliver on his own, because there is the minor constitutional irritation that Congress passes the laws, not the President. All he can do is propose or veto, he cannot impose.

It doesn't matter because we know the whole exercise is not what it pretends to be about. Campaigns use details loosely to paint an impressionist scene, not produce a photograph of it, and their goal is to produce the swoon, the seduction and then close the deal. If X or Y can find the right pitch, and the "We feel your pain" message that Bill Clinton perfected in 1992, and Hillary reprised in 2008, they know they will have a good chance of penetrating our defenses. And they are not spreading their message in a random way. It's targeted like a missile.

THEY KNOW MORE ABOUT US THAN WE KNOW ABOUT THEM

The people in the story business know more about us than we do, because marketers know what we buy, what we search for, and from all their databases and website cookies, they have our profile. They know we are middle aged, Jewish, play golf, have a fridge that is five years old, have aging parents, have just bought a new car, and have three kids in college and are putting on an extension to the garage and like to holiday in Key West. They can even find our Social Security number if they want.

Knowing us, they know our narrative vulnerabilities because to them, they reveal the marketing opportunities. It gives them a map of how to tunnel into the fortress.

> *"Here's a deal for a new refrigerator and we will throw in a whole new kitchen for three thousand dollars more-or what about a time share in Palm Beach which is cheaper than Key West and easier to get to?"*

Similarly, the Campaigns know our demographic, know what worries us, about health care for the parents and the cost of college for the kids and the stock market that is eating away our 401K; these are our areas of need and neediness right now. And a strong pro-Israel message goes without saying.

Candidates know that their challenge is to reach out to get us to buy their story as the one that will assuage our anxiety, an anxiety they have helped create. If they know more about our vulnerabilities than we do, then we are going to be suckers for their story. And if we don't think we are susceptible at all, then we are at even greater risk. We all know our soft spots and our sore points, where need and desire and ambition can all collude to create a hunger for a story that seems to understand all and offer all.

If we resist their seduction, or dare to confess we are Undecided and it's late September or we are Independent and it's October, they will not give up. Campaigns are relentless. They have a billion dollars to spend and as time gets shorter, the more desperate they become. They may have started out on the high ground of principle and foreswearing the Willy Horton way of negative ads, but eventually, campaigns revert to character assassination the more anxious they become. And we have two anxious campaigns right now. If they can't snag me on my neediness, what about my greed or even better, my fear.

NEGATIVE CAMPAIGNING- THE SIGN OF A SPENT STORY

Political campaigners are really marketers wearing the bumper stickers of their products: Obama or McCain. If they can't win you over in a positive way, then they will try and scare you away from the alternative. Negative campaigning is the sign that a campaign no longer has confidence in its own program, or believes that the opponent's weaknesses are easier to attack than laying out the advantages of their own platform. It's guerilla warfare, to wear away at the enemy, never confronting him with your full strength, but turning his strengths into negatives and hoping that at the end of this war of attrition, you will win because the electorate hates you slightly less than they hate your opponent.

VOTING YOUR FEARS OR VOTING YOUR HOPES?

Campaigns might start out in the territory of big ideas but they end in the theatre of big emotions. Emotions have a greater capacity than ideas to penetrate behind our narrative defenses to create a new neediness. And if all else fails, use fear. It works every time, and there's no end of amazing stories people will buy as solutions if we can awaken those darker fears about their own mortality.

Take January 1st, 2000 as a prize example. Someone somewhere was assiduously creating the fear that all the world's computers would freeze up with the Millennium Bug. Computer services did big business to save us losing everything and Governments spent billions. And then, nothing happened! It was the revival of a primitive story bug more familiar to the Medievals than to us moderns. And how our medieval friends would laugh to see us sophisticated Globals buying the same recycled Doomsday superstition that they did. Stories of fear are part of our natural survival kit, and so they stay in the psyche ready to be protect us from the barbarians or the flood, but if artfully triggered, they become a huge narrative vulnerability that can be endlessly exploited to support wars on drugs and wars on terror and wars on just about anything.

Beware of the person who relies on emotions to stir up the need, especially if he runs a service that just happens to offer a service to meet it. He is marketing. When someone needs us to need something even more than we appear to need it, we should hear the alarm bells ringing, that we are entering a poker game for suckers. Politics is that game by definition. Senator Conrad recently described it by quoting his father's warning to him "Never buy from a breathless salesman."

McCain and Obama's "We feel your pain," tours will buff their credentials as the common man, to seduce us into the illusion that these multi-millionaires are regular guys who also worry about their mortgages and taxes and health care when all they care about is your vote, full stop. It's that brutal and that simple. Nothing wrong with that, but to dress it up in atmospheric rhetoric is to camouflage the essential transaction. Drill down to see what is happening from our side-You get my vote if I get your story. From their side, they are politicians seeking election, so dreams are all they have to sell. Making the story transaction transparent to purpose is key to our notion of stronger consumer protection.

WHEN STORIES FOLLOW FUNCTION MORE THAN FACT

If you were a General at the Pentagon, you would be telling us about the need for the military because that's your business. You are not the Peace Corps! Or you are director of Homeland Security telling us that the security risks for another 9-11 are higher than ever, not because that's exactly true but because you have to keep the security story alive. Or you work for a drug company that trumpets some big breakthrough pill to help us all lose weight, and you know that your business can grow fat if you can sell that. To that end, you produce an info-mercial, feed it to the media who, as the story slave, your convenient host of opportunity, will play your "news" clip announcing, "Researchers may have found a diet pill to guarantee weight loss."

Maybe we expect that of the commercial world, driven by profit and not charity, but the Government has got into the same business of paying people to write good stories and float them to the media as real stories, such as good news about the Military in the Iraqi press, or the Pentagon paying its retired Generals to go on TV to talk up the war! Or even the Vice Presidential office floating a story to destroy the reputation of one of its critics. Stories are powerful weapons of war.

Instead of getting enraged at the contamination of media and government, or the total propagandizing of news, we just need to wise up and realize that this is about 'us', not them, and how easy we are to fool. Their operating assumption is that we are suckers for a good story, and using the media as their host of opportunity, they can feed this insatiable story machine all the lies, half truths and myths they need, knowing that by now we wouldn't know the difference. Look what we have uncritically swallowed in the last eight years and you realize they have a point!

We are all so sick off being lied to, but the story that should disturb us most of all is the story they have of us as consumers and viewers. Obviously they see us as narratively vulnerable which is a polite way of saying, they see us as "chumps." Their strategies wouldn't make sense otherwise. And one area we are now wiser about, the story laws of BME, (Ch-3-5) is one where they are amazingly sophisticated in first creating, and then exploiting our vulnerabilities.

THE CATASTROPHE FALLACY

We know the old preacher's trick is to tell us, "The end is nigh!" and so, we must convert now or eternally perish. It used to work, but nowadays, government and politics have supplanted it with their own "Fear of the Future" story package. It's how insurance makes its business, but not normally the business of government.

That is what made the Millennium Bug so irresistible, because no one could contradict it, and no one was prepared to be wrong, because the stakes were too high. No one wanted planes or Wall Street to crash. We were disarmed by the pseudo consequentialism of the story. Threaten someone with a future catastrophe if you want them to pay attention, and if you can scare them enough, they won't contradict you because who can contradict fear?[1]

The preacher preaches Hellfire, and the Doomsdayist describes the nuclear winter and Homeland Security warns of another 9-11, and we see it in our imaginations and so we feel it. Fear is physiological and it takes over to make even the fake feel real. No one can prove its right, which is why it's so powerful, and no one can prove its wrong, which makes it so hard to disarm, and no one can afford to dismiss it in case it is right. Any dissent can be labeled as a reckless disregard for the future.

The same brilliant narrative cunning informs the way we go to war, whether it is Vietnam and the domino's falling, or we fight the terrorists in Iraq rather than their following us here. (Another Cheney concoction) Or think about the gay marriage question and evangelists warning us that if we legalize it, marriage will be destroyed. No one can prove it, and no one can disprove it, and no one wants marriage destroyed. So it's narrative checkmate. The military hawks love this ploy because if you dare to oppose the war,

---

1 The recent Bailout Bill was an almost perfect example of this Catastrophe Fallacy, and when the markets dropped after the House refused to pass the Bill, it was not any real economic measure so much as one further sign of the story infection of fear. The Markets got spooked too.

you will be accused of not supporting the troops and putting their lives in danger. Prove it? They can't. Disprove it? You can't. Will you risk it? No.

When you want to shut someone up, concoct the lethal mixture of fear and the future, and put the burden of proof on your opponent, which is to say, you prove me wrong, when in fact the burden of proof is logically on the person trying to persuade you.[2]

The campaigns will use this tactic to perfection around the issues of the economy and taxes, or health care or Iraq or the current catastrophist narratives about energy and global warming. These predictions might be right, but if they disqualify dissent, they are dogma parading as data. The church gave that business away some time back, but trading in narrative futures by peddling some fact-proof dogmas about that future is still a thriving business.

In a later chapter, we will offer some antidotes to these poisonous story strategies, and elaborate a narrative ethic that in summary says that any story that stories over or stories out other voices is narratively unethical and a threat to the Republic of Stories where every voice has to count, especially the voice of dissent and the voice of the minority.

WHERE THE FUTURE LIES

The other counter to such stories is to state the obvious which is that every story about the future is a potential lie, and only time will tell, as it did with the Millennium Bug, or the story of Global cooling 30 years ago, and the Second Coming in 1988 when Jesus was unavoidably delayed. A Warning should be written on the label of all these stories, like you see on cigarettes, and another reminder of 'caveat emptor', Buyer Beware! Campaigns in their later phases specialize in creating insidious, incontrovertible narratives that once again play on our fears and presume that we are still Cavemen ready to run when someone shouts Bear or Bear Stearns! FDR talked about the politics of fear and he gave us the warning at his first inaugural:

> *"The only thing we have to fear is fear itself -nameless, unreasoning, unjustified terror which paralyzes needed efforts to convert retreat into advance."*

---

2 I promise that the Secretary of the Treasury, Hank Paulson, was not reading this before he went to Capitol Hill to scare the Bailout Bill through Congress.

Compare that to George Bush's post 9-11 speech. It is time to signal once and for all that the tactics of 1968 are finally unmasked, out of date and poisonous. We have enough real fears to worry about without politics manufacturing them just to get our vote.

ASSESSING THE NATION'S NARRATIVE VULNERABILITIES

If people suffering from trauma or catastrophe display hyper-vigilance, and become inoculated to some deceptions and more susceptible to others, what about a nation? Germany was humiliated after World War One, and though dictatorship is never inevitable, a nation more readily buys a story that restores national pride if they feel they have been victimized. It's the narrative vulnerability of a nation. And nations get caught up in their own drama triangles too. (See Chapter 10)

What about Russia after 1991 where they lost not only the Soviet Union, but the whole Russian Empire? Are we surprised that a leader like Putin can so capture the Russian mood for restoration? Democracy is our story for them, not their story for them! Or Iraq after Saddam Hassan? Why did we imagine that they would accept us as benevolent dictators by simply replacing a malevolent one? We blundered into a story that was ready to find scapegoats and victims, and of course, we were the designated Rescuers set up to become future Victimizers and Victims. What did we expect? And yet, we keep insisting that we know best what story other nations need. Our own story is breaking down, and we still want to export it? Countries and the affairs of nations mirror narrative vulnerabilities and Rise and Fall story cycles that any successful secretary of State ignores at her peril.

But what of the narrative vulnerabilities of the United States in 2008? Ronald Reagan invented the genre of asking, "Are you better off now then 4 or 8 years ago?" A narrative analyst, as we have already discovered, asks different and odd sorts of questions and he translates this one into, "What stories are we vulnerable to after Bush that we weren't before?" "Better off" suggests material well being which is a very misleading way of assessing progress. The UN and the World Bank now talk of the Human Development Index[3] which measures quality of life, how people are spending their lives rather than measuring their lives of spending.

---

3 Sarah Burd-Sharps et al The Measure of America American Human Development Report 2008-2009
Columbia University NY 2008

A narrative assessment of the national mood wants to know where we are most likely to buy into another story of international misadventure, (Iran, Russia?) or avoid the crisis of social security that didn't get solved, or energy policy, or health care. Blaming the President gets us off the hook, allowing us to overlook the fact we voted Bush for a second term in 2004 and a new Democratic Congress in 2006 to deal with these very same issues! A failed presidency is a symptom of a failed Congress and a failed Congress is a sign of a misinformed or disinterested electorate. "For the want of a nail, a shoe was lost, then a horse, a soldier, and finally a nation was lost."

Where did we avoid the real work in the last eight years, and how can we face up to the challenges of the future? What stories have been disqualified from the public discourse because they have been discredited, but which we might need to redeem in time for the next crisis? Presidents wear the meaning and sense out of some stories that yet, we still cannot afford to jettison.

England after World War One had no more stomach for war, and appeasement was the logical conclusion from a bloody aftermath, though we tend to look back now with more critique than understanding. Hitler exploited the aftermath story of his own nation which was the desire for vindication. And because neither weighed the narrative vulnerabilities of their history, war eventually happens. And along comes Churchill whose life story was war. It was his history and his destiny.

When Britain needed to rearm its war story, it summoned a leader who knew what it meant, (unlike Bush and 9-11. Bush knew nothing about war except how to avoid it!) Churchill knew how to reenroll the nation in its military tradition, a nation whose last experience of war was a shattering and senseless waste of life. Some stories discredited by misuse in the present, need to be reassessed but not retired. Otherwise we become alienated and inoculated from our own wisdom. One bad experience of dogs doesn't mean that all dogs should be shunned, and one ill advised war against terror doesn't mean at some future point, we might not have to use force to stop genocide or naked aggression.

The "US Invasion of Iraq" story remains one about America still willing to sacrifice its brightest and best to defend the people of a foreign land, with whom we have overly identified in their plight to escape tyranny. No other country does that! No other country is willing to spend those precious lives and all that money. The fact that the whole project was ill-conceived and incompetently carried out, does not negate the extraordinary story that it tells. It represents the best and the worst of the American story, one that we urgently need to sort out, but not one we have to throw out. 4000 lives cannot be so trivialized.

The story of how America defends itself after Iraq has become one of our more urgent narrative vulnerabilities. We need to defend ourselves, but do we need the Patriot Act, or Guantanamo, or water boarding? Do we need to spend so much on a Defense budget that means we have to choose between health and security, or between new bombs or replacing infrastructure and fixing schools? The military will make a story that serves their purposes, to make the threat as large as they think they need their budget to be. We expect that, but they should not expect us to buy it so easily after Iraq. "The Military is exhausted and depleted," and "We need to retool," and all the rest will become our narrative vulnerabilities because the military wants vindication.

The story of how America protects the freedom of its citizens is another story to review, and what is the right balance between individual liberty and national security? We have swallowed the Patriot Act whole, but it's a story that has unraveled as the story of growing government power rather than protecting citizen freedoms. We need a new story about security, one that makes more sense.

And what about the pressing needs of the nation itself? Foreign adventures seem to have consumed our resources and paralyzed our civil discourse about what the domestic priorities should be. Getting out of Iraq might be less about correcting a foreign policy blunder and more about withdrawing to get our own house in order because somewhere in these last eight years, we have lost the plot.

THAT OTHER SOFT SPOT - STORIES THAT INSPIRE

The Psalmist says there are two ways and two paths, the way of the righteous and the way of the wicked, and what he doesn't say though he knows it, is that stories can take us down either path. Stories can ennoble the human cause, or they can degrade it. The point is we get to choose.

One doesn't always have to take a negative view of vulnerability. The Buddhist tradition sees our soft spot, our area of weakness and defenselessness as also the place where compassion can grow. As much as we are vulnerable to being exploited, we are also vulnerable in a good way to being inspired and to reach beyond narrow self-interest to the cause of justice and peace and protecting our global environment.

189

The only thing worse than being vulnerable is not being vulnerable. Jesus reserved his greatest condemnation not for the sinners but for those who hardened their hearts and thought they were beyond the need for grace. The mystical tradition tells us we are vulnerable to an infinite longing that relativises all material striving, because narrow self-interest may fill a bank account but it is never enough to fill a life. Human life can only make ultimate sense if there is something more, and only in its end can we find justification for its meaning.

America is an aspirational nation, one that cherishes and monumentalizes extraordinary stories of courage and generosity. Who does not thrill to the story of Lincoln appealing to 'the better angels of our nation,' in trying to reconcile a divided nation, or the story of FDR working from a wheelchair to beat Fascism and Nazism? Who cannot stand on the steps of the Lincoln Memorial where Martin Luther King gave his "I have a dream speech," and not be moved, or witness the eternal flame that signals the perennial hope and adventure contained in JFK's challenge to *Ask not*? America and particularly Washington is a City of stories that speak for all that is the best in America, and it is these stories that Presidents and successful Candidates evoke and seek to renew.

Obama announced his candidacy on the steps of the Illinois State House where Lincoln once served, where he delivered his famous "House Divided" speech, and from where he left to serve in Washington. Obama also returned there to conduct the unveiling of his Vice President, Senator Joe Biden. Obama has the narrative intelligence to inhabit a place in order to invite us into a bigger story and touch our spirits.

He delivered his Nomination address on the 45th anniversary of the "I have a dream speech," placing his candidacy in the context of the struggle of the Civil Rights movement. This African American stands on the crest of that history, close to being the first black President. And the first night of the Convention, we witnessed moving homage to that Lion of the Senate, Senator Ted Kennedy and the Party's attempt to wrap Obama in the Kennedy mystique, the handing on of the torch to the next generation.

Senator McCain's campaign has not attempted such historic evocations. He is more the man of action than the man for carefully crafted photo-shots. The memorable moments of his story hearken back to war, but for a nation grown weary of military misadventurism, his Vietnam era, though personally heroic is not the nation's glorious past. It is a reminder of past blunders and lessons unlearned. Yet, McCain's own courage, and the story he shared so movingly at the Convention remind us of what this man is made of, and what service to country cost him.

We can be suckers, thank God, for good stories that ennoble and inspire and add to the richness of the human story. Whether we vote for Obama or McCain, let's inform them that we are not as vulnerable to being exploited again by cheap promises and by their pandering to our neediness, but that we <u>are</u> vulnerable to being inspired and to knitting the nation together again by stories that appeal to the better angels of our nature.

Surely we are ready for a new story of what patriotism looks like in the 21st century, a patriotism that amounts to more than flag pins or being a good consumer or viewer or voter. At the same time, love of country can no longer be totally collapsed into a love of the nation's military tradition, nor should a grave stone at Arlington exhaust what "to give your life" means. The story we tell the grieving families of why their sons or daughters had to die has to be a story that inspires the rest of us to live and to serve.

When our best are sent to fight and die, while the rest of us are sent to shop, you realize that our dear Republic of Stories is badly in need of a new human economy that vows never again to waste young lives, and pledges to treat all its people as its treasure.

INTRODUCING CHAPTERS FOURTEEN AND FIFTEEN

THE FOUR HORSEMEN OF THE APOCALYPSE

1- How Obama won the Presidency
2- How Obama lost the Presidency
3- How McCain won the Presidency
4- How McCain lost the Presidency

If our premise is that America's story is not working and the solution is not to make the old story work better, but that we need to find a better story, then what are the better stories on offer with our two Candidates?

Already we have watched them begin to conform to a campaign pragmatic that has made them seem more and more conventional. We thought we were going to get change but all we are getting is speeches filled with more clichés than public language has a right to have to carry. The iron law of genre that says, "This is the way it's always done," has blurred some of the fresh edges of their story. After two years, I guess, it's hard for any story to stay in shape or stay fresh.

Polls tell them how to twist this way or that to capture the swing voters, but allowing audiences to totally shape the story bends it out of shape and away from its own genius. With the bending comes the possibility of the breaking, where a Candidate loses character coherency or becomes entrapped in a caricature. It doesn't work for a novel, and it doesn't work for a campaign.

Both Candidates have compelling stories to tell and both have the potential to renew the American story. Our narrative position is not partisan, but it is certainly not disinterested. We are partial to a good story. And that's what we long for. So long as Party politics forces the Candidates into predetermined slots of the mainstream Democrat or the mainstream Republican, they wrap their unique lives in party uniforms and almost choke the potential for any new life to come into the political system.

These two candidates, by any measure, have to be the most interesting and surprising candidates of the last 50 years. This is not Gore v. Bush, nor Kerry v. Bush. This is unprecedented. People put bets on a Clinton-Giuliani match up or Clinton-Romney, because these were the monied and establishment backed candidates. But Obama v. McCain? What were the odds? They have already changed the story by their candidacy. But before we vote, we have to fully weigh and harvest the uniqueness of their stories.

If we could liberate the candidates from their Party handlers and present their stories unplugged from the noise of the polls and political pundits, what would they offer us as the stories that could reshape America's future? If they were the new maps, where might they take us? Let's road test the stories.

HOW ENDS FINALLY REVEAL PURPOSE

Because a story fits a genre, a predictable pattern of meaning making, we can play it out and even get ahead of it. If we want it to fully disclose its meaning, we have to get to the end to really understand the beginning, and where the journey was actually heading. A story only derives its meaning from the end because how something ends up tells us what it was becoming all along. We have heard "The end never justifies the means." Narrative says "The end justifies the meaning."

If the athlete wins the gold medal at the Olympics, then all her training and her sacrifices are told as, "This is how I won Gold," whereas if the person simply competes and does not make the final, the hoped for story she thought she was in, the "On the way to becoming a gold medalist" narrative has to become something else. It becomes 'How I got to be an Olympian,' which is quite a comedown from how I became an Olympic champion. The reverse also happens. One young Australian diver wasn't expected to win any medals and was content just to have qualified, but he performed so exceptionally that he was assured the silver medal, until the Chinese champion failed his last dive and the young Aussie ended up with the gold. His story had to radically change in that instant because a new end meant a new beginning and justified a dramatic new meaning. [4]

A story works from a simple formula that if Act 3 is the end, then, Act 1 and Act 2 are about "On the way to becoming the ending." It is part of the law of beginnings, middles and endings. When we apply this to the Presidential Plot, we can get ahead of history and put the desired end into the story "Becoming President" to allow us to tell the past and the present as "On the way to being elected President."

This gives us a way of road testing the narrative for its capacity to capture us and the voters and probe it for its weaknesses, because we know in the Presidential Plot that there is a winner and a loser,

---

[4] The diver's name was Matthew Mitcham and he had other stories to tell as the only male competitor at the Games who was openly gay.

and that there are only four possible stories that we already know even now are in the process of being written.

1- How Obama won the Presidency
2- How Obama lost the Presidency
3- How McCain won the Presidency
4- How McCain lost the Presidency

By using the essential facts of Obama's and McCain's lives, we can write the story of the future from where we stand now in the present. We don't have to read the stars or tea leaves; just their stories.

FOUR POSSIBLE ENDINGS

If an election was a battle of the stories, these are the finalists. We have four potential endings and we know that history will adopt the winner's narrative and transform it into a national epic, while the story of the loser will drop away. Who even remembers Bob Dole's bid against Clinton in 1996, or who FDR defeated in 1940? (It was Wendell Willkie. I knew you knew!) The loser gets consigned to the political dustbin or the trivia quizzes unless the loss is just as significant as the win, which is why we remember Dewey because he was supposed to win, and we will remember Gore because he won before he lost.

TO GET BEHIND THE STORY, YOU HAVE TO GET AHEAD OF IT

What lies at the heart of this exercise is the awareness that in the present, the future remains open and therefore meaning making can only be tentative. We think what we are doing today makes sense, but it is ultimately contingent on what happens tomorrow. I think I am writing a book on the election but that depends on whether I get it finished and get it published. If I don't, it might be that I am expounding a fuller narrative analysis of contemporary culture and media. I can plan but I cannot be sure. Only the future will validate the hopes of the present. So, in order for a story to fully reveal the pattern of meaning making that undergirds it, we have to fast forward to the future and look back. Telling the story from the future that we imagine from the present gives us clues as to what webs we are weaving and also, what stories our Candidates might be falling into. Kierkegaard said we live life forward and understand it backwards, but what he didn't say is we can get ahead of it by running it forward and reading it back.

The other feature about this process is that we can at least risk surfacing some stories of the future that might even now effect the present. What normally happens is that next year, we will have a surfeit of books that will tell us "What really happened" and if they are as revelatory as the Joe McGinnis book on the 1968 elections, they might have altered our vote had we known. Why do we get the best stories after the event when in fact, they were happening before the event, and had we known, we might have been able to do something?

It comes back to our contention that we are always in the middle of something and we are never sure of the end or its meaning, but in the case of the Presidential Plot, we do know the end, and we can use the stories and play them out to impute back into the present what might be going on. We can borrow meaning from the future.

If New Orleans had played out the story of a Force 5 hurricane hitting them, they might have been better prepared. And when you read the tragic story, you realize that they did in fact do that, but the story was buried in a scientific report that was all but ignored. Reality-a Force 3 storm-had to intervene and wake us up to our capacity for the future that we had already developed through our story imaginations but which we sadly dismissed. Some things in life are totally unpredictable, but when we know where a story is headed like a hurricane or a Presidential election, we can get out ahead of it and test the story to see if it will hold up or not.

CHAPTER FOURTEEN

OBAMA WINS!

The world will be excited that an Obama Victory might allow America to become America again and become as she has never been before.

If we keep in mind that The Presidential Plot is an Epic, then we know already that the hero who wins is the hero who either successfully invites the gods to shine on him and rescue him from the Fates and the Furies, or the hero who has the inner strength and perseverance to defy the gods and exhibit his own hidden divinity. More likely, it is a messy and capricious combination of both, meaning in common language, that he was plain lucky, right place, right time. Given that the American narrative landscape is littered with stories of the Heroic Individual rather than the lucky individual, unless one is in Las Vegas, the best fit for us is a full portrait of Obama the Hero. One cannot readily imagine a headline saying, "Obama lucky to win!" but what kind of headlines would an Obama Victory inspire?

THE HEADLINE TEST- OBAMA WINS WHITE HOUSE!

The Washington Post for November 5th 2008 reads, "The first black man to win the White House." Think of what other headlines come to mind. A headline serves as the handle of a story that allows you to pick it up in one grab and be sure that you have the meat of it. (We call it a "Grabline") Headlining can be an informative experiment, because we are asking, what would be the meat of an Obama victory, what would sum it up? Obama reclaims White House for Democrats, or Obama overcomes racist attacks to cruise to victory, or Obama ushers in New Era of open Government, or Bush repudiated in Obama landslide. Forcing people to headline their own story forces them to quickly zero in on the lead. So as narrative analysts, let's play with some Obama Victory headlines to see what we might learn about the potential of this story and which ones are the real grab-lines.

AMERICA WITNESSES HISTORIC VICTORY-THE BIG STORY

What is the biggest story that an Obama victory can become? When we think big stories, think history. Think of other big stories that echo his-a Jackie Robinson breaking the color barrier in baseball, a Catholic elected to the Oval Office, a Thurgood Marshall on the Supreme Court. Hillary spoke of 18 million cracks in the glass ceiling stopping women winning the top job but in the context of America's conflicted and tragic racial history, an African American in the White House has to be the biggest lead because it marks the end of something and the beginning of something else which, as we know from our laws of BME, always characterize the biggest stories. Something has changed and as Yeats would say, "changed irrevocably." One test for a big story is to ask, "What's historic about that?" What's historic about a McCain victory? Perhaps that the party of an unpopular President still retains the White House, but that's small beans compared to this.

An Obama victory will mark an historic change in not just the politics of America but its own sense of itself. The ghosts of the great Civil Rights leaders will be summoned to witness what will be the fulfillment of their dreams as well as validating Obama's own sense of history when he deliberately connected his campaign to Lincoln and to King and to JFK. Here is a black man who does not bring the old racial history to the White House. Rather as Booker T Washington said in a speech in 1895 about race and politics, he (Obama) will not allow "a story of grievance to overshadow a greater story of opportunity."

The speech that King gave 45 years ago, the speech that Obama deliberately echoed in his acceptance speech, has come true. America has not judged someone by the color of their skin but by the content of their character. An Obama victory will assume a larger significance than Obama, and a much bigger story than even his Presidency. His election will be made to carry the weight of historical inevitability, that this election becomes the high water mark of a tide that has finally turned to sweep down the last walls of bigotry and prejudice. On the level of symbols, it will move from the tawdry level of hand to hand political combat to the cosmic place of A Second Coming. The end of an epic signals that our hero becomes a god, and his success presages not only an inauguration but his apotheosis.

AMERICA REINVENTS ITSELF-A GLOBAL STORY

What other big stories are there? To think big, think global, think international. What will the *London Guardian* write or *Pravda* or the *Beijing Daily* or the *Mombasa Chronicle*? Son of local boy wins presidency. Or in the Jakarta *Kompas*? An adopted Son of Java wins White House.

The headlines of the world will marvel at America's ability for re-invention, that it could so radically shift from the frat boy "bring 'em on" cowboy president to the "the world as nuance" law professor, that we have moved from the pampered son of a political dynasty to a total unknown who built a power base solely on his own talent and charisma and his ability to inspire his fellow Americans to believe the impossible was possible. The world will be excited that this might allow America to become America again and perhaps be as she has never been before. Obama smartly already tested this story in Berlin and other places and knows that had the world been given a vote, he would have won by billions. Given that America craves the world's favor, that we like being liked, this victory will heal some of the hurt of being pariahs. When we feel the world likes us, we treat the world a whole lot better too.

THE POLITICAL STORY-HOW DID AN OUTSIDER WIN?

We are used to the campaign post-mortems like after the Hillary meltdown, when we had plenty of stories revealing the inner drama and her supposed lack of leadership. Hillary was portrayed as a hands-off indecisive chief allowing her team to waste energy on turf battles rather than focusing on the message. Of course, if Hillary had won the nomination, the story would have praised her truly empowering style and how she had trusted her staff to sort out their own dramas. The end always determines and justifies the meaning but before that, stories can go either way.

If the Obama camp wins, there will be a flood of books that will take us inside the campaign Situation Room and show us how they mastered the primaries, and how their tactical smarts beat Hillary first and McCain second. David Axelrod will be the new Terry McAuliffe if not the new Karl Rove. But again, when we ask ourselves what is the big story here, it will be how an unknown Illinois Senator got from being the keynote speaker at the 2004 Democratic Convention to being President four years later. This is surely unprecedented. Carter did it but he was a Governor, as was Clinton. Obama's campaign, what we are in the midst of right now, will become one of the glorious chapters in the legend should he win, and should he lose, he will have cracked a few glass ceilings in the process of how to run campaigns.

As we road test these headlines, we can already see that any story that can change history, charm the world to love us again, and reinvent the whole electoral process to make it accessible and winnable by unknowns, is a MEGA story. Obama is a totally compelling story, and notice we haven't mentioned party politics here or any issues. On its own narrative merits, this is a winner. And it's an essentially American story, new yet old, fulfilling the dream by broadening it to those who were once constitutionally denied access.

OBAMA-AN OLD STORY OF AMERICAN ACHIEVEMENT

In electing Obama, America has also opted for a deeper sense of continuity. His family circumstances marked his early life with struggle, and dislocation. His story is ready to join the Log Cabin tradition of Lincoln because here is another man who had to teach himself, who had to become his own hero before he felt his own power for good in the world. He was raised by a single mother, in a family that knew the daily struggle to make ends meet and make a life. Hawaii can now look forward to adding something else besides Waikiki to the walking tour, and perhaps even a Presidential Library sometime. And the High School and apartment where he and his Grandmother lived in the early days better be getting ready for tourist and media attention. Perhaps a new coat of paint and a plaque "Obama slept here."

OBAMA- A NEW STORY OF AMERICA STARTING OVER

Obama won because America was hungry for a new story that would begin a whole new chapter in governance. He was the beginner that matched and excited the nation's passion for a fresh start. He captured the prologic moment, sensing the opportunity in being a beginning, and he defied every stereotype. Working as a community organizer in Chicago, Obama displayed his solidarity with the working classes, rather than aspiring to climb the ladder of professional success. In his own life. Obama had a history of defying expectations and refusing to be imprisoned inside any story that would limit his horizons. He made himself up using the fragments of his diverse and disrupted upbringing and he will bring that unprecedented diversity to the White House and the nation that, more and more, mirrors the same diversity as his. Finally what we have in the White House is what we have increasingly in the country at large, someone who is not white and not WASP, not mainstream and not even mainland.

POWER AS THE REWARD OF PERSISTENCE RATHER THAN INHERITANCE

Obama exemplifies the modern story of American possibility, that you can come from a broken family without a father, you can have brothers and sisters, and step brothers and step sisters, many who live a world away, and you can be raised by your grandparents, and you can encounter racism and feel excluded without knowing why save for the color of your skin, and yet for all that, you can still inhabit the American dream and achieve its end.

One does not have to come from a family of heroes or a family of rich oil magnates or from a Boston Brahman family or have a religious calling to be President. The story of Obama as President is less about what he did and even more what America did, that America dared to choose a black President, and overthrow its history of enslavement and racism and bigotry. The world will cheer America for that choice. Obama will become America's story more than America is Obama's story. The two will be forever indistinguishable.

THE TRIUMPH OF SELF INVENTION-HORATIO ALGER RIDES AGAIN

Obama had no ready-made story to fit into and that was his youthful dilemma. His life confronted him with the choice; what is my story and where do I belong and who are my people? These are the existential choices of modernity, rather than those arising in a more traditional tribal culture of his ancestry where he would have been socialized into role before he was invited to find an identity.

That is the story of dynasties, whether they are Kennedy, or Bush or even McCain. Identity comes late to those Candidates, because they are born into duty and public service along with power, and privilege. They create their identity out of a crowded family story. But the Obama presidency is the story of how someone without that can still find an American identity and aspire to public service from an inner sense of calling rather than an outwardly imposed sense of duty and obligation.

When America chose Obama to be its leader, they repaid the choice he made to serve the South Side of Chicago, and they are saying that community service is as valid as military service as the necessary background for future presidents.

A PERSONAL JOURNEY TO HEAL THE FAMILY TRAUMA

We know the Oprah culture of our modernity translates even the most historic achievement into a family drama. Someone may walk on the moon, but some of us want to know how the wife was feeling as she watched, rather than being drawn to the engineering miracle and scientific drama that got him there. Obama's victory will thrill the tabloids and the family magazines, with two adorable Presidential Kids to obsess over, and a smart and opinionated First Lady back in 1600. What a gift. But Obama's victory is a very personal story. Becoming President does something for Obama in closing a family circle or healing a family drama.

Obama's father is a tragic figure, a smart man who never got to know his son, and his son spends his early adult life trying to find his father's story and where or if he fits into it. So Obama is this figure in search of the father and in search of the story. And that story of quest, to find what was lost is transformed into the American story of what his Mom always told him 'You can be anything you want to be if you work hard for it.' You don't have to prove your ancestry goes back to slaves to cherish freedom, or to choose the black story as your badge of pride. Obama's personal story, not his views on health care or Iraq, is what has re-ignited the story of America. Axelrod knew that all along. And to a generation of kids who have to struggle with absent and multiple dads, Obama's story is a beacon of hope.

The silent anchor to his story is his mother, who herself strives to make a better life for herself, and is an example to her son that regardless of what life throws at you, the inner determination and self-belief is what counts in the end. Obama's Presidency is a tribute to mothers and grandmothers and their role in families everywhere. Obama's Mom is the very opposite of his father, and someone who taught Obama the American story because she lived it and made it possible for her children. Though Obama's story is called "Dreams from my Father" his sequel might mention that it was his Mom, and more particularly his proud Grandmother who helped make those dreams come true.

GENERATIONAL CHANGE-THE FIRST YOUTUBE PRESIDENT

When America chooses a 47 year old unknown over a 72 year old famous warrior, you know that America is not only choosing a Candidate but that it is choosing a new generation. This leads to a whole set of other headlines that will capture the energy and excitement that has driven the Obama campaign and taken it over the top at the polls. The future is being created by the young. Today's 47 is the equivalent of yesterdays 65 when 23 year olds are inventing Google. But this is not simply about age, but about reading the mind of the generation that will shape tomorrow, reading that mind to lead and inspire it. His volunteers were young under 35's who had never before felt so invited into the political process.

The younger generation identify with this President because they know that like him, they still have everything to prove, but they voted for him because they wanted his story to be true. This generation wanted to write a new story about Washington and Obama became their Muse and their pen. The internet community he created gave the YouTube generation the feeling that they had a stake in this election like no other before. In the best form of identity politics, they were voting for themselves.

HOW CAN A CAMPAIGN MAKE THESE HEADLINES TRUE?

The best liars in the world instinctively know that the best way to sell a dodgy deal is to over-elaborate on the ending, and to help the target audience imagine the final glory and the ultimate pleasure, to place themselves there already. If telling stories is a form of lying to ourselves, then we have seduced ourselves into an exciting place called Obama Victory and in testing it out, we can clearly see it is totally compelling. I don't care who you are, we all want to buy some real estate if it includes a ringside seat to history, to hope, to a new dispensation. "We were there," we want to be able to say to our grandkids, like we might say we heard Brother Martin speak about the dream.

The other trick of a Doctor of deceit is to under-elaborate the beginning, make it totally simple and accessible. All you have to do is send 50 dollars and you will get.....and wait, there is more....just send the 50 dollars, and on top of that, we will give you....... In the case of an economic crisis, it is just "Pass that Bailout Bill," in the case of the Presidential Plot, it is your vote. Vote Obama and Washington will be changed, lobbyists will be confined to leper colonies, just vote for Obama, and not only that, we will also offer universal health care, just vote, and wait, there's more, we will give you a 1000 dollar rebate on your income, just vote for Obama.

If the Presidential Plot was in any other area than politics, we would readily identify it as a con, as too good to be true. Even Jesus would have a hard time delivering on the promises. But the willful suspension of disbelief seems to be part of the fun. We all know it's a game.

The challenge for the campaign as we move into the final month is to draw a clearer road map between beginnings and endings, to flesh out the middle. As we have said, it's where the action is though its not where the stories get told. If Obama is the Magellan or the Columbus offering us a new World, and we are willing to sign on to his quest, what are the headings, what parts of the story will reassure us that he can get us there?

And what might we imagine as the final twist in the drama that brought victory? Imagine that as we stand, he is heading to defeat, and then, there is the final reversal, that last Olympic dive that wins unprecedented scores of 10! What would we invent or wish or prophesy for the Obama story to give it the final dramatic intensity that any good story needs to keep us glued to our seats?

OBAMA-COMMUNITY ORGANISER FOR THE NATION

It all changed when Obama rediscovered the South Side of Chicago. Obama offered to become the Community Organizer of the Nation and the nation said, 'Yes, we are done with Harvard MBA's and Skull and Boneheads.' The issues that carried his campaign in the end were those of justice and equality, and how he convinced the nation that poverty could be fought through community empowerment. The campaign had stalled after the convention. It had become too predictable and pandering, too negative and feeding people's resentments more than buoying their hopes. Communism may have died but the good old class warfare playbook was trotted out as if victory would be all about middle class comrades rising in revolution. The Obama team was accused of being pessimists.

Obama's original inspiration about hope was the key to turning his Candidacy around. He found his passion by going back to the beginning and reliving his days on the South Side of Chicago fighting for the little guy. That was where his desire to run for the Presidency was born, and that is the story that finally won over the Clinton skeptics, and the Pennsylvania blue collar workers. He woke up just in time to his opponent's tactics and how damaging they were. McCain wanted to drag him into a game of hate, the divide and conquer of the drama triangle.

Obama finally found his signature story wasn't being voted the editor of the Harvard Law Review or the absence of his Father. It was in the South Side of Chicago, in a community losing jobs and kids and hope. In that story, Obama finally found his rage, his sense of righteousness, and he invited people not to be demoralized by their anger but to use it as a rallying point, where people's dissatisfaction finally bubbles over into activism, an activism that can be organized. That's what he had learned as a community organizer. This was his apprenticeship to become President. Mayors run towns and mend roads and collect parking fines but they don't start movements or start revolutions that reach across the nation.

His program was not ideologically driven, but rather an incremental and grounded approach, founded on finding and forming leaders rather than pretending to save the world with prescriptions. America voted for Obama because it wanted to renew a collaborative spirit where power was seen not as the prerogative of lobbyists and politicians, but about the power of the people to seize their own destiny, as he had done. Power, he said, must be held accountable to the commitments and promises officials make when they are given that power. That's what a community organizer does. He promised such accountability. Obama finally wanted to make the people the hero of the democracy story and he knew that instinctively because community organizing is a million miles away from the tradition of leadership that Washington exemplifies.

OBAMA-A DIFFERENT WAY OF LEADING

The other dramatic change that came late and finally turned the tide for Obama was that he did not have to defend every comma or word in his comprehensive proposals. Most of the debates were wasted opportunities about the details, and yet the core issue wasn't whether the tax threshold was 33% or 37%, but rather what type of leader Obama would be compared to a Bush or a McCain. The campaign's energy in linking McCain to particular issues meant this bigger issue got lost, and as they experienced in the debates with Hillary, people cannot long endure the minutiae of health insurance. What is the bigger story here? Not the programs but who is running them. Once campaigns get buried in the little story, they lose momentum. People's eyes glaze over. Think of the better headline "A New philosophy of Leadership to transform Washington."

That's why this election is not about two people; it's about two ways of leading. The last eight years have shown that command and control, the military chain of command, the decider in chief surrounded by yes men and shrouded in secrecy belongs to the 19th century, and not even there because Lincoln didn't do it that way, and he was Republican. You might have to run an army like that, sure, but a nation is not a military camp, and it's not a business, it's a community, it's a soul, it's a destiny that we build together, not from the top down. And you don't privilege gut instinct over sound policy process.

OBAMA-THE FUTURE BEATS THE PAST

In the final analysis, when the Obama campaign began their epic journey, they had to fight off Hillary who framed it as "experience" versus "inexperience" and was he ready for the 3am call? Having vanquished Hillary, he moved to "change" versus "more of the same." And when challenged to flesh out his program, his campaign got lost in the details. With the chance to give a speech that would be chiseled on his memorial, Obama delivered a

205

"workmanlike speech in Denver" and took the air out of the campaign. He had lost touch with his big story, his narrative capacity which was the campaign's greatest asset.

In the last month, having come under sustained negative attack from the masters of the Karl Rove School of divide and conquer, the Obama campaign looked in deep trouble. So how did Obama do it? How did he beat off that late surge from Senator McCain and how did he survive that late breaking scandal that threatened to undermine the very premise of his candidacy as being about change? (Think lobbyist money, think campaign assignations, think John Edwards, or Spiro Agnew presuming that there will be a late complication because the story needs it.)

Obama reclaimed his story, which from the beginning was not about change-that was the cliché every campaign is about, but about the future. "Change" is the cry of revolutions, Luther, Stalin, Mao, Jesus could pull it off, but Obama was not a revolutionary. Besides he did not own the change story because he didn't have a record. What had he changed? He realized in time that the McCain camp had their own story of change based on the record of McCain, calling for a change to lobbying laws, calling for a change in Iraq to add more troops, to bring change to the immigration bill. McCain wanted and got a purchase on the change story.

Obama understood the narrative logic that he was the young prince, the rightful heir, ready to take the kingdom back from the wicked and corrupt king who like any aging dictator, wants to cling to power at all costs. He was able to characterize Senator McCain as an honorable part of history, but a spent force when it came to the future. And that was the key, the battleground was not change but the future.

When the campaign moved from change to making it about the past or the future, the choice became much clearer, and Obama as character could mould the future story much more convincingly than the change story. He realized that his story needed to find its own uncontested ground and build a narrative defense against the increasingly personal attacks of his opponents.

People voted for Obama and not McCain because he was the future and McCain was the past. Obama was tomorrow, the new face of America, the Internet generation, the post modern global in a new battle against global warming and poverty and McCain was yesterday, the telephone, the typewriter, the old and noble battles of Vietnam and Cold War and Communism. But yesterday's warrior carrying yesterday's wounds was still fighting yesterday's battles.

Obama is a child of a new age and new possibility. He was born before man went to the moon, before the internet took over communications, before the Cold War ended, before the escalation of the Vietnam War. His world has changed so dramatically, and he has lived through change to see the future being born and feels a part of it. His generation gave us Microsoft and Apple and Netscape and Google. He was born the same year that JFK took office, and Clinton was shaking JFK's hand and McCain was already a young cadet in the naval academy getting ready to fight another war. Obama's Victory was the signal of a generational choice and America said yes, we are ready to the pass the baton.

America is not a place that looks back when it wants to go forward, Obama told them convincingly. The future doesn't begin tomorrow, it begins NOW and the door to it is an Obama presidency that will draw us through that portal to tomorrow. His sense is that history is out ahead of us and that we have yet to make it, rather than simply behind us and something we have an obligation and duty to relive.

FINDING THE BIG STORY AND STICKING TO IT

We have road-tested the Obama Victory narrative and it is an amazing story. When we do the same for the McCain Victory, strange as it may seem, his will equally unfold as a compelling story. But what this headlining exercise clarifies is your narrative capacity. It reveals your big stories, the ones that no matter how detailed you get, you have to hang your message on because little stories only make sense inside the bigger stories. If you tread all over your main message, you are showing you don't know what it is. If you lack the confidence that it is going to persuade people, it spells death to a campaign because if you don't really believe it, and have to keep massaging it, how do you expect us to believe it?

Getting us to fast-forward and then look back is also an exercise in visioning, which should be the expertise of a leader anyway. Without a vision, the people perish, and young men are promised that they shall see visions of the future and it's left to the old men to dream dreams of past glories. Visionaries give the present a new charge of possibility because they do not see light as the death of a star in the cold uncaring universe but rather the birth of a new sun and the potential for a new world coming into being.

Stories are maps because they are journeys and we have already placed our Obama in the epic of the *Iliad*. If he evokes that in our imaginations, we will know that our Achilles is going to make wrong turnings and they will be the price of his and our learning, and we know he will have moments of great doubt, and others will doubt him, and there will be shipwreck and loss of faith, but that's the *Iliad*, that is the journey and the journey is the destination. Earlier we quoted Tennyson's poem *Ulysses* that seemed to fit the McCain story so well. The poem we offer for Obama is Cavafy's *Ithaca*, Jackie Kennedy's favorite poem and read at her funeral.

> *When you set out on your journey to Ithaca,*
> *pray that the road is long,*
> *full of adventure, full of knowledge.*
> *The Lestrygonians and the Cyclops,*
> *the angry Poseidon -- do not fear them:*
> *You will never find such as these on your path,*
> *if your thoughts remain lofty,*
> *if a fine emotion touches your spirit and your body.*
> *The Lestrygonians and the Cyclops,*
> *the fierce Poseidon you will never encounter,*
> *if you do not carry them within your soul,*
> *if your soul does not set them up before you.*
> *Pray that the road is long.*
> *That the summer mornings are many,* [5]

---

5 Constantine P. Cavafy (1911) http://users.hol.gr/~barbanis/cavafy/ithaca.html

CHAPTER FIFTEEN

McCAIN WINS!

"Ronald Reagan said he did not want to return to the past but to the past's way of facing the future." [6]

What would be the headlines of a McCain victory come November? What would be the instant grab and story takeaway? "McCain saves White House for Republicans," or "America turns to its old hero for leadership," or "America calls on experience to chart troubled waters." If McCain has a winning story, and he certainly does, what is it?

THE McCAIN ADVANTAGE

The media have fallen in love with the Obama story, not out of political bias but more for its obvious narrative capacity. It's new and dramatic and something they can more easily feed off. So that is the first clue as to how a McCain victory would sound. It would first of all seem against the odds. And though that means in polling terms that it might catch everyone by surprise, we know from the narrative perspective that it would become the bigger story because of that very surprise. Stories that hide and then disclose surprise endings are the ones we love best. It's what heroes do-just as the giant alligator is about to devour Indiana Jones or superman is about to be zapped by kryptonite, they escape to save the day.

Great stories so reverse the ending that we realize we have been tricked into the wrong narrative. We can all think of movies like *"The Sixth Sense,"* or *"The Crying Game"* where the plot seems to be twisting and turning and taking us along for the ride until the end, when we get totally upended-nothing was as it seemed. The end rewrites the beginning and the middle. It's the BME axis again. These are the accomplishments of a master storyteller, a Stephen King thriller, and McCain's story has all this potential that an Obama story might not have, presuming McCain remains the underdog or at least is not the media favorite.

REPEATING HIS UNDERDOG ADVANTAGE

We term it the underdog advantage because not only does the downtrodden hero want to win, the story itself wants this character to win because it makes for a better story.

---

6 George Will-*Washington Post* May 21 2006 Page B-7 "Lessons for Liberals."

Let's not forget that we have been here before. The McCain campaign was dead on its feet in 2007 when staff were abandoning ship and they had run out of money. The media had all but written the obituary. Bob Shieffer from CBS had declared that, "It would take a miracle for McCain to win the early Primaries."[7] Now here we are, less than 12 months later, and McCain is heading into his party's convention to accept their nomination. The intriguing thing about McCain is that he has amazing inner resources. Remember he has had plenty of experience learning how to endure, and how to come back, so if people count him out, or if the polls show, as we would expect that he is 20 points down, that is where he is most dangerous, like the fighter pilot, ready to sneak up behind you. He saw what Bush did after New Hampshire in 2000. He is an old fox, and what they say about the old fox is what he lacks in speed, he makes up for in craftiness.

More than that, he appears to have leveled the playing field, because, according to the polls, he and Obama are currently neck and neck. The reality might well be that Obama is 20 points ahead, but no one can know that yet, and the media needs a horse race right now. They are rubbing their hands with glee, because they have a real contest to cover, and they love a Comeback Kid. A two horse race is not much of a story if the favorite is leading by 20 lengths at the first turn. Compare the drama of "How much will he win by-20 or 30 lengths?" to "Will he win at all" Stories need a contest, a conflict, something at stake, something moving, and as we have said before, if it's not there, the media will RF it themselves into their formulaic 'Rise and fall and rise' of the story cycle.

Let's road test the imaginary story of Senator John McCain winning the White House in November. How does America makes sense of that, and what is the big story on offer? Once again, we are not doing this because we have a party bias for McCain but rather the conviction that he too has a story that America could well embrace and use to shape its future. What is the promise of the McCain narrative?

Secondly, after we have expanded the stories, big and small, we will pull back and imagine how it all played out and what was the significant factor that was the game changer. Or in other words, we try to assess what was it that turned defeat into victory? What might the final drama be about?

---

7 Howard Kurtz "Campaign Storylines All Knotted Up" *Washington Post* Feb 11 2008

McCAIN-AMERICA RETURNS TO ITS CORE VALUES-A RONALD REAGAN REVIVAL

When faced with the choice of a new leader who came out of nowhere and had no depth of experience, and an old familiar face, America voted for John McCain because he was safer and because he rallied the voters to reclaim a vision of America that was founded on the old virtues of honor and duty and service and courage. McCain displayed a different sense of history to his opponent largely because he had so much more of it, but also because he knew how to use his personal story to retell the national story. While his opponent was outlining issues, McCain was telling stories. He maximized his narrative capacity and dug deep into the American stories of Individual Heroic endeavor and the Enemy at the Gates that blunted his opponent's reliance on The Beloved Community, and in a masterstroke worthy of a Robert E. Lee, he stole the Rot at the Top-Reform agenda from under Obama's nose with his surprise pick for Vice President. (See Ch.8)

McCAIN-RESTORING AMERICA'S HEROIC PURPOSE

Voters believed McCain's message that America had lost its way because it had lost its true sense of purpose, and that even his own Party had sold out its core convictions about the economy, foreign affairs and the relationship of government to the citizen. His critique of the Bush administration was that they had been seduced by the promise of big government and big money, and that McCain's reform agenda in the Senate had set a record of reigning in a runaway Republican government and calling it back to a national agenda that made sense.

His story of service and the tradition of the military, of serving a cause larger than your own self interest, was one that hit home because McCain had the life to give weight to his call. He had ballast and all Obama-Biden had was bombast. America agreed with him and Obama that Bush had squandered the last eight years, but where McCain made a distinction was that Bush's failure was because Conservatives had betrayed their own party traditions of small government, a humble foreign policy and lower taxes. McCain was not more of the same but the return of the true Conservative, a Reagan revolution. Even Obama had acknowledged that Reagan was more effective as a leader than Clinton.

McCAIN-LEADERSHIP STYLE-DECISIVE OVER CONSULTATIVE

As we saw in the Saddleback interviews, McCain's style and tone of leadership was decisive. He knew enough about the world and he knew enough about himself to know how to lead and where he would lead the country. His was not a style of "Let's talk about it," or "Let's think about that out loud." McCain convinced America that the problems we faced in the immediate future could not afford us the luxury of vacillation or political expediency. As the Russian aggression and the global market meltdown took more and more center stage, McCain's history of international diplomacy became critical, compared to his opponents who kept nuancing on the one hand and never shutting up on the other. McCain accused his opponents of having secret weapons to secure a new world order, in that Biden would talk the enemy into submission, while Obama would offer to withdraw his VP in return for signatures on the treaty. It might work for Iran and North Korea.

McCain reprised the Ronald Reagan era of leadership where America would consolidate its power and not waste it, but at the same time, it would not apologize for it. In McCain, America had once again chosen strength and conviction and a muscular foreign policy, only smarter and more pragmatic.

McCAIN-THE FUTURE IS AMERICA COMING HOME AGAIN

McCain was able to evoke the great story of *Ulysses* and the themes of return, reclaim, restore. His best story invitation to us was not to imagine a fantasyland of the undetermined future, but rather to re-imagine the stories of his grandfather and father and his own service, which were all profiles in courage and loyalty. McCain was calling America back, to return to the core of American identity deeply rooted in the stories of sacrifice and honor and duty.

He showed the nation that change alone was not what the nation yearned for, but rather what that change promised? It was a change to what? To promise something better without offering anything other than handouts and tax cuts did not address the core issue, which was not how we could be better off, but how we could be better, how we as a people could come together inspired by the government but not dependent on the government. We were the Beloved Community only because we were made up of Heroic Individuals. One is built on the other.

McCAIN-A NEW ERA OF SMALLER GOVERNMENT

The old traditional values still worked, values of self reliance and independence and States rights, and a belief in the initiative and enterprise of ordinary people. A Government that wanted to come in to more and more areas of peoples lives was a sign that the government no longer trusted the people to be the masters of their own destiny.

McCAIN-AUTHENTICITY TRUMPS AUDACITY

The McCain victory also proved the return and the triumph of idiosyncratic politics because McCain was the maverick who trusted his gut more than he trusted political operatives or ideology. He was the beef and potatoes candidate, distrustful of all the artifice of image and he also showed that comedy wins votes as powerfully as conviction. McCain mocked himself mercilessly in the latter stages of the campaign, saying that if reading a teleprompter was the main skill a president needs, then he had better think of another job. He was who he was, and the voters knew what they were voting for, that here was not only an authentic war hero but someone supremely comfortable in his own skin and also, someone who did not convey a desperation to win. He didn't have the money to compete with Obama, and he didn't have the media swooning over him, nor did he carry any great historical destiny, save that he was the oldest ever to contest let alone win an election. But he made a virtue of necessity and turned his liabilities into assets. That was the story of his life and it was the story of America.

He told America, "It's not what I say-it's what I do, and doing what I say I am going to do. I'd rather misread a teleprompter than have people misread my intentions. In the military when your life depends on the trust of others, your word is your bond and you don't have the luxury nor the time for Harvard lawyers to draw up contracts, so I don't have the facility for fine and lofty words. I am not as smart as that, but you know me, you know what I stand for, what I have always stood for, and if you stand with me, then I will stand with you, because my actions matter more than my words."

McCAIN-AUTHENTICITY TRUMPS INTELLECT

If America could vote for a George Bush for his authenticity and overlook his minimalist record or his fumbling intellect, the McCain Victory proved again that America does not put much stock on intelligence if it is not at the same time applied in a practical way. They might not have agreed with the McCain position on issues, but the result proved again that McCain's seeming lack of artifice and his slightly cynical stance to the whole process allowed him to come across as the leader who would do something rather than the leader who, for all the great ideas, would not have the courage to be unpopular. McCain had a history of risking popularity for principle. People in the heartland could relate to that. If people don't like you because they disagree with what you stand for, then

213

that's fine because this is America, but if everyone likes you, you wonder whether that person stands for anything save his own popularity.

THE FUTURE IS SEEDED IN THE PAST

When the Obama team skillfully inserted the age issue by reframing the election as the past versus the future, McCain countered by evoking the ghost of Ronald Reagan, and the stories of his own family, of what he had achieved because of the living tradition that he and his father and his grandfather had kept alive. He liked to quote Ronald Reagan when he said that a McCain Presidency was not a return to the past but rather to the past's way of facing the future. He portrayed the Democrats as running scared, and wanting to scare people into voting for Obama, and labeling their platform as displaying a lack of faith in America and a lack of respect for the deeper traditions of American initiative and enterprise. America trusts its future only because it cherishes its past. We have faced trials before and triumphed and we know we will again. America knew it was in for some trials and decided that they wanted someone they knew had been through his own and come out the stronger.

McCAIN-A CHANGE THAT REVIVES

He did not try to compete with Obama on the policies so much as argue that America did indeed need to change, but the debate needed to be on what sort of changes. He was able to describe the changes in the economy that past administrations had made that undermined America's greatness and self-belief, the harmful intrusion of government in the market place, the profligate waste of funds and corruption, the dependency creep making people believe that they could no longer solve their own problems.

America was once the booming economy that led the world, and McCain promised that he would lead the country back to that. We were once the voice of moral character in the world, and now we are the laughing stock. We want to change back so we can reclaim our true identity. Once our military were the best and we treated them the best, but that changed when we loaded too much on them, and as good as they are, they cannot fight three major wars at once, using militia. We need to change that. America will stand tall again and no one will be able to bully us.

McCAIN-THE GREATEST GENERATION STILL TO LEAD AND EXPERIENCE STILL COUNTS

A McCain victory would also signal that America is not ready to hand over the reins of government to a new generation just yet. They wanted an older and wiser and steadier hand on the tiller. There are major generational changes in the culture that Obama reflects, but deep down, every American wants a fair deal, wants a good job and a home and a family and good health care and though not expecting a perfect world or a perfectly risk-free life, citizens have a right to expect they can walk the streets at night and feel safe and don't have to send their kids to risk their lives in foreign theatres of war. McCain's grandfather did that, and his father did that, and he did that, and three generations is surely enough to make sure we don't use up another three generations.

The final retort to Obama's candidacy was that he could not promise what he did not have, and he did not have it because he had not lived through enough of it. On the other hand, if Obama rallied the younger generation, McCain gave voice to the baby boomers who increasingly felt sidelined, considered to be too old to have any real say. McCain elevated wisdom as a prerequisite for leadership, and made grey hair and his craggy face and limp into assets. He could not only tell people that he feels their pain, he could honestly tell them that he is still feeling it.

Experience doesn't necessarily mean knowledge, nor does age and achievement mean expertise. What a successful leader needs is not just knowledge but wisdom-he needs to be the wise sage, a Merlin character. It is a wisdom that can take a longer view of history, a broader view of what it takes to create real change, and knowing the hard way that what everyone acclaims today as an instant success often in the longer view turns out to be a disaster, and vice versa. You have to be around long enough to know that and it's called wisdom. That's what America needs now more than ever, not the short term but the long view.

McCAIN-A NEW WORLD BUT THE SAME OLD ENEMIES

Here is what I would imagine Senator McCain delivering as a message that helped win him the presidency:

"Senator Obama grew up in Honolulu and I am sure he has been to Pearl Harbor as I have and seen the oil still leaking from the wreck of the USS Arizona. That would remind him of the patriots and of his own grandfather, and it always reminds me that what my Grandfather fought for, and what my father fought for, and what I fought for, but which, even now, in our own day, has still not been secured, a true and lasting peace.

I am here to make sure we finish that job, because even while the world is building better satellites and faster internets, the old plagues of hunger and disease and ignorance and tyranny are still with us. And I cannot feel I have finished my life's work in public service without one last time, offering my life and my experience to help lead the American people into a world that finally finds ways to eradicate these ancient enemies.

If the battles were all totally new, if it was interplanetary and Star Wars and all the rest, then, sure, as my kids will tell you, the Old Man can't even handle a keyboard because his wrist is frozen, so let someone younger handle that. The younger generation have the world in front of them and they have everything to prove, just as once we did, that they are worthy of shaping America into a more perfect union, and we know they will, but the thing about our generation is, we have nothing much left to prove because we have seen it all, but now, we have everything to give back.

Maybe if the enemies are all new, then Senator Obama is new and he is the better leader to deal with that, but I know that the new enemies are the old enemies, the same we faced in Asia, the same in the Middle East, ignorance and fear, and the same as the Cold War, and it all seems to be coming back with a vengeance. It was the great President Roosevelt who named the four freedoms- freedom of speech, freedom to worship, freedom from want, and freedom from fear, and anyone can go to the FDR memorial in Washington as I love to, late at night and instead of thinking, aren't they great old fashioned words from 60 years ago, NO, you realize, he is still speaking to us today, and remember he was a leader that America elected four times, and he was never too old, and he was someone who from the age of 30 couldn't even walk upright.

He had the inner courage because of what he had to endure, and that is why America trusted him. So, my friends, I ask you to trust the wisdom that life has taught me and my generation, and that it is never too late for the virtues of service and sacrifice, and no one is too old to lead, or too young to serve, and the values that keep America America, that keep America at its best, are values that united the aging Benjamin Franklin and the young and precocious Thomas Jefferson. Campaigns can divide us but our deeper values as Americans unite us not because they are new, not because they change but because they are ageless.

Sometimes, in moments of crisis, the new generation is not about age but about who is willing once again to commit their lives and their blood, sweat, and tears to summon America back to its founding vision and restore it to the glory that is its destiny."

WHAT TURNED THE McCAIN STORY INTO TRIUMPH?

The next part of this exercise is to imagine that a month before, that McCain was clearly going to lose, that he was 14 points behind and that some lobbying scandal or some mutiny among his own campaign management had distracted them and that they were off message and just throwing negative ads and digging themselves into a deeper hole, and then suddenly, there was a late intervention, something changed the story and transformed it in those closing days, and made the country finally end their romance with the Obama Biopic and return to the McCain chronicles of an old warrior. We shifted back from the Iliad to the Odyssey.

THE STORY OF THE FATHER

Given that both Candidates told their biographies as Father Quests, we suggested earlier that electing either Obama or McCain was going to take America into a Father story, whether we wanted to or not. McCain is the Father figure and Obama is not. Obama is too young, or at least too young looking to play a paternal role. The turning point was not the campaign itself but the international scene that suddenly erupted into Part one of the next Great Depression coupled with a new Cold War fought over currency.

The heating up of the rhetoric, the stand off between NATO and Russia, the EU's economic collapse and its ineffectual role, the history of frozen conflicts that suddenly thawed, all this increasingly turned the eyes of the voters to a world of danger that was not just that of terrorists, but the return of big power politics big time. Russia signed a peace agreement with Georgia months back and has still not withdrawn, flouting the rule of international law. The collapse of the oil prices, the investment retreat from Moscow, a run on the banks in London and Geneva all put the world economy on the edge, and China retreated from the dollar and called in the US debt. As Robert Kagan [8] writes, if history ended in 1989, it came back with a vengeance in 2008.

---

8 Robert Kagan, <u>The Return of History and the End of Dreams</u> Knopf 2008

THE RETURN OF AN OLD ENEMY MEANT THE RETURN OF AN OLD WARRIOR

We are prisoners of our experiences, especially those that involve life and death and shape us in the cauldrons of war. McCain is a warrior, and he will only truly inhabit a story that maintains him in that role. It's that pugilistic, no holds barred, take it or leave it side of him that shows you he's been in past situations where he had everything to lose, and so, what has he got to lose now by being blunt or honest? You know the value of life when you have come so close to death and are, ever after, freed to live dangerously.

He might lose an election, that's all. And if he wins it, it's because there is still a Warrior role to inhabit, that war is still on the agenda. Old Warrior summoned back for last battle is how Hollywood might play it, or the last Harrison Ford movie, that he had one last 'Raiders of the Lost Ark' in him, but you need some bad guys and some threats and foreign adventures. McCain is the old Churchill, discarded and belittled, who is called back to lead because the nation needed a leader who knew war and knew how to win them.

While Obama and his experts tried to nuance their response to Russia and Iran and North Korea, McCain was able to make it sound like uncertainty and inexperience. McCain as Commander in Chief finally was able to make full use of his military experience and speak to how he and thousands of other veterans were victims not only of Communist aggression but of the incompetence of the Pentagon putting troops into an unwinnable war, and a war that they helped to make unwinnable. And why it was unwinnable was because the political leaders then as now did not have a clue what an American life was worth, because they had never seen war. America did that with Bush and they cannot afford to make the same mistake as they will with an Obama president, who McCain said had seen the street battles of the South Side of Chicago, and that was about his only war experience.

The Iraq war was once going to be the defining issue of the campaign. It was one that first of all seemed to favor Obama, and then, with the seeming success of the surge, to favor McCain. But the economic news made war secondary, until the final act when Russia turned on Ukraine and demanded Poland remove the US missile shield and China came debt collecting.

Suddenly American woke up to a more dangerous world. Churchill's book about Britain in the late 1930's was entitled "While England Slept", and JFK did his thesis on the same theme calling it "Why England Slept." The book about this time in our history might well be entitled, "While everyone was watching the Olympics and the Conventions," because Russia was arming the South Ossetians and Abkhazi's, carving out their territories as part of Greater Russia and rattling the sabres at Ukraine and the former Soviet states. NATO was impotent; the EU ineffective, emboldening Russia because it realized that no one had the guts or the army to challenge it, and America was too distracted by the romance of the Obama candidacy.

Why America finally chose McCain's story is because the nation needed a father figure. We wanted someone tested in the line of fire, and we couldn't afford another playboy, or another callow youth who will have to have his training wheels on. Bush was too busy playing volleyball with his athletes to notice that Putin was busy redrawing the map of Europe. There was only one candidate who understood what that meant. Bush looked into Putin's eyes and saw his soul, and McCain looked into his eyes and saw KGB.

FULFILLING THE FAMILY PROMISE

A Candidate always has an Oprah story. With McCain, one can write the story of a dynasty; that this naval hero, who had a grandfather, hero of World War Two and his father, hero of the same war and commander of Vietnam, and he, the son who did not command much, save a jet squadron and a prison cell, now, after serving all his years in the Senate, finally is elected commander in chief, and that like a good fairy tale that does things in threes, the youngest son outdoes the father and the grandfather.

He is finally vindicated, he measures up, and he surpasses. From POW to POTUS would be the Hollywood biopic. Finally, in a time of war, America calls up one of its sons from a family of tested warriors, steeled and fired in the crucible of war, tested to the limits of endurance close to the edge of death, and now, this hero is called from his elder statesman duties on the floor of the Senate to lead the country out of war and out of economic darkness. If Cincinnatus could be called from the farm to the Senate, McCain is called from the Senate to the White House.

It is a compelling story. And what would make it more so is that this is the campaign that was written off a year or so ago, and here is the candidate who beat the young charismatic Romney and the 9-11 heroic Giuliani and the film star Fred Thompson. He was the underdog, and no one gave him a dog's chance to beat Obama. Winning it will remind America that is does not vote on popularity or age, but on values and character.

HOW DID HE DO IT?

What finally turned the tables? Obama was the favorite, but that in the end worked against him. McCain having come from behind for most of his life, proved formidable once again because he took more gambles than the Obama team, and finally because the gods of war smiled on him again with world events taking the agenda away from the home scene. Who knew we were heading into another depression and another Cold War? In the end, people were not willing to give the nation into the unsteady hands of an untried leader. It wasn't as if the nation was saying never, but rather saying, not yet. Obama's will be the stronger President one day for having come so close this time and living to fight another day.

CHAPTER SIXTEEN

OBAMA DEFEATS McCAIN DEFEATS OBAMA

*"Victory has a thousand fathers;
defeat is an orphan." JFK*

If we can use our imaginations and follow the map, the trajectory of the Candidate's stories to an imagined victory to reveal their narrative capacity, we can also do the opposite and move each of their stories forward to an end that sees them defeated. The stories of Victory will see either one of them crowned as the hero of their story while defeat, though not their goal, will also see one of them at least starring in his own tragedy. So, these stories are equally sprung for either ending. Each will produce a great story. Yet, by doing this exercise, we explore the narrative vulnerability within their stories as distinct from the narrative vulnerability we spoke of in Chapter 12 which was more about our weakness for a story.

In the epic genre, why do heroes fail? Either the Gods are against them and it was a futile struggle all along, or the hero was deeply flawed and undone by blindness to his own hubris, the Achilles heel, or it is a combination of both, meaning that they placed themselves on the wrong side of history.

We have explored both winning narratives and expanded on why both of them are compelling in their own way. Either candidate would easily grace the annals of American Presidents. But the point about stories is that if both could win, both could just as easily fail. The failure would lie in the campaigns lack of ability to get their story out there, or their uncertainty as to what story they wanted to go with, or they allowed their story to come undone so that the story being promoted didn't fit their words and images. They exposed a fatal contradiction that the opposition was able to seize on and use as a wedge to break open the narrative coherence of the candidate.

THE CATASTROPHIC REVELATION

We can also do the catastrophe scenario and imagine that our candidates are all set to win in a landslide and in the final weeks, something happens that dramatically turns the tables. Remember, that is the Candidates' worst nightmare and a stories greatest ambition, to catch the audience in the last chapter with a total reversal. Stories that work have this predictable surprise in them and in doing this simulation, we are again probing the story for any potential flaws, or what might come unstuck at the end.

We need to remind ourselves of our earlier work about sorting out the plot and finding the right cast and knowing that the drama requires heroes and villains, spoilers and losers and that the drama triangle is going to map out many character reactions and roles. Also, though we will talk about them separately, this is the one story. If McCain won, the story is Obama didn't win, so why? And the answer is that Obama lost, so that the real story may not lie in the victory, but rather in the defeat.

We also want to apply our new narrative tools to examine how Obama or McCain may have misunderstood the law of beginnings middles and endings, and that is what got them unstuck, and also, think of the drama triangle and who got landed with the Victim-Loser role. Lastly, we might assess how they read or misread the narrative landscape of the four basic American stories.

##

OBAMA IS DEFEATED IN A CLOSE ELECTION!

Imagine this as the headline? Having heard the compelling story, his history breaking candidacy and the attraction of a young, zealous, smart Senator from Illinois, fed to us by a media swooning for his seductive promise, what could possibly have happened?

Were the fates against him, or he was too callow and shallow, as a younger man, and his opponent successfully locked him inside that caricature, or was it a combination of both? Let's flesh this out to explore the narrative vulnerabilities in the Obama epic.

If Obama fails to win, it will be a bigger story than McCain winning, because he has the inside running, like the favorite running in the Derby. As a candidate and as a story, he looks like a winner. The part he auditioned for needed someone young and vibrant and fresh and unknown and new, and someone who in himself was the new story he talked about for American politics. He had all that and more.

TOO NEW, TOO UNFAMILIAR-THE BRADLEY EFFECT

This sense of surprise might give us the first clue about what happened, in that he was too new, he was too unknown not in respect of America not knowing his story so much as having no story to predict or judge what his performance in the Oval Office was going to be. America liked him but not as President. Given that America was not only voting a candidacy, they were voting history to put the first African American into the White House, perhaps the

Obama candidacy was still too prophetic, and the racial fears he awakened were still too strong. He was a victim of the Bradley effect, where voters give the politically correct answer to the pollsters and it turns out to be the opposite of their actual voting intentions.

TOO MUCH THE SAME

There could also be the sense that he was not so new after all, that he was the "same old, same old" sell-out, money driven politician, with overbearing ambition and hubris, someone who actually gave off that elitist air and a fatal sense of inevitability, which we might now call the Hillary effect. The fact that his acceptance speech looked more like a coronation than a nomination, two months before the vote, turned as many people off as on.

Converting celebrity into votes is something a Reagan and a Schwarzenegger could do because they established themselves as actors first and parleyed that later into ballot box success, but to do it all at once and to become a celebrity because you are running for office rather than a celebrity running for office distorts what people imagine the celebrity meant. People almost universally applauded his Candidacy, but when it comes to someone running the Government, that is a different question and one that the Obama campaign didn't manage to answer. The Paris Hilton ad will be forever remembered as the fatal flaw, for when you set yourself up to be ridiculed, you are exposing your narrative vulnerabilities. Mockery is a deadly weapon in campaigns, and explains why, though we forget most of the substance, we still remember moments such as *"I knew Jack Kennedy"* or *"There he goes again."* Obama proved he was famous enough to be President but the people also wanted proven competency after eight years of the opposite.

TOO INTELLECTUAL

Television is not kind to intellectuals unless they are witty or so eccentric that at least they entertain. Obama clearly had the ideas and the skills, but given that the story machine that relays the message to the voters is TV/Internet, Obama could not break through the received impression that he was too remote, and he did not connect with his swing voters who wanted to get a sense of how he felt rather than what he thought. It was John Kerry and Al Gore all over again.

They were turned off by his intensity and his earnestness, which they translated to be either pure ambition or worse, taking himself too seriously. People felt he was not in touch with the full palette of emotions and he needed a funny bone transplant. Though he got blanket coverage for his Denver speech in August, two months later people remember what they saw but nothing of what they heard. There was nothing to take away, compared to what Biden had shared with his charming stories of Amtrak or the speeches of both Clintons. Obama did not tell his story in a way that his listeners could experience or emotionally connect to. What they connected to was the spectacle and the historic occasion and Stevie Wonder and John Lewis. Who wouldn't? But he did not get them onside because his stories did not take them inside. That's what a good story always does.

TOO GOOD TO BE TRUE-TOO ELITIST

Obama had millions of dollars to create a spectacular campaign which is exactly what he did do and people watched the spectacle from Denver with rapt attention. But the effect proved counterproductive because it all looked too good to be true. Obama never came off as real and the staging of the campaign kept him in the demigod mode. The Greek pillars at the football stadium gave the opposition and late night comedy shows a useful weapon to make Obama seem ridiculous or grandiose. And instead of dismantling the celebrity project, the campaign made a fatal miscalculation adding Denver to Berlin. It gave the 'anything but epic' McCain something to pivot on when it came to running his convention which they could not afford to be as spectacular because they did not have the money or the technological trickery. Yet it came across as more real, less orchestrated, not as many bells and whistles, and we even had protesters and environmentally friendly balloons. A Convention without balloons is like a birthday party without ice-cream.

CLAIMING MORE COMPETENCE THAN HIS CV ALLOWED

What made Obama such an amazing candidate was his freshness and his commitment to bring a new tone to Washington that promised to disarm the political posturing and partisan bickering. But when the harsh necessities of campaigning took over, Obama reverted back to an old style politician, as negative and partisan as the people he earlier had criticized. He also revealed his immaturity in showing a propensity for taking things far too personally and getting prickly. His campaign stooped to a level of spite and pettiness that undermined the message that this was a new style of politician. This was a Chicago politician at the end of the day. McCain could carve out the higher ground and his ad congratulating Obama on the night of his acceptance speech, though seen by many to be a cynical ploy, revealed what a civil campaign might actually look and sound like. And it came from McCain.

Obama could not be who he was, because the media demanded him to be everything but that. He could have said he refused to repeat the mistake of the Bush administration that prided itself on having all the answers even when they didn't even know what the questions were. When you don't claim to have all the answers, you at least realize you have to consult. Shoot first, Aim later, Ask last, is no way to run a foreign policy. But Obama's campaign got sidetracked in the swamps of policy, an area that Obama himself loved, but which had killed Gore's nerdy campaign and knocked Kerry's into the dustbin with his deadening devotion to details. Also, the Democratic machine did a Gore on him, assessing that Obama's real personality was not good enough for prime time and he had to adhere more closely to Democrat orthodoxy than was natural. He would win running as a traditional Democrat rather than running as Barack Obama. Nicholas Lehman writing in the *New Yorker* in July 2000 wrote of the same phenomenon with Gore.

> *"The people around Gore, and evidently the candidate himself, seem to believe that to present him to the voters as he really is-a serious man who, at every juncture has pushed himself hard, who cares about doing right, who has developed passion and expertise, who has a sense of the world, who has devoted himself to public life-couldn't possibly work."*[9]

Having to pretend that he was this 60 year old veteran locked inside a 47 year old body, Obama trashed the asset that won him the early votes, that here was someone new, someone not claiming to know it all. He needed to soften rather than get harder against McCain to show he is flexible and can listen to all the stories. It's not for him to come out with certain solutions so much as demonstrate a way of listening and collaboration which, because Bush didn't listen and didn't collaborate, caused half the problems in the first place. Sometimes the substance of leadership depends on the style of leadership. Obama did not make the case.

He had to make himself vulnerable to inoculate himself against the charge that he is another out of touch liberal living in an ivory tower. Being too smooth, too smart talking, too handsome and too cool for school added to a perceived sense of elitism. Perhaps the

---

9 Nicholas Lehmann "Gore without a Script" *The New Yorker* July 31, 2000 p.57

campaign should have adopted the practice of the greatest Persian carpet makers who it is said, always weave a tiny mistake into the pattern to remind them and everyone else that they are not God and perfection is not theirs to aspire to.

In the end, Obama the new story got tempted back into the old playbook, the tried and true campaign story which, with 300 million plus dollars, he could try to tell better and with more panache and special effects. But it destroyed his greatest asset, that he was different. With victory so close, his campaign gurus could not let him take the risk of ditching the negativity, and disarming McCain with a storying style that said that what McCain offered was a start and full of good intentions but that it wasn't good enough or didn't go far enough. The narrative strategy of storying your opponent into your story rather than always being oppositional was the new way, the path he started out on but he lost his nerve and with it, his advantage. He got down and dirty as the party chiefs told him he had to. Obama was reduced to the same old story and the denial of the promise of Obama, whatever he said about the promise of America.

OUT OF TOUCH VERSUS ABOVE MY PAY GRADE

His own campaign had set up the age story trap that was the obvious one when you had a 72 year old versus a 47 year old. McCain was out of touch, and he didn't even know how to do email, didn't have a blackberry and he couldn't remember how many houses he owned. The Obama team labeled it that he was confused, hoping for a Gerald Ford moment that Eastern Europe was not Communist or that McCain wouldn't know his Sunni from his Shia. But it backfired because the McCain team set up the opposite trap, that Obama was too out of touch, too elitist and too much the liberal, too lacking in experience, and they used his own words against him. If he was not prepared to answer straight on abortion, and it was above his pay scale, then his answer to the invasion of Georgia, or his willingness to negotiate unconditionally with Iran which even Hillary said was naive, and his idea that Jerusalem was to be given over to Israel, that this all fit into the narrative trap of Obama the unprepared versus McCain the out of touch and McCain won that battle.

OBAMA UNDERMINED HIS OWN 'CHANGE' BRAND

Obama's actions about resigning from his church, ending his friendship with the Rev. Wright, letting his VP Vetter go and changing his mind on the public funding of elections made him vulnerable, because these filled out an alternative plot that here

226

was a very normal scheming, unscrupulous politician, bent on winning power at any cost. As the Obama campaign gained momentum on its message of change, the more conservative it became because the party knew they could easily jeopardize their lead. Obama seemed to run against his own brand because his rhetoric of change and audacity did not mesh with a campaign that demonstrated little audacity and no change.

His was a normal aggressive, no holds bar campaign to win, and there was little originality shown in the programs which were all loaded up to win voters rather than convince voters. He played it totally safe with his VP choice whereas McCain took a huge risk but it was a choice that re-enforced his maverick and reformer credentials. The Obama campaign reverted to the conventional rather than the transformational. Even his Acceptance speech that won such approval repeated what Nixon had said in 1972, about renewing the promise of America, and what Clinton had said in 1992, about a new promise, and what Bush had said in 2000. It is as Didion said, that we suffer from amnesia because instead of saying we have heard it all before, we say-How original.

PLAYING IT SAFE

When people aren't sure, they revert back to the tried and true. Obama failed to make people feel secure when they looked at the world as it was unraveling and thinking of his hand on the nuclear button. It wasn't that his candidacy wasn't compelling or didn't inspire a whole new generation of voters, but Obama did not close the deal. His candidacy was a split candidacy from the start, and the Hillary supporters never forgave him for not selecting her as his VP. McCain's VP if for nothing else, was a good pick because she reminded folks, 'Why didn't he pick Hillary?' He never closed the deal with the Democratic voters in the swing states and he never closed the deal with the nation. People in the end go back to what they know. They did precisely what he did with his campaign; go back to the Safe Mode, which is the default position when you are not sure.

BEATEN ON A CONTESTED AGENDA OF CHANGE

Obama wanted to win on the theme of change and reforming Washington, but McCain stole the ground from under him with his own history of reform and change in the Senate, risking so much to pass the McCain-Feingold reform, or push for more troops for an unpopular war, or reform immigration. And when McCain named his VP as an outsider and a reformer, it made Obama's VP, his safe pick, someone who did nothing to add to the central theme of the

Obama ticket. It was a defensive choice to shore up the foreign affairs credentials, but it blunted his message of change. You don't pick a Senate veteran with 34 years insider experience if you want to change Washington. As Obama said, you bring change to Washington, say from Alaska, not the other way around. Obama's story got lost or was effectively countered.

LACK OF A BIGGER STORY

When Bill Clinton stepped up to the podium at the Convention, the media were fixated on his speech and hopeful that he would fuel their melodrama of, "Will the Clintons spit the dummy?" What they got instead was vintage Clinton and the clearest and crispest argument for change in the history of the whole Obama campaign. What the Obama team did not pick up on was how Clinton first of all, assessed the situation, or in narrative terms, declared the middle, 'This is what we are in the middle of right now, here are the figures about real income and here is where we will continue to head unless we make a dramatic change of leadership.' He declared the middle and declared it an end. When Obama made his great speech about restoring the promise of America, he didn't do enough to ground his case or to even realize that Clinton gave him the core for the speech he needed to give. He needed to story the middle to make the case of a necessary and urgent change now, to alter the ending.

RUNNING ON "YOURSELF AS THE PLATFORM"[10]

Obama kept saying that the election was not about him but about the people, and as a piece of effective rhetoric, it always won applause, even though it is one of the cringe clichés of politics. But the whole way Axelrod staged the campaign gave the lie to that. What the nation was voting on was him; he was the program. Inviting such close scrutiny means that the voters finally tire or start to feel there has to be more than the candidate. They ask what is he going to do? Obama did not energize the nation with any new vision of where America should be heading apart from a change in tone and style and though that could be radical in itself, it did not have the feel of substance about it because he didn't.

He missed his best opportunity in Denver when the occasion was begging for him to update the "I have a dream" speech; we wanted to hear how his Presidency would be both the fulfillment of that

---

10 "The message is becoming dangerously self-referential. The Obama campaign all too often is about how wonderful the Obama campaign is." Joe Klein quoted in Charles Krauthammer "The Audacity of Selling Hope" *Washington Post* Feb 15 2008 A-21

dream and the start of a new dream. He could have given a speech that 45 years later, people would still quote, but he decided instead to cave to the pundits and the experts and give a workmanlike list of programs. We never got his vision of the future that gripped him enough to grip us. He built the set for an epic speech, and for a defining moment, and it was perhaps all that regardless of what he said, but if ever there was a moment when America was ready to hear a Reagan-esque or Kennedy-esque clarion call, it was then. Where was the New Frontier, the New Deal? He wasted too much time pillorying his opponent rather than elevating the election to something beyond the party politics that he said he would change. You can't change it by engaging in it. What kind of new America was he fighting for? What was his dream beyond the safe party line? As a moment of tragic irony in the story, it offers one of those moments that even history will remember as a lost opportunity. 38 million people were tuned in.

Denver played into the other suspicion that was the blowback effect of his campaign, the feeling that Obama was oversold. With 70,000 in Portland, and then 200,000 in Berlin, followed by 85,000 in the Coliseum, no, the Acropolis, no the Invesco stadium in Denver, he had the drawing power of royalty and every state was blasted with relentless Obama ads. Campaign Obama had zillions to spend and everyone kept repeating the mantra that America still didn't know him well enough to trust. In fact, the reverse was the case because in the end, the nation knew his biography too well and his vision too little. The connection between his life story and the vision he had for the country was not made, or made in a way that seemed forced. It reminds one of the story told about a parliamentarian giving an important speech in Westminster, and the text had been marked up by aides to give cues for delivery such as hand gesture here and take off glasses there, and for one large section at the end, it had the note, "Argument weak, shout like hell!" Too much had the reverse effect of delivering too little from an otherwise great campaign. In overselling, people felt the same way as they feel with overenthusiastic car salesmen, the more they exaggerate, the less the quality of the car. Quality in the end sells itself.

PLAYING THE VICTIM CARD IN THE DRAMA TRIANGLE

We examined in Chapter 10 the drama triangle, and the Presidential Plot is not only set up for heroes and villains but also the game of Victim, Persecutor and Rescuer. Why Obama lost in the end might boil down to how he got sucked into this dance by taking things too seriously with the attack on his patriotism, and whether he was American enough, and whether his wife was loyal enough. He came across as thin skinned and too much the victim. He presented himself as the Rescuer who would elevate the tone of the Presidential elections and get us away from all the partisan bickering, but once the Republicans or Hillary put him to the test and accused him of everything, he felt his story and his honor were under attack rather than his staying above it. He didn't understand the deliberate McCain tactic of audacious provocation. Every time McCain had Obama complaining about lies and negativity, McCain knew he had struck home, knocked his opponent off message. He went for the jugular causing Obama to play Victim, pleading for the sympathy vote and thereby showing people his unfitness to command.

MISREADING THE NARRATIVE LANDSCAPE

We have said that reading the narrative landscape is an essential skill for the would-be leader, and we outlined the four main stories (Ch. 9) in the American story. Normally, the Democrat stakes out the Beloved Community, that we are all in this together and everyone is equal, and the Rot at the Top, that Washington is broken, and power and wealth has to be redistributed to all, and not just held by the Heroic Individual i.e., the reform agenda. Republicans usually stake out the Heroic Individual when it comes to guns and wealth and the role of government versus the citizen, and the Enemy at the Gate, the threats to security.

Obama thought in the beginning he had no contest on the security issue as the earliest critic of the Iraq war and extra credibility with the Beloved Community given his background. But Iraq fell off the radar with what seemed to be a successful surge and troops coming home, and McCain trumped him on the reform agenda making change the contested story. What Obama needed was an uncontested story scape, and he got outfoxed. It was a similar move that Bush took in 2000, combining the Heroic Individual with the Beloved Community with the phrase, "Compassionate Conservative," squaring the circle and leaving Gore looking like a square. Once Obama had retreated from the story of change he had staked out, he allowed McCain to counter attack and turn the story on its head. Obama got out-storied.

WHEN IT ALL FELL APART

The catastrophic moment for the Obama campaign, when it looked all but won was the debates with McCain, and the repeat of the Saddleback effect where McCain was such a decisive speaker and Obama came across as a Law professor better suited to the Supreme Court than to the White House. Obama had never had to fight at this level before, nor had he anticipated how strong McCain would be. Obama was calculating but McCain was instinctive. And finally, Obama seemed tired, bored with the process and on the edge of campaign burnout, while McCain found a second wind with his VP selection. George McGovern asked Barry Goldwater once what he had learned from his drubbing at the polls and Goldwater replied," Don't get exhausted. It's lying out there ready to trap you and make you do all sorts of half-arsed things."[11]

LESSONS TO LEARN NOW

When you play it out to the end, and then realize that you are still in the middle, that Obama sill has time to shore up his story or defend it from such depredations, or realize that he has to swing back to defend an exposed flank on Reform, then the campaign has a new way to map the campaign and strengthen their claim to having the best story for America's future.

When you watch international yacht racing such as the America's Cup with the old 12 meter boats, you soon learn that the lead yacht tries always to tack to block the wind from the rival's sails and as they come close to the finish, a fierce tacking duel happens as the yacht behind tries to tack and tack in hopes that the lead yacht, which must cover each time, fouls a line or messes up. So long as the leading yacht covers the challenger's every move and keeps the wind in their sails, they win.

Obama staked out "Change" and "Reform" and caught the early winds of change blowing in the electorate, and McCain coming from behind moved to cover him with a stunning VP pick and reviving the Maverick label by 'dissing' his own party in front of all the party faithful at the Convention. McCain's audacity was breathtaking.

Obama can tack to cover this, but seems unsure how to, and in the hesitation, the wind goes out of his sails and the challenger picks up that wind and takes the lead. The Obama campaign will waste too much energy in a tack for tack contest because it needs uncontested space which, in our read of the narrative potential, is the future versus the past. McCain can compete on change, but on the future, his is a face and a style that just doesn't work. McCain and change-yes, but McCain and future, No.

If Obama can take some courage from McCain's risk-taking and lose some of his timid handlers, he might dare to stake out the future, not with the tired old style class politics and hand-outs that

---

11 Ed Pilkington "The White House Losers" *The Guardian Weekly* March 29,2008 Page 29

he did in Denver but with something much bolder. What is the new America he wants to lead us into which of its very nature leaves orthodox Democrat agendas and orthodox Republican shibboleths sounding like 19th century astrology? He has to tell us in one compelling image or phrase. Ditch the clichés! It has to sound more than just a new tone or a makeover. Gore used a good tag of re-inventing government that might do service. Lastly, Obama needs to read some good science fiction to feed his imagination about the future and he needs to be inspired by McCain. As my friend Tom Wheeler[12] says, audacity is a force multiplier, "L'audace, l'audace, toujours l'audace."

##

WHY McCAIN FAILED!

November 5th and the headline is "Obama in a landslide, McCain concedes." So what happened? Where did Senator McCain lose it, or was it always a long shot for the ruling party to be returned when the incumbent President and Party were so unpopular. We don't have to be partisan to confess that this is probably the headline we are expecting, whether we are Republican or Democrat. So how would it play out? And what is there to be learned now that might still help shape a campaign?

YOU CAN'T FIGHT HISTORIC INEVITABILITY

The designer of the new and controversial World War II monument here in Washington, Friedrich St. Florian, said that the best compliment he received was from someone who told him that it looked like it was always meant to be there, that it didn't look new or an encroachment on the Mall. The Obama candidacy had the same effect. Once it wrapped itself in the "I have a dream speech" and the celebration of Civil Rights 45 years after King's speech, it was a juggernaut and there was little that McCain could do. They say that when an idea's time has come, it is unstoppable and Obama was able to paint himself as the inevitable candidate. If anyone dare vote against that, they were voting against the relentless tide of history, that King had said, always bends towards justice. For as much as McCain tried to make the case for his candidacy to be a Martin Luther type reformer of a corrupt and discredited GOP church, and appointing a woman as VP in his own attempt at tempting history, he was never going to beat the Obama ascendency. What was remarkable is that he made it appear to be so close.

---

12 Tom Wheeler Leadership Lessons from the Civil War Doubleday 1999

THE FUTURE OVER THE PAST

McCain and his seven houses and the counter-plot of the Obama campaign, that he was an old man, and that he got confused, or that he wasn't wrong so much as just out touch allowed the Obama campaign to story every slip and every stutter as more of the same. And the repeated Bush-McCain labeling worked to keep in people's minds the last eight years and their hunger for change. It was the Dick Cheney trick of mentioning "Saddam and 9-11" enough times that the brain builds the neuronal link. People in the end thought McCain was Bush's VP. So the Obama Team made their characterization of McCain as old and out of touch stick, and he fleshed out the image with his contradictory words and erratic or impulsive behavior. And so long as Obama made the case that it was about the future, and about real change, then McCain was not going to get called up for the part. 72 year olds don't get leads anymore unless they are playing a role for seniors.

MONEY COUNTS MORE THAN CHARACTER

When you compare what Obama had at his disposal as far as money and supporters on the ground to Campaign McCain, one might not have to look much further, because in the States where the final votes counted, Obama outspent McCain by a huge margin. He could get the ads out, he could train and commission more volunteers, he could target more niche markets and he could harness the new technology, whether through YouTube or Facebook or text- messaging to get the base excited and out knocking on doors, and registering voters. The explosion in under 35 voters was a phenomenon all by itself, and it was the Obama phenomenon.

A FOREIGN POLICY OF TEMPER TANTRUMS!

McCain had well established the Maverick brand, and it was one he needed to accentuate to create some light between the Bush administration and himself. But Obama turned even that into a liability by branding Bush as the original maverick of the international community, someone who was determined to go it alone, no matter what the cost. Maverick also describes the personality of someone no one wants to work with them. And once the Obama campaign could link that Maverick to the testy and sometimes enraged Candidate who loses it in moments of stress, the electorate had second thoughts about trusting the Commander in Chief to someone who might be trigger happy, or still suffering from some shell shock and inclined to take a far too bellicose approach to the world. McCain was portrayed as the Mad Hatter who, as soon as you mentioned North Korea, he would yell, "Off with their heads!" Iran? "Off with their heads," Russia? "Off with their heads." The world was too dangerous to put a hot head in the Oval office. Mavericks as world leaders have to go the way of dinosaurs because one man can't run the country relying on his gut feelings anymore. Bush did that, and McCain, "his VP" wants to do the same.

McCain and his campaign had craftily exploited some of the Obama excesses by using the tool of humor and satire. The Obama campaign returned the compliment in their Maverick send-up of McCain with shotgun and black hat transposed into the old James Garner frames, and using the theme song and words of the old Maverick theme song:

> *Who is the tall dark stranger there?*
> *Maverick is the name.*
> *Riding the trail to who-knows-where*
> *Luck is his companion*
> *Gamblin' is his game.* [13]

Locking McCain in the old story of a funny, crazy, risk-taking cowboy from the 50's, which the new generation don't remember but had fun discovering, and reviving the comic reverie that the older ones still had for Roger Moore and James Garner, it used humor to lampoon McCain and associate his Candidacy with a joke. After that, no one took him seriously because they kept seeing this Maverick as that old cowboy and once they thought cowboy, they were thinking Bush, and all the reasons for change.

FIGHTING AGAINST THE FAIRY TALE

We have stressed all through our narrative analysis that our language gets its life from stories and that whether we remember it or not, the language always does. Words like 'Kingdom' and 'Power' are drawn from stories where the role of the heroic Prince who inherits or overthrows the King is not a part for an older man. If I tell you the story of the Prince and the Princess, you immediately imagine these characters as young, rather than an aging Prince like Prince Charles who is still waiting to ascend the British throne. The Princely role in the British imagination has been assumed by a younger Prince, Prince William. If there was a narrative story for why McCain did not win the White House, it was because he had too heavy a weight of stories sedimented in the language to disrupt and overthrow. For the same reason, the media who are writing

---

13 http://en.wikipedia.org/wiki/Maverick_(TV series)

their celebrity stories of the latest star or starlet are not into the genre of aging celebrities or politicians, unless they are selling Viagra. McCain was a counter-cultural Candidacy, and though Obama's was too, in the end, the character part went to the younger Candidate whose character was more suited to the role.

THINGS FALL APART

If we imagined that McCain had it all but won coming into the final weeks and then, something went horribly wrong and cost him the election, what might it be? He could well have a messy VP melt-down, or he may flub a line in the debate or some other scandal may surface, but the coup de grace might be as simple as a fall and having to limp around the last week of the campaign and not being able to disguise the lack of energy and agility. Mind you, it might have to be quite a fall or accident because McCain looks very sprightly for 72, and if he was racing Joe Biden to the podium, McCain might even give him a run for his money despite the good form Joe displayed the day he literally ran on to the stage in Illinois when his VP Candidacy was announced.

LESSONS TO LEARN NOW

The McCain campaign never expected to be taken as seriously or to come so close to upsetting the Obama Assumption to power. The story of his Candidacy is 'One surprise against the odds' after another. What McCain did with his VP selection is what he needs to do once more as the election date closes in and the economy continues to falter. There is still time to crawl back from the precipice by connecting policy to his own experience, and reclaiming the narrative ground that Senator McCain dominated at the Saddle Back Forum. When the nation is facing a major crisis, what matters is not whether the leader has a Harvard degree in economics, but whether he has the leadership style to steady the ship of state, and not be afraid of acting decisively and making the unpopular calls. If the Obama campaign continues to promise everything, it gives McCain a chance to pivot and to steal a play from the Clinton playbook, which is to level with the voters and dare suggest that we might be in for some tough times ahead, and when the times get tough, the tough get moving. Turning adversity into opportunity defines McCain personality, and it is one that he now needs to turn into his policies and leadership.

CONCLUSIONS

Doing this exercise makes it seem that the narrative advantage is with the Obama story, meaning that there is much more to talk about if he wins, and even more to talk about if he fails. That is because the Obama candidacy links into more stories and bigger stories, and it threatens to disrupt the patterns of meaning making we use to make sense of the Presidential Plot. It will take more explaining. No matter the result, the acceptance speech in Denver marked an historic marker, and regardless of McCain's acceptance speech, his nomination for all its surprise, is not a genre breaking candidacy, unless he wanted to make it about age, and he has not. Perhaps he will in his concession and claim that he put 18 million plus cracks in the ceiling barring pensionable old men from higher office. His heroic quest will deserve an heroic end, just as Hillary's did.

DEFEAT IS NOT THE END OF THE STORY

There is an ancient story told about the old man whose sons were kidnapped by invaders and when a friend said consolingly, "What a tragedy!" he sardonically replied "Perhaps. It might be bad news and it might be good news but one never knows." A few years later when the village was about to starve, one of those lost sons returned with food and saved the community and another friend visited to congratulate him saying, "You must be very proud-to have your son back as a hero." And the old man said, "Perhaps. It might be bad news and it might be good news but one never knows." And six months later, because their village was the only one still with food, it became vulnerable to bandits who plundered it and left half the village dead, and when a friend came to the old man to console him saying, "What a tragedy," he said "Perhaps. It might be bad news and it might be good news but one never knows."

The story is a reminder that when we imagine what it might be like to lose, that does not mean that the story ends in failure. If Barack Obama had won his first attempt at electoral office when he ran against Bobby Rush for a House of Representatives seat in Chicago, he probably would still be the Representative for that part of Chicago because, as Mark Shields pointed out recently, Senate campaigns have to be statewide and are very hard to launch from a Rep seat that is so uniform a constituency. One may have to lose to win and one may have to win to lose. If Obama is not ready, and he wins and totally makes a mess of it, what does that do to the next African American candidate? Think of Hillary and her defeat. She may run again, or someone else might but she is probably right when she says that whoever the next woman candidate is, she is going to have an easier time. Without a Hillary defeat, would there have been a Palin Candidacy? Rest assured a few million other working women will now aspire to the role and we will certainly be more used to the Women President story by then.

Other lives are forged in failure. Think of the homage that the Convention gave to Senator Ted Kennedy, who has served so nobly in the Senate for so long. Yet his whole career is built upon the tragedy of his family and his own tragedy of failing to win even the nomination, when he ran for President. Or we remember Al Gore and how when the Supreme Court defeated his Candidacy, he launched a new life as the environmental prophet that he always was, and a Nobel Peace prize later, he probably has as much power as he could ever want or imagine with a mission to save not only the nation but the planet.

When one looks at the story and asks what might be the bigger story at play here that we don't even yet see, it gives one a narrative modesty before declaring what is good news and what is bad news because, as the old man said, one never knows and we don't know what the story means until it ends. Yogi Berra would say, "It ain't over till it's over," and Robert Penn Warren wrote equally eloquently in <u>All the Kings Men</u>:

> *"If anything is certain it is that no story is ever over, for the story which we think is over is only a chapter in a story which will not be over, and it isn't the game that is over, it is just an inning, and that game has a lot more than nine innings."*[14]

---

14 Robert Penn Warren <u>All the Kings Men</u> Harvest 1996 p. 354

CHAPTER SEVENTEEN

THE REPUBLIC OF STORIES

"Tradition contributes in a basic fashion to ontological security insofar as it sustains trust in the continuity of past, present and future, and connects such trust to routinised social practices."[15]

The election campaigns travel the country making the claim that "Washington is broken," and that partisan politics blocks the Congress from doing the people's business. It's a script straight out of the old Presidential Plot whether it be 1888 or 2008, but what if we took it seriously, what would it mean in narrative terms?

Washington isn't working because its story is broken. It doesn't make sense any more. The people who govern no longer seem to work in a world of shared meaning. They refuse any responsibilities to weave a web of shared understandings that would knit the Republic back together. If we are to remedy it, we have to mend meaning. We have to find a better story, one that works, rather than trying to tell the same story better which is what we argue has characterized the Presidential Plot for these last 40 years.

We have to re-invent government by making it meaningful again. The Presidential Plot is an alluring story that grips a nation for a year or more, but even it distorts the machinery of government that was invented by the founders when they signed the Constitution in 1789. If government is a story, it is never the President's alone to tell. In fact, the over emphasis on the executive branch is a measure of the narrative creep of his role. He was never meant to tell the whole story, or bear all the blame. An "Imperial Presidency" was meant to be a contradiction in terms, though today, it reflects enlarged presidential rule, to the detriment of the other arms of government. What happened to Congress? What happened to the Supreme Court?

We have lost our way because we have lost the sense that there are three tellers of the national story and three guardians of our national destiny. It is not partisanship that breaks the system, but rather, it is people opting out of their narrative responsibility to together create and tell a coherent story, the big story, the story that keeps *We the People* at its heroic center.

Partisanship replaces the big story with the small story. It stalls the narrative in the middle, so that we never get to an ending, and

---

15 Roger Silverstein <u>Television and Everyday Life</u> Routledge 1994

laws are not passed. The architects of governance are more skilled in blocking a bill than getting it to resolution. And the conflict never rises to that sense of national urgency or emergency that would force it to be solved. Sectional interests and short term goals are entrenched in a system which is ruled by party politicking and lobbying. We end up being imprisoned in stories that are too small or end too soon to do justice to the larger imagination of the nation and its continental reality. It was never meant to work like this.

The founding fathers had a narrative instinct when they set up the three separate branches of government because they knew that the big story of a nation could never be told by one person or one party, and it could never be summed up for all time by any one time. They were founding a Republic that they hoped would survive the shocks of history and not collapse back into tyranny that, in times of crisis, the governed seem to tolerate to their detriment. That is why they shrewdly empowered three different arms of government, and gave to each one a different and yet shared responsibility for telling the one national story.

Each arm was to represent a different segment of time in the unfolding story of the Republic and to have a different relationship to and responsibility for that history. The Founders knew as students of Aristotle that a story to be complete had to have a beginning, middle and end, and they knew that if America was to be like Rome or Athens, it needed a glorious past, a vibrant present and an heroic future. Only then could America both rival and revive the epic of the Republic that was Rome.

To look at what was once the landscape of Washington on to which they mapped this vision, one could accuse them of getting a little carried away with their own grandiosity, especially when they named a little streamlet near the future White House, the Tiber. But they read and knew the great stories of the past, and they knew how to make the provincial stories of Thirteen single States into one national story, and one that would keep on working long after they were gone.

Knowing that the national story had to balance the promise of the future with the demands of the present and the traditions of the past, they instinctively gave each of these roles to a different arm of government, not simply as checks and balances but because a story that sacrifices one to the other is a story that will not work in the best interests of the Republic. They were creating a big story, not only to cover a huge geography of space, but an epic with a grand geography of time to match.[16]

How can one tell the American story in a short story, or in episodes that are disconnected and competing when it is meant to be "e pluribus Unum," out of many voices, one story. Remaining open to the broadest sweep of time and place is the way that any story finds its own renewal, keeping it open to the future and yet still anchored and in touch with its original intentions. The story of America is the story of pre-history and Native America, of 1607 and 1776, and 2008, and the story of 2050 and 2110. It is the ongoing story, and in 2008, though our own grandiosity would have us forget, we are but another chapter in that unfolding.

A GOVERNMENT FOR THE TIMES AND THE THREE TIMES OF GOVERNMENT

Thinking in this narrative way invites us to no longer divide up government in strictly partisan terms, or having a Democrat in the White House and a Congress split between Democrats and Republicans and the Supreme Court swinging between its conservatives and liberal justices. In a national narrative, their real constituency is the <u>one</u> national story of government to which each of them has a core contribution to make, a contribution not based on party loyalty but on what part of the national story they have to represent and inject into the imagination and memory of the Republic.

So let's forget for a moment about party and ideology and think of the constituencies of time that each of the arms of Government must preserve, protect and defend.

- **The President's** natural constituency is the <u>future</u>, (Vision)

- The Congressional constituency most apt for **the House** is the <u>present</u> (Contemporary Concerns)

- The **Supreme Court's** natural remit is their vote on the <u>past</u> for today. (Tradition)

- The **Senate's** critical constituency is oversight, to protect <u>credibility</u>, <u>continuity</u> and build <u>coherence</u> in all the other parts of Government (Review and Edit)

---

16 Think back to Ch 3 on The Genre as Epic

We don't pretend that this is exactly what Jefferson or Adams were about, nor is it a narrative reading of the Federalist Papers, but it attempts to give a fresh way of describing the functions of government to find a better and more sustainable story than the one we seemed to be trapped in at the moment.

THE VOICE OF THE PAST-THE SUPREME COURT

While America is in love with the idea of change and innovation, the Founders placed Law at the heart of government through an institution that was dedicated to protecting what did not change. The Court was minimally described in the Constitution but it evolved into a third, independent arm of government. It was committed to a consistent and coherent reading of the Constitution to guide the modern government and ensure it never lost touch with the founding vision.

As we described in the law of beginnings, middles and endings, (Ch. 3-5) a leader like a Columbus can only negotiate through those testing middle passages by reminding the crew why they set out in the first place. Generative power resides in the beginning. The Supreme Court cherishes the Founding traditions of Constitutional Law that it interprets through precedent. The Judges look back to see how they can fit a presently contested law into the larger story of the Constitution and the Bill of Rights that enshrines the values of the Declaration of Independence.

Where else in Government would we find nine legal scholars hibernating in their Roman temple devoting all their time to hearing cases and then retiring to research arcane gun laws of pre-revolutionary America and what was in the mind of Thomas Jefferson when he put a comma rather than a full stop after a clause? These are our Priests, the Scribes of our Temple, devoting their lives to the law and keeping it alive by offering authoritative interpretations to either validate or strike down the legislators and lower courts. Because the President and the Congress are prone to be caught up in the pressing needs of the day, they are easily tempted to ignore the founding fathers. The Supreme Court's mandate is to speak for them, and the three centuries between then and now. As Jaraslov Pelikan said about tradition when applied to the Christian faith:

242

"There ought to be somebody who speaks for the other 19 centuries. Not everybody should be caught in this moment. I'm filing a minority report on behalf of the past."[17]

Chief Justice Roberts believes that every case in law is a story and the Court, in expounding the law and what it meant then and what it means now, has to excavate those stories and the various layers of meaning hidden in the language in which it is expressed. What did the founders mean by Militia" back then compared to what we mean now? What did "Cruel and unusual punishment" mean and how does it guide us to determine whether water boarding is cruel and unusual? The only way they can get back to those meanings is through stories because words only come alive in stories.

The law is meant to be a boundary or a limit, as in a fence around a cliff marks off a limit, a warning, that if you go over that margin, you will go over the edge. In story terms, the American Republic is based on certain rights and duties and whatever laws governments might pass to solve current problems, the court is vigilant about whether the new law enhances or extends the old story, or whether it threatens to undermine those originating values. Roberts was always taken by the idea of a judge as a referee, clearing up any ambiguities and helping to create a more coherent body of law given that the USA prides itself as a nation of laws not people. If so, they had better be clear laws. [18]

EXTENDING THE FRANCHISE TO THE ANCESTORS

One of the core principles of narrative ethics is ownership, knowing and respecting whose story we are telling, especially when it is not originally our own. The Supreme Court ensures that Benjamin Franklin and Thomas Jefferson and John Adams are still in the story, some 190 years after they passed on. They might not have expressed it as part of their idea of democracy, but when we re-describe America as a Republic of Stories, their voices are still primary because it is their story before it is ours. The great G. K. Chesterton argued how tradition actually extends the franchise of democracy.

> *"It is obvious that tradition is only democracy extended through time. It is trusting to a consensus of common human voices rather than to some isolated or arbitrary*

---

17 Jaroslav Pelikan in 1983 interview with the Christian Science Monitor quotes in *Washington Post* May 17th 2006 Obit Page B-6

18 Chief Justice Roberts June 2007 in a personal meeting with interns and the author

record...Tradition may be defined as an extension of the franchise. Tradition means giving votes to the most obscure of all classes, our ancestors. It is the democracy of the dead. Tradition refuses to submit to all the small and arrogant oligarchy of those who merely happen to be walking around. All democrats object to men being disqualified by the accident of birth; tradition objects to their being disqualified by accident of death. Democracy tells us not to neglect a good man's opinion, even if he is our groom; tradition asks us not to neglect a good man's opinion, even if he is our father." [19]

Paul Ricoeur, the pre-eminent philosopher of narrative, expresses it this way:

"Tradition represents the aspect of debt which concerns the past and reminds us that nothing comes from nothing. A tradition remains living however, only if it continues to be held in an unbroken process of reinterpretation." [20]

Ricoeur also points out that the role of Tradition is to be the voice of what the poet Langston Hughes called, the "dreams deferred."[21] The history of the Constitution is not just a timeless law, but also a promise, what Martin Luther King Jnr. called a promissory note, that it is still waiting to be cashed, and America, the land of promise that Obama spoke so eloquently about in his acceptance speech, is still not complete. It still contains an unfinished future, as witnessed by the Supreme Court who at first declared slavery legal, and later repudiated their own ruling, or more recently, judging that habeas corpus is a non-negotiable part of the American story even in times of war. The Constitution is still our map and our compass.

The past is not over, and as William Faulkner says, it's not even past yet, because we are still trying to understand its promise. Ricoeur calls the past "a cemetery" of broken promises, promises that must still be kept:

"It is principally the founding events of a historical community which should be submitted to this critical reading in order to release the burden of expectation that the subsequent course of its history carried and then betrayed. The past is a cemetery of promises which have not been kept. It is a matter of bringing them back to life like the dry bones

---

19 G.K Chestertron <u>Orthodoxy</u> Image 1959, Page 47-48

20 Paul Ricoeur <u>The Hermeneutics of Action</u>-Richard Kearney Sage 1996

21 Langston Hughes poem "A Dream Deferred"

We go 'Back to the future' because we still have not exhausted the dreams that are contained in the founding imagination and that, after all, is the sign of a great story in that we can keep going back to it to find new meanings. A story exhausted with one reading is not much of a story.

LIFE TENURE MEANS STAYING FOR A LONGER VIEW

The founders wanted to protect the court from the pressures of contemporary urgency by giving them tenure dependent on good behavior, and tradition has translated that into life tenure. And the Judges themselves, though accused of being the most secretive arm of government, protect themselves very assiduously from media surveillance by not allowing cameras or having press officers giving daily updates. The media do not get the access that they take for granted with the President and the Congress. As we argued in chapter Nine, the court displays a canny narrative understanding of their role and chooses to minimize any possible media contamination. Audience amplifies and media distorts and while their decisions inevitably go through the media spin cycle, they let their decisions speak for themselves. Why else spend months crafting them?

Being appointed for life means the Judges can take a longer view of the nation's affairs. They become the voice of the past, its living experts because they live it, and ultimately, they will have more of it than any other arm of government. Where else would an 88 year old Judge Stevens, or a 75 year old Judge Ginsberg have such a decisive voice in government? There have been older Senators, but they are one vote in 100 rather than one vote in 9. These are the most significant appointments for life within our structure of government, and seen in the light of the heated debate about term limits then and now, this life tenure is a critical feature of the Court giving them an indispensable role in the three storied architecture of government.

PROTECTING AND RENEWING THE BEGINNING

The court is there to protect the contribution of the beginning to the story, because if we forget why we first set out, if we lose the originary inspiration, we are in danger of losing the plot and losing our way. We can look back to the power of the beginnings that we

---

22 *Op cit.*

wrote about in chapter 3 knowing that this is the job of the Supreme Court in the story of governance.

It's not as if they can do this alone. No, the story also has a middle that the Congress must attend to, and it has a future that the President must articulate, but too much power resides in the beginnings to ignore. It is our Torah, the Ten Commandments, the Beatitudes, the Talmud, and the Koran. The Bible tells the story of King Josiah whose nation had fallen on hard times, full of violence and assassinations. Then, the Court rediscovered a copy of the original Covenant hidden away in the Temple, and the King by realigning his state with its Founding Law, was able to restore the kingdom to its original faith and its true identity. (2 Kings) Walking the marble steps of the Supreme Court building in Washington, one can sense the ghost of Josiah.

"In the beginning was the story," says the Gospel of John, and the people of any faith know that the secret of renewal when an old story seems dead, is not to jettison it but to go back and revive the original vision. If Washington is broken, we need to go back to beginnings and therefore, the Supreme Court has an indispensable part to play in getting Washington working again.

It is the Court that normally swears in the President at the inauguration with the pledge, "To preserve, protect and defend the Constitution," which means the best way to serve the people is to serve the law. If the President is the decider, the Court is the preserver, and in so doing, provides the anchor, the ballast, the center of narrative gravity, to steal a phrase from Daniel Dennett, for our national story.[23]

PRESENT IN THE MIDDLE OF THE PRESENT-THE HOUSE OF REPRESENTATIVES

If stories give life to words and words are echoes of the stories they once lived in, we can always get clues about what story we are in from everyday language and from our ritual use of words. For instance, when the members of the House of Representatives answer the roll call, they answer, "Present." And truly, they are in the story of the Present, not the past.

---

23 Daniel C. Dennett, The Self as a Center of Narrative Gravity (1992)

.

The members of the House are elected to serve for two years, and so, they are at the very opposite end of the time scale to the Supreme Court. If the founders wanted the members to be visionaries, then they certainly did not give them much time. Members have to be rooted in the present and the pressing concerns of their constituents, and they had better be because they are always less than two years away from the next election. As Tip O'Neill said, all politics is local and your political security rests on your next vote, not your last.

A story has a beginning, a middle and an ending, and we are always usually somewhere in the middle and so, the time zone of the House is this middle passage. As we said in Chapter 4, the middle is the messy part, it's where we all get lost, trapped or sidetracked. When we see no beginning or end and we have no long view, the present becomes an obsession because it's all we can see. We forget where we left from, and we forget where we are going. We are stuck in the conflict de jour, where the goal is more about making sure your side wins, or the other side is blocked from winning, and as for the national story? What is that?

The role of the Congress, at least in the House, is to be in the middle and to measure that middle, to tell us what we are in the midst of, and to be the people who read the temperature of the electorate, always assessing what is working and what it not. But as with any middle, they are only as effective as the beginning and the end. A failed Congress is both a symptom and a cause of a failed Presidency. In 2008, while the campaigns love to gloat on the poor approval ratings of the current President, they forget that the Congress is as much a part of his failure as he is of Congress's because they inhabit the same story.

GUARDIAN OF THE FUTURE –THE PRESIDENCY

"Without a vision, the people perish," so says the prophet and so say all the Harvard gurus who write on leadership. What is leadership supposed to be about? Once, it was thought to be the hands-on role, but now that is described as the manager's role, and considered a waste of the genius that a leader is supposed to bring to any organization. "Leaders establish the vision for the future," says John Kotter, "and set the strategy for getting there; they cause change. They motivate and inspire others to go in the right direction and they, along with everyone else, sacrifice to get there."[24]

---

24 John Kotter <u>Leading Change</u>. Boston, MA: Harvard Business School Press, 1996.

A leader and hence a President is supposed to chart where we are going, motivate us to sign on, and bring everyone together to work to get us there. When he swears the oath of office, he says, "I will faithfully execute the office," signaling that the beginning of his administration always begins in that future tense, and that is where it needs to stay.

He gets elected for four years, and then a possible four more. Eight years is almost a decade to implement a program, and to take a country from here to there; from dependency on oil to independence, from decaying infrastructure to renewal of schools, bridges, roads, from discriminatory health care to universal health care. Eight years is time enough to make a difference, and make changes that your successor will find hard to reverse if you have been successful. And eight years is an agony if you are a dud. Has he gone yet? We are allowed four years for voters' remorse.

In a Westminster system, Parliament can decide this morning that the Prime Minister has exceeded his Use-by date, and they can vote him out this afternoon. The Founders, for all their great wisdom, left the loophole that an ineffective Chief Executive could freeze the whole national story by overstaying his welcome, and since he can only be removed by force of impeachment, the danger of a stuck story is always present. Then the future can't come soon enough.

When you face an ending, it does wonders to focus your mind on the future. What next? So, it is no surprise that President Bush has become obsessed with the future of late because soon that's all he will have left of his presidency, and how his record plays in the years to come.

He has mentioned the future a few times, telling us, "The future will be better tomorrow," and that, "He has made some good judgments in the future." But President Bush, having been banished from relevance in the day to day politics of the elections, claims that posterity will be kinder to him and we tend to agree, because regardless of history, he is certainly right in terms of a story he is still in the middle of.

He knows that only the future can tell the full and fair story of his Presidency, because Presidencies only truly reveal themselves in the tomorrow that they helped shape. Therefore, it is incumbent on any President while in office, to keep telling the nation the story of his vision of that future. Given that the Report Card that counts is delivered 10 years after a president leaves office, that is where a President needs to be thinking all the time. It should not just dawn on the President in the waning years of his term as he belatedly tries to garner a reputation for posterity. Rather this was his job all along.

Narratively speaking, the Presidency is absolutely pivotal. Who will write about the impact of the 110th Congress in years to come? Who cares? A Congress does not define an era, and it's not their constitutional role. Nor is it the role of the Court. We only remember the Supreme Court when we think they have got it all wrong, such as gone and elected a President in place of the people, or become so pharisaically strict that they have strangled the life out of the Constitution. But a President matters. He has the lead role in making the national story work.

For a President to be trapped in partisan politics or to be more concerned about the small story of getting re-elected rather than the bigger story of _why_ he wants people to re-elect him is to degrade the role, and turn it into something it was never meant to be. It was meant to be a story whose previous chapters are named _Washington_, and _Jefferson, Lincoln_ and _FDR, JFK_ and _Ronald Reagan_, names that belong as much to the future as they do to the past.

Only the President gets to deliver the State of the Union Speech which is an annual report card of where the President thinks we are and where we still need to go. He has the bully pulpit to cajole and reassure and challenge, in the way that an FDR steered the nation through successive crises of depression and war. The burning question any potential President needs to answer is, "Where do you want to take us?" All the other details of particular issues and programs must be part of that. Take us to the moon. Take us to into a New World Order. Take us to the Great Society. But set the sails and take the ship out of the harbor.

If the mandate of the future that a Candidate seeks from us is not clear, then the Presidential Candidate is reduced to some slick salesmen with a bag of tricks wanting us to buy him rather than the vision with which he seeks to re inspire the nation. It _is the vision thing_, and what Ronald Reagan described and enacted, what America means and what it needs to mean again. If the Candidate cannot articulate that vision, he should not be elected. If elected and he does not deliver, no matter what immediate fallout we may feel in terms of economy or jobs, the Constitution makes us stand and watch a failed presidency tragically squander our future. The national story is currently stuck in a dead-end because we are stuck in a dead-ended presidency. The General Patton School of leadership says, 'Lead, follow or get out of the way.' In Washington, it is the reverse "Lead, follow, or get in the way!" No wonder the nation longs for the future to start again. And with a new President, we have a chance to unfreeze the story.

THE SENATE AS THE HOUSE OF REVIEW

The Founders made the Senate to be the States' House to make sure that in one house, there was an equality in representation with two Senators from each State, whatever the size. (of the State- I hasten to add) This was also the American version of the Roman Senate, the House of Elders. They are elected for six years, and it is the Legislative body that has to approve or ratify treaties and other key appointments. As an ingenious invention to reassure the small states that they would not be overwhelmed by the larger ones, the Senate acting collegially, has the responsibility of melding fifty stories into one, and ensuring the citizens of Alaska are as represented and included as the citizens of New York in the national project.

The Senate is also the referee, the Editor-in Chief, the Head Reviewer of the national story. If it is not working, they alone have the power to take steps to remove those who are obstacles. And though the House can impeach a President, only the Senate can vote to have him removed, and in the same way, they can remove a member of the Judiciary.

In our narrative model, the Senate acts to make sure that the three arms of government are working in a coherent way to create one story of governance that makes sense to the citizen. When the Executive oversteps his power, the Senate has the power to call his administration to account, and even act to remove him if they feel it is a high crime. Narratively speaking, it is a high crime to act in any way that seriously undermines the core credibility of the Presidency, and murders the meaning of his office. The corruption of meaning, of language, the spreading of nonsense as law is the capital crime here. The Senate has the same powers and duties with the Supreme Court. They can impeach a Justice and narratively, a high crime would be to interpret the Constitution so broadly that it can mean anything, or so narrowly, that it means nothing that is relevant to citizens' lives. The Senate has to keep the story of all arms of government connected and credible. They have to protect meaning to keep Government meaningful to the nation.

The Founders in their wisdom and their deep skepticism about power, created a system within a system to answer the age old conundrum of who guards the guards? If the three arms are elected or appointed to be guardians of the American story, who gets to oversee them and hold them all accountable? The Senate. The Senate straddles both future and past as the House of review, and Senators are rightly given high status in the Republic because they too can enjoy longevity in the role. Someone like a Senator Byrd can remind us what a "real Senate speech" sounds like, or a Strom Thurmond could remind us that even a former Governor who supported segregation can reinvent himself to become an elder of the Senate.

WORKING TOGETHER FOR ONE STORY, NOT ONE PARTY

When one arm of government gets hi-jacked by partisan loyalties that causes them to abandon their obligations to history and their duties to the future, or locks them inside the present day scrap for the spoils of power, they should be sent to a narrative boot-camp and reminded of their duty to make the whole story work again for the people. Congress should be held as accountable[25]for Washington being broken as they would want to hold their President or the Supreme Court.

When the President has no vision or is not borrowing meaning from the future, pressure comes on the other arms of Government to usurp his role. The oft heard critique of the Supreme Court is that they legislate from the bench, and it is not their job, but it may not be their fault for all that. Judicial activism can be a symptom of executive indolence. For instance, if a Congress that has been bought and paid for by tobacco lobbyists won't change the laws for the sake of the nation's health, then it is left to citizens to use the law to sue the tobacco companies to drive them out of business. And the Supreme Court can be a willing and important accomplice of that change. So too in selecting a President. If the Florida Supreme Court were going to make a ruling that might decide the Presidency, did anyone think the Supremest of Supreme Courts in the land was not going to get involved? Rehnquist didn't wear the three stripes on his robe for nothing.

If one arm of Government doesn't do its job, the other arm is pressured into doing it, or gladly seizes the opportunity, except for Congress itself, which has a recent history of surrendering much of its deliberative power to the Court and to the President. Yet for their efforts, they are rewarded by the obstructionism of both President and Court reducing the House at times to little more than a debating society. Storytelling is a team sport. When the

---

25 The whole principle of <u>accountability</u> is a narrative concept, meaning to be expected to give an account of, or tell their story so it makes sense in terms of responsible choice

story is as big as the nation of 300 million people, then, it had better be polyphonic if not always symphonic. So what would it look like if it did all work together?

If the president can create the compelling vision of the future, then the acts of Congress are the prologue to and implementation of that future, and the Supreme Court is there to protect that future with all the law and wisdom of the past, to say that this desired future is part of the original promise that was within the constitution all along.

As the nation faces new challenges, the genius of the Founders gave us three options on where to look for the wisdom and the know-how to respond.

- Will we use the <u>past</u> to solve this issue? Then we look to the Courts.

- Will we use the <u>present</u> to solve this issue? Then we look to Congress.

- Will we use the <u>future</u> to solve this issue? Then we look to the President and his Administration.

When a president runs his government by polls, he is abusing his role, sacrificing the good of the nation for the quest to hang on to power. Or if he is polling, he needs to be polling the 5-10 year olds and finding out what they see as the future, or new Moms and Moms-to-be, because that is the constituency that the President is there to serve. He is not there to worship the present or to open up a quarrel between the past and the present, because as Churchill said, that is a sure way of losing the future.

WHY WE ARE VOTING FOR THE FUTURE

A Candidate for the Presidency must tell us about the future, and give us his dream. To get bogged down in the details as Hillary too often did, gave off a counter message. As someone said, she was running for Chief Operations Officer, and Bush ran for Chief Marketing Officer, but the President is the person not running the ops or the ads, but driving the vision and the values. They know that and they teach that at Harvard Business School, but I guess the country is a pretty unique company to run when you are expected to be the new JFK, Ronald Reagan, FDR all rolled into one. Yet, smart Presidents succeed by stealing their predecessors' best ideas and giving them their own contemporary spin.

A RESPONSIBILITY TO HISTORY AND THE FUTURE- NOT TO THE PRESENT OR TO PARTIES

The Founders never planned for political Parties to exist the way they do today and in fact, Jefferson and Washington were suspicious of interests that could form parties to dictate to government. But they did want certain stories represented by the way they set up the three arms of government. The President as CEO belongs to the Party of the Future, and the Congress-House of Representatives belongs to the party of the Present and the Supreme Court belongs to the party of the Past, while the Senate is the all important glue between them all, charged with the job of making the whole story work, and work meaningfully for the people.

This means that we might need to dramatically revise our job descriptions. The Supreme Court doesn't just need lawyers but historians and archaeologists and former Presidents and Senators. Why not Carter and Bush Snr on the Court?

In the White House, enough of the lawyers and professional politicians. We need poets and visionaries and prophets and artists and musicians. Constitutional lawyers and Senators are rarely visionaries. Where is our Vaclav Havel? Or why not draft Leonard Slatkin for President! Or Maya Angelou or Toni Morrison?

In the Congress, we need pollsters and sociologists and mayors and teachers and welfare workers and policemen, and folks from the local community like the Red Cross and the Scouts and the PTA, people rooted and grounded in the reality of the present rather than in the politics of any one party.

Finally we need more storytellers in Congress who can tell it like it is (House), who can tell it how it could be (the President) and who can tell us how it used to be (Court). And over all these, we need more astute elders and editors (Senators) who can do for Government what Max Perkins did for Hemingway or what William Shawn did for *The New Yorker* magazine, to help us find and craft a better story that makes sense, that works, and that allows the people to have a determinative say in their future.

Only by sharing the storytelling roles between past, present and future, between beginnings, middles and endings, and between the Court, the Congress and the Presidency, can we get a sense of direction and purpose back into our government.

Finally, let's translate all this back into our immediate task of finding the right Candidate to be our next President.

MORE THAN MOVEMENT, BECAUSE DIRECTION IS ALL

A nation's leader has to abide by this same law of Beginnings, Middles, and Endings if we as a nation are to once again make sense of where we came from and where we are going. Single-Issue politics and campaigning on the clichés of 'change' or 'reform' are too stale to do justice to the irrepressible optimism that the country feels about its future, even in the worst of times. America only knows one direction and that is forward. Robert Penn Warren in <u>All the Kings Men</u> describes the epiphany of his main character, Jack Burden, who finally realizes reality is not about something static, but it is about connection and direction.

> *"Reality is not a function of the event as event, but of the relationship of that event to past, and future, events. We seem here to have a paradox: that the reality of an event, which is not real in itself, arises from the other events which, likewise, in themselves are not real. But this only affirms what we must affirm: that direction is all. And only as we realize this do we live, for our own identity is dependent upon this principal."* [26]

Traditional campaigns want us to judge Candidates by the content of their character, their position on issues, their past experiences, but Warren suggests we need to judge character by the dynamic of direction. Who you are now as a Candidate is one thing, but it is only part of the more important story of who you are becoming, and what you will become if we elect you President. We voted for Clinton as a young, untested Governor and he matured and produced years of prosperity, and we voted for Bush, a conservative, unspectacular Governor who became the biggest spending, most militarily adventurous President in 50 years.

The laws of BME can get Washington working again in a forward direction, with the three narrative arms of government playing their respective roles, and if the President understands his Constitutional role is also a narrative role, he can be the critical catalyst to a stronger national story. What he will become is what the nation will become, and where he is moving is where we will move. Direction is a function of plot, and plot is a function of the narrative logic that connects beginnings, middles and endings. A

---

26 Robert Penn Warren <u>All the Kings Men</u> Harvest P. 384"

President has to fit into that three storied architecture of government and he has to energetically move and inspire that story forward into the future.

CONCLUSION

When you understand the system of government as a Republic of Stories, you clearly get quite a different view. That does not make it right or wrong but it makes it narratively intelligent and that is precisely the point. The government can only work if the story works. If the story doesn't work, then that signals a fundamental breakdown in meaning making, that things don't make sense anymore because they are not going anywhere, and no matter what individual initiatives work, there is no center to the whole, and things fall apart, as Yeats predicted. We need the coherent story. We need the big story that inhabits and enlivens the little stories. As a manager friend from Lockheed Martin loves to quote to me, *Leadership is meaning making in a community of practice.*[27] If the breakdown is at the level of meaning, then is it any wonder that we as citizens feel powerless and stuck.

America is built on a common set of shared stories that best transmit their ideas and ideals by being embodied in the heroes and heroines of the Republic. When we hear the cliché, "A nation built on shared ideas," we know that those ideas most come alive in the living stories of our history. I can give you a lecture on the concept of freedom so you understand it, but I can tell you about Lincoln and Martin Luther King or Harriett Taubman and you will feel it and breathe it, you will understand it from the inside.

Stories contain the philosophy that most feeds the masses. Nations are built on stories, and wars are fought because of stories, and peace is brokered through stories. This is not a nation of ideas, and not even a nation of laws, but a Republic of Stories and so the stories that the President and the institutions of government are meant to enshrine, and to grow, and give witness to, are critical. If the state of America now is not working, it is because its stories are not working. We have to stop just trying to tell the old stories better. We have to find better stories to tell, we have to reconnect the three primary tellers as designated in the Constitution, reweave the plot to connect the beginning to the middle and the middle to the end, and pick a Presidential Candidate who will provide the vision to move the whole nation forward. If *"Direction is all,"* it's time to get moving again.

---

27 Drath, Wilfred H.; Palus, Charles J. Making Common Sense. Leadership As Meaning-Making in a Community of Practice. Center for Creative Leadership 1994

CHAPTER EIGHTEEN

BECOMING STORYWISE

Humankind has always been a 'sucker' for a good story. When you read about Adam and Eve, what you discover is not the story of Original Sin so much as the story of Original Gullibility.

We are all suckers for a good story, and our narrative vulnerabilities, as every con man knows, reside in the fact that we more willingly suspend our disbelief if we want the story to be true. Let's face it. Like Dick Cheney and most of Congress, we wanted Saddam to have WMD's, and like Pat Tillman's family, we would have wanted our loved one to have died courageously, rather than in a senseless accident, and we desperately want that new house regardless of the 0% deposit and 100% loan from Fannie Mae that is too good to be true. We invest our credibility in the stories we want to be true. Then, exposing the lie threatens <u>our</u> credibility. So lies become entwined with our sense of self, and our sense of the world. And that's why they stay so entrenched.

THE ORIGINAL SIN OF SEX, LIES AND VIDEOTAPES

When a story told as true unravels as a lie, we might unravel with it. Dangerous stuff! Yet, it's why people get invested in lies and why they persist in them. Our Vice President will never give up believing Saddam had WMD's or that Iraq was part of the 9-11 plot. Why would he? He has to go on believing his own credibility, even if we don't.

Lies always seem to shock or surprise us. Remember Kenneth Starr and Clinton's "I did not have sex with that woman," scandal. Fox News and other Cable news Channels made righteous indignation into an industry, but as one great storyteller of the past asked, 'Who among us dare cast the first stone?'

Instead of lamenting this endless litany of misconduct, Enron, Bear Sterns, Iraq, Guantanamo, leading to another predictable O'Reilly Factor rant, we might remind ourselves of the ancient stories of humans coming to sticky ends. Then, we might remember that humankind has always been a 'sucker' for a good story. Read Genesis Chapter 3 and Adam and Eve. What you discover is not the story of Original Sin so much as the story of Original Gullibility. If we are suckers for a story, it's because we always have been. We can't help ourselves, and that's always been our excuse and we are sticking to it.

The fall from grace was falling for the serpent's story, "You too can be like gods." (Genesis 3, 4) Serpents talking should have been a giveaway clue that this was a dodgy deal! But Satan fooled Eve, and Eve fooled Adam and both of them tried to fool the headmaster in the sky by telling him some lame "Dog ate my homework" excuse or "Blame someone else" or "Mistakes were made" because "There was no controlling legal authority!"

Excuses, excuses, excuses! But excuses are nothing but the exculpatory stories we chose to tell someone else trying to sucker them into our story, to cover up the way we were suckered into someone else's. It's recycling the lie. The book market in Washington at the moment is flooded with 'Story as Excuse,' memoirs from a host of ex-White House staff. They have titles that even Adam and Eve would be proud of: "What Happened," "The Price of Loyalty," "At the Center of the Storm," "All too Human," and "Against all Enemies." They take plausible deniability to a new level and make a high art of retrospective coherency!

Excuses aren't just stories, they are choices. And if the fate of the nation and the fate of the free world are at risk because we are still so persistently story-stupid, then we need to wise up. We need to become Storywise. We can't afford to be suckers anymore!

THE PRACTICE OF NARRATIVE

That has been the sermon throughout this book, and what I need to do now is pass the collection basket and have an offering hymn and clear out- before you ask me what to do? But we can't afford to leave it there, when we have less than two months to elect a new President and we have a billion dollar story machine assaulting us at every moment. How do we resist? What does it mean to become Storywise? That is another book all by itself, but let me give you some of the flavor of our work over the last 20 years and some clues that might protect us in these critical few months ahead.

'TAKE TWO' ON THE WMD INTERVIEW

The old morality by which we are used to judging stories, the true/false evaluation no longer works. We have to take so much on faith, and we lack the resources to know if Obama actually said this or McCain did that. We weren't there, and we rely on our witnesses, the journalists and media hosts, who are people we give our credibility to but who seem to deserve it less and less because they are taking sides.

258

To protect ourselves from deception when we cannot vouch for the truth content of a story, we have to develop other ways that can catch a story that is told to us for its deceptive purposes. A story is a work of art, and there is good art and bad art, just as a film is a story and we know a good film from a bad film. Unfortunately, the good film does not mean it is true, and the bad art does not mean it is false, but there is an ethics that can be derived from understanding the aesthetics of stories and storytelling. What we see in art is the product, but behind it is the artifice, and when we focus on that, we can see more readily the artist's real intentions. Applied to stories, what we need to hone in on is 'The story of the story,' How did this narrative get created, by whom, and why?

The McGinnis book The Selling the President begins with Nixon taping a personal address that will appear on prime time TV as spontaneous and engaging, but when you go behind the scenes to watch the artifice behind the art, you see how "artificial" it all is. We see take after take when Nixon and his producers experiment with tone and length to get it looking just right, with that sparkle and directness. But it is produced and aimed and delivered so that all we see is the illusion. Roger Ailes made sure that no press was allowed behind the scenes to witness all the bloopers.[28]

Let's take a more recent case. Vice President Cheney came on television to deliver his now infamous WMD story. That was the product, the art. We were not in a position then to know if it was true or false, but if we were Storywise, we could go back there with Dick Cheney and Tim Russert in their *Meet the Press* interview and explore the artifice in such a way that we might detect that this story was bogus, or at least that it was a narrative full of other agendas besides facts, and we should have known that even back then.

What questions might we have put to Cheney? Russert was great at catching the guest in a contradiction, "You said this then and you are saying this now. How come?" That is the old cross-examining trick that most professional politicians can adeptly rationalize away, though Russert could make the unwary squirm. On March 16th 2003, Tim began his Cheney interview by accepting the premise that war was imminent and positioning himself inside and onside   with   the   VP's   story   using   questions   such   as

---

28 Joe McGinniss Selling the President Penguin 1988 Ch.1

- *How close are <u>we</u> to war?*
- *What could Saddam Hussein do to stop war?*
- *So bottom line, he would have to disarm completely and leave the country?*

When he goes on to challenge Cheney to justify going to war against a country that did not attack America, the Vice President moves into his brilliant 890 word uninterrupted fabulation of, "We have been attacked by bad guys on 9-11," and "Saddam is a bad guy," and therefore, "Saddam must have attacked us, or wanted to," and ipse facto, "We had better attack him back before he gets those evil thoughts again." Cheney presents an amazing list of untested and unchallenged assertions, *"We found ample evidence....We see evidence of...We know that they...We are also confident that...There's no doubt...There's absolutely nothing to restrain them...We know in fact...We know...We know...We know...We know.*[29]

Hindsight is easy, but so much of this story is carried on the authority of the Vice President alone. He is the omniscient narrator, and the call sign for that style of narration is "We know" which he uses 19 times! We never know <u>how</u> he knows and we never know who the WE is. Russert doesn't probe that, but actually assumes the same position, "How close are WE to war?" he begins. A narrative approach would move in exactly the opposite direction, not into the story but out of it, to view it as a language construction with a headline *The story of WMD as a clear and present danger that will justify launching an attack on Iraq.*

Let's re-imagine that interview, opening up some different avenues of inquiry that focus on the 'story as story' and 'the story behind the story.'

Mr. VP, lets be sure I have your story straight. The story I heard you tell is.......and to make sure I get it, give us your headline. What is the core story here?

When confronted with a complex narrative, to ask the headline is to ask for a heads-up of what the lead is, so that we don't get lost in the details, which, in a story like Iraq, is where the whole Administration got lost and we followed.

---

29 Interview with Vice-President Dick Cheney, NBC, "Meet the Press," Transcript for March 16, 2003.
www.mtholyoke.edu/acad/intrel/bush/cheneymeetthepress.htm

What I want to ask you about is the story itself, not you personally and I do not want you to feel you have to defend yourself, because, and correct if I am wrong, you are not a key actor in this story. Correct? You are its voice but you are not the source of this intelligence?

Television is gripping when it gets personal, but the first move for a narrative inquiry it to be sure that it is not personal. This is about the story of the story, not about the VP. The strategy is to make some narrative room by the interviewer inviting the VP and himself to be outside looking in. Also, it is important to identify that the VP is relaying a story that is <u>not</u> his, and therefore he does not have authority as witness, only as interpreter. That is vital to declare from the outset because a witness carries the authority of being there, and we had better pay attention. But the teller who is an interpreter means he is just like the rest of us interpreters, and his burden of proof is to show that being VP means his interpretation is intrinsically better than mine or yours? Interpretive authority is always secondary and derivative, unless perhaps you are the Pope or the Supreme Court with historic claims to interpretive expertise.

IT'S NOT YOUR STORY

Mr. VP, This is not your story as in you are not the witness with any authority of firsthand experience, so I am wondering how it became your story? You keep saying "We" but who is the "We"?

WHOSE STORY IS IT?

Who else is telling this story? The White House? The Secretary of State? Whose story is it? Has it come from an official report? Or your office? The military? The President? Who put all its pieces together?

Why knowing story ownership or sponsorship is critical is because facts follow function. If this is the Defense Department's story, we know it is about war, or if it is the CIA, it is to do with terrorism. The media practice of unsourced quotes and information blocks us from making this critical assessment. When I know where it came from, I can better guess the story behind the story. If we are prevented from assessing the story behind the story in terms of origin and ownership and purpose, we immediately need to be suspicious about the reason for not telling us. What is that story?

One of the sources Russert uses in his questions is *The New York Times*, but it was a story Cheney's office had leaked to the Times days before, so one of Russert's so called independent and authoritative sources was Cheney himself. How neat! Cheney seemingly knew how to run the game better than the dean of Washington political journalists.

WHOSE POWER IS EXERCISED IN TELLING IT? THE STORY OWNERS?

Who authorized you to tell it, or whose power is being exercised here as you tell it? Clearly the administration sanctioned you coming on to tell it but do all of the people you are quoting know they are witnesses in your story? The President? The Secretary of Defense? The Speaker of the House? The informants? Are they all aware how you are putting this together?

WHO IS LEFT OUT?

Whose voices are heard and whose are silent or ignored? For instance, Iraq, Saddam, the Pentagon, the Army, the CIA, our allies, the UN, the children of Iraq, Iran? The Kurds? Turkey?

WHO WOULD BE MOST LIKELY TO CONTRADICT IT AND WHY?

We don't have any information to contradict the story but who would be telling the opposite of this story? And why? And why would they say you are telling your story in opposition to theirs? For instance, what would Saddam's story be?

When we are confronted with such a high stakes story as this, it is critical to explore the possibility of a counter story to see if it could make as much sense. If the VP wasn't willing to even countenance this possibility, you immediately get clues as to his agenda. The fact that any alternative makes no sense to us might be a story about us, not about our so called 'enemy,' because let's face it, war makes no sense to either party unless it is the only viable alternative. Why else put precious life at risk? Unless we are talking about a discretionary war? Sadly, most wars are acts of national advancement rather than desperate acts of self-defense, and that is why wars provoke wars more often than they prevent wars. David Halberstam writing about the Korean War highlighted how totally wrong our assumptions about the enemy were in that conflict.[30] Pre-emptive ignorance starts more wars than pre-emptive threats, though they might amount to the same thing!

---

30 David Halberstam <u>The Coldest Winter -America and the Korean War</u> Hyperion. 2007

WHERE IS IT POSITIONING US?

If we accept this story and act on it, what follows? Where is this story taking us-if this is the prologue, what is the epilogue? War?

Someone tells us a story not just to tell us a story but for a purpose that lies outside of the story. The purpose is to take us somewhere else, and three days later in Cheney's story, the Military went to war. This story was a ticket to Baghdad.

WHO STANDS TO GAIN AND WHO STANDS TO LOSE?

Who is most likely to be directly effected by this story if we follow it through to its logical conclusion? Both positively and negatively? Who wins and who loses?

WHERE IS THE VICTIM'S VOICE?

Some people stand to be negatively effected by this story, so where is their voice in the story? How are their views and concerns being represented?

If there are key people in the story who have no voice, you know that someone is left out, and secondly, if these voiceless ones are the ones most likely to be effected by the story's proposed action, you know you are hearing story suppression, a contradiction of the narrative ethic. Warning sirens should be going off.

WHAT IS THE STORY OF THE MIDDLE? (See Chapter 4)

A story primarily crafted to persuade us draws its listeners into the energy fields of the end and the beginning even though the messy unstoried bits are in the middle. Can you flesh out the middle? Say we do invade Iraq-what then? How long, 3 months, a year, when, where and what happens between now and the end?

To watch a classic case of the end devouring the middle and triggering the precipitous beginning is to replay Colin Powell's case to the UN where he supplies pictures as evidence of rocket launchers and mobile laboratories which we identify on the strength of the story, not on the examination of the prints. They were so hazy, and how would we know what to look for anyway? When I tell you a scary story, the first thing you think you see afterwards is a ghost, but it is only the curtains moving in the breeze. The story made you see it, nothing else.

THE STORY OF TRIUMPH-WHO IS THE HERO? (See Chapter 14)

If you succeed, what story will be told and who is the hero? And what do you think the success will be attributed to? And what will be the biggest obstacle that the hero will finally have to overcome?

Over-determined stories allow you to read the future, play it forward to read it back for narrative coherence and vulnerability, just as we did with the Presidential Plot. A war story is only going in one direction. Even Tim Russert knew that.

THE STORY OF TRAGEDY (see Chapter 15)

You say that failure is not an option but I am afraid that it is always a possibility, and so, take us through how you would deal with failure? What would that failure story sound like? And who would be the villain or what would be the reason for the failure? And what would be the one thing that in the end might get in the way of success?

NARRATIVE VULNERABILITIES (see Chapter 13)

The nation at the moment is still reeling with the 9-11 attacks and we are hence narratively vulnerable to stories of conspiracies and revenge and blame which all make sense of our feelings but might not be a good guide for mapping the reality of the world out there. If we put those strained feelings aside for the moment, would we be banging the war drums quite so loudly?

THE GENRE IS WAR STORIES (see Chapter 6)

You are basically telling us "the cause to go to war"' story but we know all war stories contain a mixture of truth and half truths, and hidden assumptions that establish the case. So knowing that's how a 'casus belli' functions, that its purpose is brinkmanship, to push us to the edge of acting, how would you grade this one on the scales of certainty and urgency remembering the Gulf of Tonkin and the SS Maine and the Cuban Crisis. How certain are you of the evidence, and what factor moves it from serious to urgent and urgent to imperative?

My parents lived through the Blitz in London during World War II and they would tell us of how important it was to be able to identify the planes flying overhead in a London sky as to whether they were German bombers or British bombers. My Aussie father flew with the RAF and it was even more critical for him. Identifying what is coming at you is pretty important before you act. It is the same with stories, and identifying the genre, because certain genres like war stories or medical break-through stories or company profit stories are functional narratives constructed in certain ways to get specific results. War stories have to be about threat, about enemies, about urgency to act. Once we identify the species, we are drawn to the story's construction rather than totally taken in by the story of impending destruction.

A FUTURE STORY IS A LIE BY DEFINITION

Every story about the future Mr. Vice-President is a lie by definition, and when it comes to our case history of Vietnam and Korea, we know how truth is a casualty of war, which is not to say that just wars aren't fought on good lies. But if Saddam did not have WMD's and we had not suffered the terrorist attack, would there still be a case for taking him out?

IT'S ALSO A DETECTIVE STORY (See Chapter 6 on Genre)

You have quoted all sorts of disparate sources and informants and it sounds like The Bourne Identity, or a James Bond movie, that has to pull all the pieces of the jig saw together, but what we all know about mysteries is that sometimes we get the wrong guy, or that the story is deliberately told to deceive. So, could this story surprise us, could Saddam not be the bad guy but the real villain wants us to blame him? Or could Saddam be bluffing? What might you not know now that could overturn your story?

WHAT DOES IT MEAN TO YOU-DECLARING SELF INTEREST?

Though Mr. Vice President, this is a story about Iraq, we know that every honest story seeks to make transparent the purpose of the teller and the interest of the listener. This is a huge story to be covering because it feels like the build up to war and any responsible journalist wants to get as many sides of the story as possible out to the public so they know what is at stake. I wonder if I can ask you the same question- Why is this story so important to you? What are your purposes in coming here today to tell it on Meet the Press and what's the desired outcome?

TEXTUAL ODDITIES-SMOKING GUN-MUSHROOM CLOUDS

Your Colleagues, and Secretary of State Rice used this fetching phrase that we don't want 'the smoking gun to become a mushroom cloud,' and that is so striking, not only because it is a bit of a mixed metaphor but it is so poetic-who came up with that?

265

People think that Cheney used this expression but it was actually Rice and Rumsfeld and President Bush. When a piece of language, a phrase like "axis of evil" suddenly leaps out at you, unless the interviewee is Mark Doty or Robert Frost or Alice McDermott, be suspicious. It's a sign of craft and craftiness. Likewise when six commentators go on the talk shows and all of them say in response to former White House Press Secretary Scott McClellan's expose, "That is not the Scott we knew," you know they are reciting a script, not telling a story. Reminds you of the performance art of an election campaign.

SWITCH AUDIENCES (see Chapter 9)

Can we experiment with the audience here, and ask if you were telling it to a group of Moms whose sons are going to be the first ones called to fight on the front lines, how could they makes sense of losing a son in Iraq? Or if you were speaking to a group of 5 year olds in Bagdad, some of whom might be collateral damage, how would you help them make sense of it? What is the story that can defend the loss of life which is the awesome burden of all war stories?

The stories that justify an action or excuse a non-action are important in our moral repertoire to help us make sense of human life, but the story that has to justify a life in its totality, and why someone had to sacrifice it, is a story that carries a much greater burden than the excuse of why I was late for football practice. If life is the stake, then life has to be clearly at stake. Otherwise, it does not make any sense. When one knows the stories of World War One and Vietnam and our earlier Mexican and Indian Wars, one is forewarned that war stories are mostly narrative non-sense because the people whose story it is become its silenced victims who never get to tell it.

We have <u>our</u> story of Vietnam, but if we could interview the 56,000 names listed on the Vietnam Wall, what would they say about it? *Dulce et decorum est pro patria mori*[31]. I wonder? Or the 618,000 dead of the Civil War? Or the 112,000 from World War One and the 406,000 of World War Two? Military cemeteries and memorials pay silent witness to stories that war first of all uniquely qualified these victims to tell, because they suffered it more than anyone else, but at the same time, it tragically disqualified them from ever telling it because they did not survive to speak anything but silence. Perhaps by Act of Congress, we might demand that every future

---

[31] A reference to Wilfrid Owens bitter and ironic poem about World War One "How wonderful and sweet it is to give your life for the fatherland." His poems survived a war that he didn't.

declaration of war has to be made at Arlington Cemetery, not on *Meet the Press*, so that VPs and lawmakers and Presidents who have never known war, realize the awful and real consequences of their decisions. War for all its rhetoric is a death sentence.

CREATING NARRATIVE ROOM TO EXPLORE THE STORY

This might give you some ideas of how a narrative analyst probes not only the teller of the story and his or her motive but the story itself, treating it as an artifact, a construction of meaning in language that uses words that find meaning in stories hidden within stories. To go on the attack with the VP only seals him into the story by forcing him to defend it. Curiosity is more revealing than criticism. What you want is to create narrative room so you can peel back the layers of meaning in the story to see whose interests it is speaking for and against. And we can do that simply by looking closely at the story itself without having to look much beyond it.

Mind you, if Vice President Cheney knew he was coming on to *Meet the Press* for a literary analysis, he would have gone to Fox. But the project of a narrative ethical approach is to make us Storywise, to save us from future wars that are choices excused by stories. Next time, we will probe the stories to reveal those hidden choices. The media is accomplice to every story they repeat because they are accomplice to every choice each story conceals. Three days after Cheney went on *Meet the Press*, the invasion was launched, and his efforts were exposed as part of the softening up process. Cheney knew he had to secure the bases. Blanket bombing before the army hit Baghdad, and blanket media coverage for the folks at home. Truth is the collateral damage of war.

A PRIMER FOR NARRATIVE ETHICS

We call this a narratively ethical approach. It examines how a narrative conceals choices and creates implied audiences, how it stories us as potential listeners, how it creates its own economy of power, and how it presents a particular point of view. Stories position us to respond in particular ways and those that are built to deceive reveal themselves in this process because they cannot pass the transparency test.

I tell my tale to move you inside the story, and once I get you there, if the story is an effective vehicle of transferring experience, you feel what I feel. You are on side, and on my side. If I want you to be scared that Obama lacks the experience to lead, I tell you a story of his failure to do X or Y, and you absorb it so that when I finish, you might still think he's competent, but I have made you feel anxious through the power of my story, and I know your thoughts will eventually follow your feelings. So even as I listen with empathy, I need at the same time to protect myself from story contamination that will switch off any narrative critical faculties. I need to honor my feelings but refuse to give them ultimate authority.

We listen with one ear inside the story and the other preparing ourselves to move outside the story as an appreciative listener instead of an empathic listener. To listen with feeling is to experience a story's power, but to respectfully place oneself outside of the story critically unmasks its power. People who want to con us want us to make the first move and not the second. They want us to be seduced by the art, rather than notice the artifice. This is the core of a listening laboratory process we call Narrative Room and which we teach in our Narrative Practitioner Program.

Let's apply this approach to the Presidential campaign and the tit for tat storywars that would have us believe that Obama is ambitious and dangerously liberal, or that McCain is senile and out of touch. Why are they telling us all this save to get us to assume a position that favors them, and gets us to vote for their Candidate? Once you declare that we are not dealing with truth here, that these are all fictions, we can relax the indignation muscle that gets overworked anyway, and turn on the narrative intelligence to feel a story first for its power and then weigh its real effects as to how its meaning is a force of language, a force that is not irresistible.

The Center for Narrative Studies teaches an ethics[32] that derives from our use of stories, and it allows us to assess whether a story is unethical or not. Here are our some of our working principles and assumptions.

- Everyone has a story.
- Every story is worth telling.
- Every story is a choice
- Every story makes sense in its originating context. If we don't make sense of a story, it might be because it makes no sense of us.

---

32 The challenge to find an ethics for media is one even Churches are grappling with. Recently Pope Benedict XVI wrote "We must ask, therefore, whether it is wise to allow the instruments of social communication to be exploited for indiscriminate 'self-promotion' or to end up in the hands of those who use them to manipulate consciences." Robert Mickens "Pope calls for info-ethics to guide the world's wayward media. *The Tablet* Feb 2 2008

- No one has the full story.

- We hold the narrative rights to tell our own story over someone else telling it for us, especially without our consent

- We are part of one another's stories. You are part of my story and I am part of yours. We live story-entwined lives.

- No one is ever in just one story.

- No one story can ever capture or do justice to the fullness of life as lived.

- No story is innocent. Stories have effects on identity and destiny for which we are accountable as both tellers and listeners.

- Stories serve purposes other than truth, and follow function as much as they follow facts. If facts are a perfect fit for the story's function, suspect that function is overriding facts. E.g. War stories use fact to create war, Drug companies use facts to sell cures, Corporations to sell profitability

- Any story that 'stories-over' or 'stories-out' the people the story is most likely to effect, is narratively speaking, unethical. The voice of the person most effected, whose interests are most at stake, needs to have some determinative say in the decisions most affecting them.

- The authority of the first hand witness in the story is different from the authority of the witness outside the story and the authority of the outside witness decreases with the distance from the originary story event. The authority of the witness is qualitatively different from the authority of the interpreter. Witnesses can offer unique accounts while everyone else is an interpreter, and though we privilege witnesses, there are few privileged interpreters.

- We have to claim and win narrative authority over our lives from those who assume they know our story or who have the power to impose it or its meaning on us.

- The Higher Power or divine storyteller knows all the stories and that is why all the ancient faiths believe that God is compassion-he who knows all the stories, he alone understands.

- The narrative ethical position is always, "I must be able to tell the story in front of the people most likely to be effected by it." That is what **accountability** means in narrative terms.

WINNING INTEREST ISN'T THE SAME AS EARNING INTEREST

I have to get your interest in my story first, if I am to sell it to you, and sell whatever comes with it. And "interest" is a good term to use, because, just because you win my interest does not mean you represent my interests, or have my best interests at heart or that I will earn any more interest if I buy it.

A good and simple question to ask is, "Why are you telling me this?" because it is asking someone to declare their real interest in the relationship they want me to have, not to them, but to their story. If people try to disguise their self-interest, or if we don't have an honest grip of our own, we are prone to be exploited. Honesty in stories is less about truth and more about declaring a self-interest up front. If the seller doesn't, we should. By declaring your interest you invite the teller to make theirs more transparent and if they can't own that, then you know you are likely entering a dangerous zone of deception.

If the Vice President told us that his only concern telling us about WMD's was his deep concern to protect the fatherland, we can tell immediately that he is not totally transparent to the politics and the power of his telling a story which, three days before going to war, was more about a fait accompli than an honest exploration of choices. Secondly, it would be assuming that we would buy such an explanation, which is to say, he relied on his power to draw us into his web, *"We know...Tim, We know...Tim"* nineteen times he said, and drawing us inside meant we would be on side. Russert began the questioning with, "How close are WE to war?" which put him embedded inside the story to begin with, and that's where he put his viewers. It was classic story seduction.

EXPOSING DUAL NARRATIVE RELATIONSHIPS

Narrative analysis exposes other dubious ethical practices such as dual relationships. We endure this every day without anyone noticing or calling anyone to account. If I am sitting on a Board of DrillBabyDrill Oil Company and I am also a key player in devising the Government's policy on oil, we clearly see a conflict of interest, and I have to give up one to do the other. I must declare my interest, for to hide it is to already invite accusations of double dealing. Likewise, in the ethics of therapy, students are taught about why dual roles are wrong, to ensure that therapists cannot be exploiting the vulnerable people they are supposed to be helping.

In narrative, we must be vigilant to guard against a similar conflict of interest, because if the teller has an interest in the story other than simply being it's teller, if he or she is invested in a particular outcome which they do not declare, then we know we are being deceived by this very lack of transparency in the storytelling act, without having to worry much about the factuality of the story. Why else would I lie or obfuscate about my need to tell you the "truth?" There is no such thing as a disinterested telling of a story. It only works if there is interest and it is only honest when that interest is declared.

CALLING YOU A LIAR, THEN PRINTING YOUR LIES!

Let's demonstrate how these ideas can be applied by using a current egregious example in a newspaper story. Recently, the *Washington Post* has written trenchant and probably justified editorials calling Russia for its lies and its aggression against Georgia. Their headlines roared, *"Russia's Delusion-A flurry of Russian presidential statements on Georgia mix lies with a dangerous new doctrine."* And they ended the editorial with, *"This is the rhetoric of an isolated authoritarian government drunk with euphoria of a perceived victory and nursing the delusion of restored empire."* [33]

Strong words, but the only problem was that the day before, they printed a 'Russia Beyond the Headlines' Advertising Supplement with headlines, "Georgian Bombs Rained on Us," and "Russia acts Decisively in Georgia Conflict," and "Russian Foreign Minister faults Western perceptions of Conflict." The Russian editor explained that *"This is why Russia launched its operation to force Georgia to agree on peace."* [34]

That last sentence is simply brilliant, with its shades of "Nixon meets Orwell" and bombing as a strategy of peace! Senator Henry Jackson advised Nixon to tell the American people that he had only bombed Vietnam in order to get them back to peace negotiations.[35] To have *the Washington Post's* name written at the top of what they themselves described as "drunken rhetoric" and "delusional," is to ask the question of media as to how they can allow themselves to

---

33 *Washington Post* "Russia's Delusion" August 28 2008 p. A-18

34 *Washington Post* Supplement Russia beyond the Headlines" Aug 27 2008 H-1 H-3

35 See Wikipedia Operation Linebacker II

be the undiscriminating host of opportunity for stories that are pure propaganda. I guess they got paid to print it, but we know they are lies and the Post know they are lies, (because they told us) and yet, that did not stop them from printing eight pages of it. The editorial hand must not know or care what the advertizing hand is doing. But it's a lesson on how to destroy your credibility and make a joke of serious journalism. They should at least make it look like advertizing rather than a proper part of the paper and print it in Pravda pink.

INSIDERS PRETENDING TO BE OUTSIDERS

The dodgy dual relationship also rears its ugly head in the broadcast media. Some former key staffers of the current White House are writing Op-Ed columns or doing political commentary on the elections and issues related to government. They know their stuff and much of the time, they have great insights, but when it comes to topics of policy that they were directly involved in, they clearly have an undeclared interest in the story.

Even if these ex-Staffers didn't happen to agree with a controversial Bush policy, say dismissing lawyers from the Justice Department for being the wrong Party, their professional credibility as policy advisers would preclude them from making an honest and disinterested assessment. They are going to story themselves in a good light, clearly, as tellers who are also in the story. And that is the key to the narrative dual relationship, tellers who are also in the story but who remain invisible. The media should at least declare the interest, and tell us, "X was part of the Bush policy on Y that X's Op-Ed is objectively praising as unstintingly brilliant." Or perhaps one should be as honest as Winston Churchill was when asked by a young journalist if he thought history would be kind to him, replied, "Of Course," and when asked to explain his certainty, said, "Because my boy, I am writing it." And he did.

First person narrators are known in literary analysis as unreliable narrators, and third person narrators are called omniscient narrators. Translated, it means third person stories are told by God, or someone pretending to be God, and first person stories told by someone inside the story are normally going to be epics of self-hero-ization and vindication. In the media, former insiders have this platform to tell totally self-serving accounts of politics, or "objectively" assess Candidates from both Parties, etc, and they can disguise their purposes by the claim of the public's right to know. (See Chapter 12)

Once we can identify a dual relationship, we can at least protect our imaginations. But when the tellers or the media cultivate this dual relationship and serve it up to us as legitimate news and commentary, we know the media is corrupted, or that they are bigger suckers than we are, and that we are fools to be fooled.

THE STORY OF PURPOSE MADE TRANSPARENT

Presidential campaigns are telling stories that distort and deceive and slice and dice the facts and create the fictions with the declared interest or purpose of getting your vote. One way to translate the strategy and reveal the assumptions behind the campaigns is to express it in terms of simple purpose. Let's make it as transparent to purpose as we can:

"You think I will vote for you because you told me that Senator McCain couldn't remember how many houses he has?"

"You think I will vote for you because you told me that Senator Obama doesn't wear a flag pin?"

"You think I will vote for you because you told me that Senator Obama is acting like a celebrity?"

"You think I will vote for you because you told me that Senator McCain is a close ally of President Bush?"

As you watch all the ads for the next 60 days, attach to each one this stem,"You think I will vote for you because......" and for a lot of them, you might even add, "You think I am so silly that I will vote for you because..." "You tell me that Obama used the word 'lipstick' referring to a pig." Or "You tell me that McCain has had some skin cancer."

When you lay out campaign stories as purposeful acts that are told to influence behavior, you expose how primitive many of them are, and how they presume that most audiences are stunningly stupid. Sure, we will vote against Obama because he has no flag pin-that's a big deal, or sure, not remembering how many houses you have is an indictable offense. Fannie Mae and Freddy Mac made the same mistake and it cost the country billions!

When you take the emotions out of it, and the smarmy voice-overs and the grim music, you expose the ads as gossip parading as serious political debate. "Did you hear that the neighbor is running a brothel?" "No, who told you?" "Did you hear the VP Candidate's daughter is pregnant?" "Did you know that John Edwards had an affair?" It is demeaning that campaigns and media in tandem would aim their ads at the lowest rung of Neanderthal intelligence and that we would suffer them as we do.

They want to turn us into voyeurs, trying to titillate our viewing, in the style of Kenneth Starr's exposition of Executive Exertions outside the Oval Office. Yet, we are not stupid and though we might not be able to always give a reason, we eventually get a gut feel for who is more authentic and who is taking us for a ride. Fool me once, shame on you; fool me twice, shame on me. Though George Bush couldn't say it straight, we know what he meant and after Katrina, we tended to agree with him.

PEOPLE NEED TO HAVE THEIR SAY

The narrative ethical position is built on the assumption that people have a right to have a determinative say in their own life and in what effects that life. How can my story make any sense to me if my voice isn't genuinely in it? That should be the mantra guiding all the candidates. Stories that don't allow us to have our say, stories that mimic the adage, that children should be seen and not heard, or slave's bodies should be counted as 3/5ths but their actual lives don't count, clearly contradict the principles of justice and equality, but equally, they contradict the principles of ethical storytelling. Why do we tolerate stories in which we don't count, where our voice is drowned out by someone else's ambitions or suspicions that have nothing to do with our own legitimate intentions for our own life?

SERVING FOREIGN MASTERS AND ALIEN PURPOSES

The great Russian philosopher of language, Mikhail Bahktin taught that we need to be careful of words because we don't know where they have been, and so too with stories, we don't know who told them before to whom and to what end. When someone repeats a story as theirs when it is in fact a story originating somewhere else, (Dick Cheney) we know that someone has made themselves the host of opportunity for carrying that story to us. And just as we don't let total strangers into our houses, we shouldn't let strange and unowned stories into our heads. We need to be vigilant and ask, "Who benefits by you telling me this story?" If it is clearly me, thank you, I didn't know my house was on fire, but much of the time, it is not told for my benefit at all. We should never presume it is a disinterested act.

The beauty of narrative analysis is that we do not have to make it personal. Michael White used to always say, "The person is not the problem, the problem is the problem," and our revision of his rule is "The person is not the story. The story is the story." The critical shift is to separate the story from the teller, to treat it like Terry Pratchett does, by imagining the story has a life of its own and has come down to us through a chain of tellers. Let me repeat what Pratchett writes,

> "Stories exist independently of their players. If you know that, the knowledge is power...So a thousand heroes have stolen fire from the gods. A thousand wolves have eaten grandmother, a thousand princesses have been kissed. A million unknowing actors have moved, unknowing, through the pathways of story....Stories don't' care who takes part in them. All that matters is that the story gets told, that the story repeats. Or, if you prefer to think of it like this: stories are a parasitical life form, warping lives in the service only of the story itself." [36]

Because stories gets so disconnected from the occasion of their first telling where perhaps motive was much clearer, one has to always remain skeptical. "Why are you telling me this?" is a simple but disarming question. If we passively listen to a story and go on to repeat it without any critical assessment, we could be quite innocently doing the devil's work. That is the power of gossip. If I get you to tell my story, like Orwell realized in his great essay, "Politics and the English Language", I am exercising an authority over your mind and your imagination without you even knowing. Stories make the best Trojan Horses that invade our imaginations, build colonies of influence and can hi-jack our brains. We worry sometimes quite obsessively about what we take into our bodies and are rightfully wary of what can make us sick. We need to be equally vigilant about what we take into our minds because stories can be just as deadly. If we sound like a consumer protection body warning about contaminated milk or peanut butter, we mean to. As someone said, we want to be the Ralph Nader of stories.

SOME OTHER READY-TO-USE MAXIMS

When I conducted the seminars on the Presidential Plot, we handed out a whole series of front pages from recent newspapers and asked folks to apply some other little narrative tricks and principles to the news that was being fed to them by the mainstream media. They apply the principles of exception or contradiction. So let's try some of them:

---

36 Terry Pratchett <u>Witches Abroad</u> Corgi 1991 Page 8-9

- **Any prediction about the future by definition is a lie-** how can it be true when the future is unknowable? The fact that any prediction has perhaps a 50-50 or less chance of becoming true does not make it a fact. So whenever you read a prediction, or see the subjunctive verbs "may" "might" "expected" "fear that" just contradict it. For instance, a headline from today's paper reads *"Raid's Outcome May Signal a Retreat in Immigration Strategy, Critics Say."* Take out a marker and write, "And it MAY not." This is speculation parading as news. It is not news!

- News only becomes news when it can be trumpeted to be NEW, and while that is easy when its hard news such as an earthquake or a plane crash, so much else is only new because we have forgotten the last time it happened. (see Chapter 12) So to test how new the news is, add the tag **"AGAIN"** to the headline and see if it works. For some, such as *"Titanic sinks in Atlantic"* AGAIN, we quickly realize that this IS news. But for most other headlines, "Russia attacks Georgia" AGAIN, we will hear the echo of earlier stories that invisibly feed the meaning machine, and we deflate the headline for its claim to novelty.

- Another option is to add **STILL** to see if the change is really a change. *"Fed deciding if interest rates to rise."* Becomes "Fed STILL deciding if rates to rise," and it would appear that it is more likely, "Fed ALWAYS deciding if interest rates to rise", so what is the real news here?

- Another is to use **CONTRARY** to test the deviance, meaning we seek to reveal what moved or changed that made something news. To every headline, put in front of it CONTRARY TO WHAT HAPPENED BEFORE, or CONTRARY TO WHAT PEOPLE BELIEVE. What is the contrary that makes the news news? If it dilutes or destroys the headline, then you know you are in the story cycle of the news, rather than reading anything new. "New Orleans to assess preparedness to Hurricane Gustav" becomes "CONTRARY TO WHAT HAPPENED BEFORE, New Orleans to assess preparedness for Gustav." Well, they haven't stopped assessing after Katrina so this is not a big deal. On the other hand, putting CONTRARY TO WHAT HAPPENED BEFORE "Democrats nominate African-American Candidate for Presidency" It stands up because it stands out. That IS news! CONTRARY TO WHAT HAPPENED BEFORE, "Former Military Hero elected President" is a big deal but it is only new for those who forget our last war hero was President, George Bush Snr.

- Headlines love to make sweeping claims to catch our attention. "Most immigrants not getting health insurance," or "Most Hillary supporters still unconvinced," or "Most blue collar workers don't get Obama," When you see MOST or ALL or MAJORITY or any other such boast about a majority, it is easy to test it for hot air by tacking on **EXCEPT WHEN IT'S NOT**. "Most Immigrants not on health insurance except those that are," and "Most Hillary supporters unconvinced except those that are." It defangs generalizations which claim knowledge that is hard to prove or disprove and only work because they are vague. 'Most' can be 50.1% or 99.9% and as my teacher used to say, "Never trust any generalization, except this one."

- Stories in the news make sense because they inhabit a larger story, or it fits into a larger pattern of meaning. Remember little stories gain meaning from big stories. The headlines will presume that rather than state it, and it's the hidden but common ground of assent that a reader/viewer and a writer/presenter must share for meaning to be made. But the hidden assumptions are often where the power of a story is hidden. Surfacing the assumptions allows us to test the story behind the story, or what is holding it up. So, after each headline, add....**ASSUMING THAT**....."Racism and Prejudice and Gender politics can be lurking behind seemingly innocent comments such as, "How can a mother of five with an infant be Vice President?" assuming that? Assuming that Parents with young kids can't be competent leaders? Assuming that women and not men are supposed to stay at home and look after the kids???!!! Here are some other examples.

"McCain risks unknown as VP" ASSUMING THAT... someone was unknown but unknown to whom? And risk for whom? And risking what exactly? And does it assume other choices to be less risky? And who assumed their opinion deserved to be news? etc.

"Obama plays it safe with his VP pick" ASSUMING THAT... someone is safe but what makes for safe? And what is at stake? And this is a particular point of view, an opinion so who assumes it is news? etc.

277

OTHER GAMES TO DISRUPT THE SEDUCTIONS OF STORY

Wittgenstein said his mission as a philosopher was to battle against the bewitchment of our intelligence that happens through language. A narrative analyst might adapt that and say that our job is to battle against the seduction of our imaginations by means of stories. The techniques suggested above are little prompts to keep some space, some narrative room for choice between us and the story, and make us realize we don't have to buy it; we don't have to always be suckers for a good story. Remember the secret of staying connected to a reality community is to "Mind the Gap" between the story and the reality. Anyone who has been on the London underground hears that warning at every stop.

Other fun games can work too, such as nonsense's like placing the headline in a different exotic place. Try putting "In bed" after each one, so "Putin threatens Georgia "in bed" or Obama attacks McCain" up a tree". After every quote, add to "he said, holding his breath." "McCain said Obama was not ready" holding his breath, or "Just pretending," to add irony, or "I want you to believe this because the very opposite is happening," or "I want you to believe this to give me time to actually work out for myself what the hell is going on," or "And If you believe this, you are sillier than I thought you were."

The media are playing a game with stories so why should they have all the fun? The old alchemist's quest of turning lead into gold has become the modern quest to make falsehoods credible and believable, and once we can do that, we can sell you any story we want. Obama the Muslim, McCain the Traitor, Palin the Russian Spy, Gore the idiot, Bush the genius, Nixon the Magnificent.

EXERCISE ON THE PRESIDENTIAL PLOT

Applying this to the Presidential campaigns, let's try a few of the stories the media have fed to us from the campaigns to put them under the scrutiny of a narrative ethical approach.

HEADLINE: ***Obama has a radical black Pastor who says 'God damn America,' who says 9-11 was our fault, and this Pastor married Obama to Michelle and baptized his two children***

- Why did you choose to tell me this story?
- Whose story is it and do they have any voice in your version of it?
- Who does this story benefit and who might it disadvantage?
- Where does it want me to go?

- Is the story loaded with a moral-something is bad, or something is good? And if I believe it, what judgment is the story wanting me to internalize as mine, and if it is not mine, whose judgment is it?
- Does it invite my curiosity or my criticism? Is the tone, "Isn't that curious" or "Isn't that terrible?"
- Is my indignation muscle all a twitch or What is the emotional pay off for my accepting it?
- What assumptions does the story make about me? That I would approve or disapprove?
- Does the story invite me to check it out for myself or accept it on faith? Can it be checked out independently?

Your story detector will quickly tell you that someone is selling you this story rather than telling you the story. Its facts are not a function of the story being told but of the story being sold, that you are meant to be outraged, and question Obama's judgment, and add this to the unfolding narrative of his lack of patriotism.

And should you get interested to Google the sermon in question, you would see how it is taken totally out of context, and though Rev Wright's sermon is controversial and challenging, it was meant for church, not prime time. Plus, Rev Wright was not running for President last time we checked. Usually the press are exposing Candidates weaknesses of the flesh, but this marks a totally new trend in exposing Candidates weaknesses of the spirit, to fall for a fiery preacher. Just as well Martin Luther King Jnr. wasn't preaching, or even running for President because he preached even more provocatively.

Most white folks, it seems, have never been to black churches, or the sermons in their churches have lost the good old hellfire and brimstone tradition. When you are selling salvation, damning someone is part of the softening up process before you sell them grace. Reverend Wright was not speaking policy, foreign or domestic, but simply impersonating Isaiah who accused Israel of being a nation of murderers and whores! (Isaiah 1.) And Isaiah makes Rev. Wright sound like a sissy!

HEADLINE: *McCain defines middle class threshold at 5 million dollars and forgets how many houses he has, and says the economy is sound showing he is totally out of touch*

- Why did you choose to tell me this story?
- Whose story is it and do they have a voice in your version of it?
- Who stands to benefit and who is disadvantaged?

- Where is it taking me?
- Is it inviting me to judge or inviting me to accept a judgment already made?
- If I absorb the story and the judgment it contains, whose judgment have I just swallowed if it is not mine?
- What does the story assume about me?
- Does it expect me to approve of disapprove?
- Does the story invite my curiosity or criticism?
- What does "out of touch" mean? What would "in touch" look like?
- Is it inviting me into the righteous position so I can enjoy being indignant and what is the emotional pay off here for me?
- Does the story invite me to check it our for myself or expect me to take it on faith?
- Can it be checked out independently?

If one did check out the 'Five million dollar' reference at the Saddleback Forum, one would find that it was a joke, and that McCain actually predicted that the Obama campaign would twist it into a serious statement of intent. When you see the original and then the story the opponent is telling about it, you see clearly exposed how tenuous a campaign's commitment is to any sense of honesty! Or else it reveals that one party doesn't have a sense of humor to know what a joke is.

Both campaigns seem to be weaving webs of deceit and innuendo that undermine each Candidate's claim to integrity. Campaigns have become character assassination machines. The Nixon team would feel flattered that the lessons of 1968 live on. Truth and reality don't matter, it's the invented truth and the virtual reality you can create with the stories you tell that matters most, unless we get Storywise and then we can't stop noticing the story of the stories and we can better protect ourselves from political campaigns or governments trying to manipulate our consciences.

CONCLUSION

The great moral philosopher Alasdair McIntyre writes in his seminal work <u>After Virtue</u> :

> "A central thesis then begins to emerge: man is in his actions and practice, as well in his fictions, essentially a story-telling animal. He is not essentially, but becomes through his history, a teller of stories that aspire to truth. But the key question for men is not about their own authorship; I can only answer the question 'What am I to do?' if I can answer the

prior question 'Of what story or stories do I find myself a part?' We enter human society, that is, with one or more imputed characters -- roles into which we have been drafted -- and we have to learn what they are in order to be able to understand how others respond to us and how our responses to them are apt to be construed" [37].

Over many years of teaching, I have found that I have creatively misquoted McIntyre's question to be, *"Before I ask what am I to do, there is a prior question I must answer which is 'What story am I acting out of?"* which in a way is a better fit for the purpose of deciding what is an ethical action from a narrative point of view.

What stories are we acting out of? Are they working for us? If not, where do we find better stories? These questions alone could cause a revolution.

37 Alasdair McIntyre <u>After Virtue</u>, Notre Dame 1984 p. 216

CHAPTER NINETEEN

AFTER THE BALL IS OVER

"This work continues. This story goes on. And an angel still rides in the whirlwind and directs this storm."[38]

On the morning of Tuesday, January 20th, 2009, the new President will be sworn in by Chief Justice Roberts on the back-steps of the Capitol, which since Reagan's time, have become its front steps. The move was made because it allowed for a bigger viewing theatre for the thousands assembled on the Mall. And perhaps for old Father Abraham to get a distant glimpse of his new man.

> *"I do solemnly swear that I will faithfully execute the office of President of the United States, and will to the best of my ability, preserve, protect and defend the Constitution of the United States."*

It is the ending, and it is the beginning. The future begins here.

"With a simple oath, we affirm old traditions and make new beginnings," said President Bush back in 2001. JFK expressed it, *"Symbolizing an end, as well as a beginning - signifying renewal, as well as change,"* and he goes on, capturing in his words, all the narrative power of a new beginning:

> *"All this will not be finished in the first 100 days. Nor will it be finished in the first 1,000 days, nor in the life of this Administration, nor even perhaps in our lifetime on this planet. But let us begin."*

After the oath, the president will become the Orator in Chief, as he outlines the dream for his presidency, and connects it to the dreams of the Founders. Should this President turn out to be a great leader, these might be the words that will be chiseled on the marble adorning his future memorial. If ever a President knows he is speaking to and for the future, it is this one speech because, if it captures the imagination, his words will live in memory and always re-inspire the national conversation.

For JFK, it was *"And so, my fellow Americans: ask not what your country can do for you-ask what you can do for your country."*

---

38 Bush Inaugural Address January 2001

For FDR, it was *"So, first of all, let me assert my firm belief that the only thing we have to fear is fear itself."*

For Ronald Reagan, it was *"In this present crisis, government is not the solution to our problem."*

It is no surprise that these are probably the most worked over words a President gets to deliver. They set the tone, they are the national Prologue. In the beginning was the Word of God, and then the President said..."

You can be sure God will get mentioned at the beginning and certainly at the end, and homage will be paid to Lincoln and King and JFK and the previous President. And all the great words from our greatest stories will be given a new life in the new voice of the President; "Freedom," "Justice," "Peace," "Promise," "Faith." Only this time, this is no stump speech. This is the real thing. The nation has given him the power to make those words come true again. That is why we elected him.

The sobering thought though, is that no one will remember what you say here, to quote Lincoln, unless you do something that makes them come true here. And you can only do that by living the story you tell so that ordinary Americans feel the effect of that in their own lives. Bush gave a great Inaugural Address in 2001, but no one remembers it because the reality of the last eight years has reduced it to mere words, and perhaps worse, turned his lofty sentiments into accusations about dreams betrayed and opportunities lost. He said:

> *"We have a place, all of us, in a long story--a story we continue, but whose end we will not see. It is the story of a new world that became a friend and liberator of the old, a story of a slave-holding society that became a servant of freedom, the story of a power that went into the world to protect but not possess, to defend but not to conquer. It is the American story--a story of flawed and fallible people, united across the generations by grand and enduring ideals."[39]*

This can be a moment to live in history or it can be mere rhetorical window dressing but regardless, it marks the fairy tale end to our Epic. At long last, we have our new Head of State.

Next comes the luncheon in the Capitol. Since the President's laws have to pass here if he is to govern effectively, the least they can do

---

39 President George W Bush Inaugural Address January 2001

is begin in a true spirit of national unity, and break bread together. Then the Presidential cavalcade rolls on to Pennsylvania Avenue for the Victory parade to finish up at the Executive Mansion at 1600. It will be bitterly cold and if he is brave, the President might walk for a few blocks, provided his security detail lets him.

Then the President and the First Lady in all their finery head out in the evening to attend as many of the Inaugural balls as they can. The First Lady's gown will draw much attention and the sight of the First Couple on the dance floor will thrill the on-lookers, proud to see such a fetching couple as their First Family. And so, the day of triumph ends appropriately in an evening of pomp and splendor, as the President starts to get used to hearing "Hail to the Chief" as his entrance antiphon for every formal occasion from here on in.

But after the Ball is over, the limousine might not become a pumpkin, and the horses might not become mice, but our new Head of State returns to a quiet White House just waking to the dawn of a cold winter morning and as the sun comes up, the Fairy Tale ends.

His first working day begins in the Oval Office with security briefings and the urgency of filling the vacancies of what amounts in size and budget to ten multi-nationals, finding CEOs and managers and secretaries and assistant secretaries for each of them, and some 3000 other political appointments that are essential if the government is to start working again under his leadership. There are judges to appoint and ambassadors to dispatch and friends and donors to reward for their efforts to get him elected. And for the thousands of Americans in uniform, he is the new Commander in Chief who has pledged to keep them safe and get them home. Whatever the glamour of winning the highest office of the land, it is soon a distant memory as the real work begins.

Presidential elections, like this one in 2008, are the re-enchantment of America, when it stops worrying about the business of governing and entertains the possibilities of what might lay just over the horizon, the new Deal, the New Frontier, the New Contract with America, the Great Society, the bridge to the 21st century, the renewal of the Promise. The Future seems to have taken over and hope is the coin of the realm.

For that brief shining moment, a new America is again possible, only to slowly unravel, as all our hopes invested in one man prove to be totally beyond any man, but hopes that we and he have conspired to entertain. He is the change we wanted to believe in, but soon, we will see our demigod's wings melt the closer he gets to the sun, because of the intense heat of every day governance.

He will have to deal with a fractious Congress no matter what party wins the majority. He will meet regularly with the ego-maniacal media ever eager to become the storymakers, not the story tellers. He will have a Supreme Court aging and split as if there was a San Andreas Fault line hidden at the heart of the Constitution. For a hundred days, at least, the honeymoon will cushion the new President from the dull thud of reality but then, it all changes.

All those stories, that Washington is broken, that politics is too rancorous and partisan, that legislation is nothing but compromise and pork and gridlock; these were all the stories of the Presidential Plot that helped get him elected because he promised to change all of that.

But in 2009 and 2010, our hero will come crashing down to earth, because great heroes are made for great tragedies. And it is part of the President's hidden contract with the story, the part it demands he play. All those election clichés will have been forgotten long enough for them to reappear as new. Washington is broken, but now, our hero broke it, or was broken by it, and once again, our leaders have failed the country. Another election cycle will loom, and it will be time to dust off the "How to get re-elected" story kit. It will be time for campaign managers to revive the story cycle, rise and fall, rise and fall, and the re-enchantment of America starts all over again

We will willingly conspire once again in the Fairy Tale of a future and forget that we have been here before, and nothing much has changed, that it is as it ever was. It is The Presidential Plot, the story to overthrow a government by seducing a nation again into its most comforting fictions. The fact that election 1968 sounds like election 2008 and 1988 and 1980, or that Joe McGinnis's book The Selling of the President can serve as insightful a guide today as it was 40 years ago, tells us that this story is badly broken, like a broken record, and we remain its victims.

All Inauguration Day, January 20th, can give us is a fix for our romance addiction, like the happy ending that America craves in the movies. We will soar on the wings of great rhetoric and ritual, but that will only mask what can only be a hopeful but uncertain beginning. It is a beginning doomed to disappointment because we have elected a demigod and he can only rule as a mortal. We have created a fantastic novel, a *Great Expectations* for a hero to fly heavenward, only to find that our hero comes crashing down and the real story is about pride and prejudice, and the getting of wisdom. The story that elects a President is the story that can as quickly destroy him once in office. It just doesn't work anymore.

It is what Lincoln knew when the nation was torn apart over slavery, that old broken story of America. He strove with all his power, to create a new story, not rejecting the best of the old, but reshaping a better more inclusive story for America to internalize and live out of. At Gettysburg, he called it 'A new birth of freedom,' and he knew what America had to do to be able to even conceive of it. He said we had to first free our imaginations. He told Congress in 1862:

> *"The dogmas of the quiet past are inadequate to the stormy present. The occasion is piled high with difficulty, and we must rise—with the occasion. As our case is new, so we must think anew, and act anew. We must disenthrall ourselves, and then we shall save our country."*

"Disenthrall" is an amazing word. "Thrall" means "to enslave mentally or morally, to captivate, hold spellbound." To disenthrall ourselves is to stop being such suckers for a good story, to realize as Lincoln did back then, that the nation was living out a lie, about a freedom that it proclaimed to a people it enslaved.

A kingdom divided against itself cannot stand, Lincoln said, and he meant that when we countenance blatant contradictions such as a free nation tolerating slavery, we are creating an insane world, a world that no longer makes sense. Stories and lies can cover it over for a while. "Subordination is the Negro's natural and normal condition." the South said in 1861, just as they said that the levees in New Orleans were holding, but reality wreaks its revenge because as Herman Melville said, *"Reality outraces apprehension."*

Reality, political or otherwise, in the end will not allow you to be for lobbying and against lobbying, or for a security that destroys liberty, or a Clean Air Act that adds to the pollution, because you are tearing apart the very fabric of meaning. It makes no sense and it destroys language, our precious tool of sense-making. The corruption of politics then becomes an epistemological problem because deceit degrades reality and destroys the relationship between language and meaning, between action and consequence. We get used to nonsense, non-sense.

The American Republic today is trapped in another broken story that proclaims power to the people, and continues to treat them as victims, and denies them any effective way of having their voices heard. We cannot long endure as a nation if we continue to allow our politicians or our media or our cheer leaders for war to seduce us again into wasting our young people's lives and our hard earned tax dollars on a folly, a fable, that exploits our fears and shamelessly targets our narrative vulnerabilities. Lincoln told us our imaginations were diseased and imprisoned in the dogmas of the quiet past. The new work of freedom in our dangerous world demands a new imagination and that is where we must begin. Our case is new and so we must think anew and act anew. The old stories won't do.

A few months before the election, we still have time to wise up to the Presidential Plot, and if you don't get to read this before November 2008, there is still time before we get swept up again into this fairy tale in 2012. If we can imagine America as a Republic of Stories, not a Republic of Parties, and if we can teach the media a narrative ethic to restore and restory the people's trust in what is real, we can free ourselves of our modern slavery to old stories and worn out practices.

A latter day visionary, the former Librarian of the Library of Congress, Daniel Boorstin, wrote a powerful book called The Image in which he echoes Lincoln's call:

> *"Nowadays everybody tells us that what we need is more belief, a stronger and deeper and more encompassing faith. A faith in America and in what we are doing. That may be true in the long run. What we need first and now is to disillusion ourselves."* [40]

Joe McGinnis quoted that way back in 1968 in his futile plea for something to change. Back then, as now, the Presidential Plot gets a candidate elected as this book has tried to show. But it is not a story that has anything to do with making him a good or better President. We are electing a Fairy Tale King to govern a Magic Kingdom and once elected, the Magic Kingdom turns out to be a blow up toy for kids. Reality breaks the stories because the stories pay no respect to it. The levees of New Orleans still cannot defend their fair city from hurricane force because even now, we do not have the stories to repair them, or make them stronger.

WE HAVE A FOUNDING STORY, NOT A FOUNDING MYTH

The founding myths of most other countries begin with "Once upon a time," and they tell of wolves and giants and gods and kings and

---

40 Daniel Boorstin The Image Vintage 1992 Page 6

barbarians. They even go back to pre-history, to the imagined time before time and to Adam and Eve in the Garden of Eden.

But America's founding story is radically different.

There is no "Once Upon a time," no Romulus or Remus, no Rainbow Serpent. Though we have done our best to mythologize it, to turn it into an epic to rival Rome and Greece, and monumentalized it into marble Parthenon's on the Mall, it is no myth. It is a story rooted in real time and real people and it is a story whose language deeply respects the reality of power and its formative influence on our national identity. Our story begins with three key words, *"We the people."* There is no other great and enduring national story to compare with it. As with any story, the power is in the beginning, and what a beginning!

Our founders installed the uncommon common man and woman in the pantheon of our gods. Kings and Emperors were the enemy. Our Gods are invoked at the beginning and the end of public proceedings, but then told politely to keep their divine noses out of our story of government. We don't do Kings and we don't do Gods. The hero of the American story is *"We the People,"* or it was meant to be. But Hollywood and the media and government and election campaigns, all parts of a military industrial story complex, have seduced us into a different story where gods and kings abound.

Every election, when the Presidential Plot takes over, the people, the heroes of the democracy story, are relegated to bit players or stage props[41] on platforms sitting behind plastic Candidates created for the camera but not for real flesh and blood citizens whom these wannabe heroes aspire to serve. Candidates are manufactured to play the lead in the Presidential Plot which feeds our fantasy, but which ignores the deeper longing America has for a new birth of freedom. It will be new not because it has solved every problem or achieved every lofty goal but because finally it is real again.

As Lincoln bends his head at the Lincoln Memorial to see past the Washington Monument to watch the 44th President of the United States get sworn in, he will repeat his message to his beloved Republic that once more needs emancipation by thinking anew and acting anew, but imagining my Lincoln, I know that he would do

---

41 "The average citizen has come to feel rather like a deaf spectator in the back row, who ought to keep his mind on the mystery off there, but cannot quite manage to stay awake. He knows he is somehow affected by what is going on.. Yet these public affairs are in no convincing way his affairs." Walter Lippman quoted in Richard Harwood "So Much for Washington" *Washington Post* July 15 1997

something else as well. He would lean forward, and in his high pitched voice and that silly grin on his face, he would say, "Listen Johnny," or "Hey Barack," "Let me tell you a story."

CHAPTER TWENTY

THE PRESIDENTIAL PLOT-THE GAME

What Obama knows, what McCain needs to know and what Hillary didn't know!

"You've read the book-Now play the game."

Have you heard these latest election headlines? Test yourself to see which ones might be true, and which ones might not be?

- **Why Obama can't possibly win**

- **Why McCain will win in the greatest upset since Truman**

- **How Karl Rove and the Republicans intend to steal this election**

- **Why Obama remains a closet Muslim**

- **Why McCain is anything BUT a war hero**

- **McCain's plane not shot down-Thought he was landing!**

- **Bush vindicated in Iraq-Americans apologize for dissing d'W**

- **Obama sabotaged a Gore-Powell ticket**

- **Obama couture-he listens to Hillary's fashion tips**

- **Strategist says terrorist attack would have to kill more than three thousand to aid McCain**

- **Obama will establish a department of Youth**

- **Another gay Congressman found making hand signals in Senate bathroom-says it was a bi-partisan gesture**

- **Swift Boat Veteran finances rebuilding the Titanic**

- **October Surprise to happen in September,**

- Society for the Reputation of Pigs sues Campaigns for discriminatory disparagement and being anti-pork

- Michelle Obama says she's always been proud of herself

- Bush says history will reveal true WMD's –As in "We Misjudged Dwaya."

- Obama's flag pin engraved with secret Koranic verse

- Pig farmers producing new line of lipstick

- Hank Paulson bailout to pay for Hillary' campaign debts

- Lobbyists paid big bucks to get anti-lobbying measures passed

- Major Lobbyist resigns from McCain team to save his reputation

- Obama break-through on Middle East- will give Palestine back to Israel

- Chief Justice Roberts willing to intervene if McCain loses count of his votes

- Kenneth Starr, Scooter Libby and Gordon Liddy to be indicted into Heritage Foundation's Hall of Fame

- ACLU wants new trial-claims Saddam hung unfairly

- Rumsfeld unsure of Memoir title-'I told you so" or "I told the so and so,"

- Osama in Torah Borah press release backs his namesake to win

- McCain raises retirement age to 85

- Palin reveals Bridge to Nowhere was going somewhere when she supported it

- Fred Thompson deciding if he will run in 2020

- Some make it happen, others watch it happen, and Scott McClellan asks 'What happened?'

- **Osama attempts to save McCain a trip denying he is at Hellsgate**

- **Biden misses Amtrak train home and holds 8 hour pep rally at Union Station instead**

If any of these headlines have grabbed your attention, then you display a healthy curiosity about the presidential elections.

You also display a strong sense for a good headline grabber. You appreciate that while the impossible in politics can take a few weeks or months or years, like getting out of a war, or saving the planet, the absurd can happen every other day, especially in an election year. And as they say, anything can happen in Washington, and it frequently does. Besides passing laws, which is a bit of a rarity.

None of these headlines are totally outside the bounds of credibility, though some are clearly tongue in cheek. None are beyond imagining, even in fun. Some of them would make darn good stories that would spice up an otherwise predictable, and typically over-hyped Presidential election.

With this book, we want to inaugurate a new game called the Presidential Plot. It's also an experiment in viral marketing.
First get your friends over on a Friday night with a few packs of Budweiser, to watch *Inside Washington*, *Shields and Brooks*, *Bill Moyers* and *the Factor*. Then create a list of possible and improbable headlines that you would love to see steal the news.

Imagine Mark Shields discussing whether Obama's Department of Youth is going to be part of Homeland Security since everything else is, or is it just those hormonally charged kids under 18. Or David Brooks saying that Sarah Palin could well secure the Hillary vote for McCain because her family seems as normal as Hillary's. Then imagine Nina Totenberg and Charles Krauthammer discussing whether retrying Saddam matters if he is dead, and whether this is a *habeas corpus* case.

Next, put these headlines on your blog, one at a time. Provocatively title your blog, "The Real News," or "What people aren't telling us," or "The conspiracy they don't want you to know about." Or use the old fashioned oral method of transmission, by testing them with your friends at the water cooler on Monday morning. Be sure to use a casual tone, "Did you hear that McCain wanted to give his acceptance speech from a rooftop in New Orleans amidst Hurricane Gustav?" or, "I heard the rumor in Chicago that Obama is so superstitious that he wears a Michael Jordan jersey underneath his shirt."

Now, when people say, you are lying, give yourself plausible deniability with this alibi; 'You did hear someone spreading this crazy rumor in Chicago,' Just don't tell them it was you. Utter it once, so you can then reliably quote yourself subsequently, and give yourself the shield every good journalist does, as the unnamed source. Or say it was an anonymous tip-off from someone who knows what he is talking about, as you clearly do! Technically it's called lying, but no one else calls it that these days so you don't have to either. You are just having fun and also protecting your sources and the First Amendment. Like Judy Miller.

Then, wait and see if Drudge or MoveOn.com or any of your headline gobblers pick it up. Experiment and learn how to make the headline plausible to both hard line liberals and hard boiled conservatives. Be an equal opportunity story-monger. Also, learn how your headlines have to fit the story that someone out there has already half imagined for a candidate. That Obama thanks Christ he is a Muslim, or McCain forgot he has Alzheimer's. Or be so original and outlandish that people make it true because they want it to be true.

Try "McCain will appoint Obama to his Cabinet as secretary for Hope-Based initiatives," or "Obama to replace Biden in VP debate with Palin." Also, each one should have a little irony concealed in it, such as, "Giuliani can't remember all the details of 9-11," so that you can at least defend yourself later, to say that the story did have a hint that it was only a game, after all.

If any of them get mentioned in mainstream media, we will give you a special Obama flag pin, (he has plenty these days) and if any come true, we will give you the Rush Limbaugh Poet of the Pundits award. And all prize winners will join Libby, Cheney, Bush and other awardees at an event in the Building Museum in 2009 to open their new exhibit, "Tall Ships, Tall Tales and other Election Curiosities." We hope Scott McClellan will present the awards and then tell us what happened, when he has had a chance to think about it.

Ultimately the experiment will prove the central premise of our book The Presidential Plot, that we are all suckers for a good story! And you will be doing what the media and politicians together have been doing in this town since 1790! Plotting to be President. Now that's a story. So start playing now before reality comes up with even greater fictions that we wouldn't otherwise believe.

SELECT BIBLIOGRAPHY

Boorstin, Daniel   The Image-A Guide to Pseudo-Events in America Vintage Books 1987

Brooks, Peter   Reading for the Plot Harvard 1984

Chamberlain, Murray; Thompson, Paul

Narrative and Genre of Communication-Contexts and Types New Brunswick 2004

Chambers, Oswald   My Utmost for His Highest Fleming Revell NJ 1935

Chesterton, G.K.   Orthodoxy Image Books New York 1959

Crynulnik, Boris   Talking of Love on the Edge of a Precipice Allen Lane 2007

Doctorow, E.L.   Poets and Presidents -Selected Essays 1977-1992 Papermac Toronto 1993

Dyson, Freeman   Weapons and Hope Perennial 1984

George, Bill   True North Jossey Bass 2007

Gergen, Kenneth   Realities and Relationships Harvard 1994

Kagan, Robert   The Return of History and the End of Dreams Knopf 2008

Kearney, Richard   Paul Ricoeur-The Hermeneutics of Action Sage 1996

Kotter John   Leading Change Harvard Business Press 1996

Lehmann, Nicholas "Gore Without a Script" *The New Yorker* July 31st, 2000

Manguel, Alberto   Homer's the Iliad and the Odyssey-A Biography Atlantic 2007

McAdams, Douglas   The Redemptive Self-Stories
                                    Americans Live By Oxford 2006

McClain, John with Mark Salter

                                    Faith of My Fathers –A Family Memoir
                                    Random House 1999

McGinniss, Joe   The Selling of the President Penguin
                                    1988

Milbank, Dana   Homo Politicus-The Strange and
                                    Barbaric Tribes of the Beltway
                                    Doubleday NY 2008

Obama, Barack   The Audacity of Hope Three Rivers
                                    Press New York 2006

Obama, Barack   Dreams from My Father- A Story of
                                    Inheritance Three Rivers Press New
                                    York 2004

Ornstein, Robert; Ehrlich, Paul

                                    New World New Mind Touchstone
                                    Books New York 1989

Pratchett, Terry   Witches Abroad A Discworld Novel
                                    Corgi Books UK 1991

McIntyre, Alasdair   After Virtue Notre Dame 1984

Rapaille, Clotaire   The Culture Code Broadway Books
                                    2006

Silf, Margaret   Roots and Wings Darton Longman
                                    and Todd London 2006

Silverstein, Roger   Television and Everyday Life
                                    Routledge 1994

Vonnegut, Karl   A Man Without a Country Random
                                    House 2007

Warren, Robert Penn   All the Kings Men Harvest 1996

Wax, Steven	<u>Kafka Comes to America</u> Other Press 2008
Wheeler, Kip	<u>Notes on Epic</u> web.cn.edu/kwheeler/documents/Epic.pdf
Wheeler, Tom	<u>Leadership Lessons from the Civil War</u> Currency Book Double Day NY 2000
White, Curtis	<u>The Middle Mind Why Americans Don't Think for Themselves</u> Harper SanFrancisco 2003
Zohar, Danah	<u>Spiritual Capital</u> Berrett-Keehler 2004

ABOUT THE AUTHOR

P. Andrew Costello is an educator, writer and social activist from Australia. He founded *Rosies-Friends on the Street*, a youth-to-youth volunteer organization that for the last 20 years has continued to serve homeless youth in six major cities along Australia's east coast. Paul's studies with Michael White, founder of narrative therapy, inspired him to come to the United States to research narrative method and its applications to community renewal and organizations dealing with conflict and change.

In 1995, Paul founded www.storywise.com, the Center for Narrative Studies, (CNS) in Washington DC and currently serves as the Director of the Center. CNS offers training programs for narrative practitioners and a narrative approach to knowledge management, media, and community renewal.

For the past ten years, Paul has been the director of The Washington Ireland Program for Service and Leadership, www.wiprogram.org a peace and reconciliation program that brings 30 university students from all communities in Northern Ireland and Ireland to the United States every summer for internships and intense leadership training. He has been publicly recognized by the 110th Congress and by the Northern Ireland Assembly for this important work. Paul frequently lectures at universities nationally and internationally and was a lecturer in Business Studies at Trinity College, Washington and has worked with The Catholic University of America in their summer schools. He holds degrees in Literature, Theology, Education and an MFA in Creative Writing from American University. He is currently writing a book on the lessons learned from the last ten years in Northern Ireland.

THE CENTER FOR NARRRATIVE STUDIES (CNS)
www.storywise.com

"Shaping the stories that shape us"

CNS offers regular trainings and workshops in Narrative Ethics, Living Stories and Narrative Room, and consults to organizations seeking renewal. Their faculty also speak at Conferences and facilitate corporate retreats. If you would like to invite a speaker from CNS or want to know how CNS might be able to help your organization or community, please email paul@storywise.com

If you would like more copies of this book, go to

http://www.lulu.com/content/3972295

###

THE REPUBLIC OF STORIES-THE NARRATIVE BLOG

You can get a regular Narrative Commentary on public affairs provided by www.storywise.com at the Republic of Stories at their new Blog site http://www.storywise.com/wordpress/ Join the conversation.

###

A LIVING STORIES PROJECT

If this book has got you thinking about *the Republic of Stories* and inspired you to comment, or to offer your own story that you believe Washington needs to hear that will help get Government working again for the people, please send it to
republicofstories@gmail.com